THE
ILLUSTRATED
HERBAL

THE
ILLUSTRATED
HERBAL

PHILLIPPA BACK

HAMLYN

To My Husband

Acknowledgments
Special photography on pages 1, 3, 9, 12, 15 by Jan Baldwin
with stylist Hilary Guy.

The herbs on pages 18–157 were specially photographed by
Angelo Hornak with the kind permission of the Royal
Horticultural Society, London.

The publishers and author would also like to thank the
following for their help.

Michael Boys Syndication and Camera Press Ltd for the
photographs on pages 7 and 11 respectively.

Daphne M. ffiske, Herb Nursery, Rosemary Cottage,
Bramerton, Norfolk.

Culpeper Ltd, 21 Bruton Street, London W1; and Bill
McHugh, Herb Farm Manager at Culpeper, Wixoe, Suffolk.

Editor Camilla Simmons
Art Editor Lisa Tai
Designer Clare Clements
Production Controller Maryann Rogers
Picture Research Judith Schecter
Illustrations Russell Barnett

Publisher's Note
All the remedies in this book should only be taken or applied in
moderation and for a limited period of time. For any condition
of a serious nature or which shows signs of complications, a
doctor should be consulted. Use preparations fresh, and always
follow the guidance given for storage.

First published 1987 by
Hamlyn Publishing Group
Bridge House, 69 London Road
Twickenham, Middlesex TW1 3SB

and distributed for them by
Hamlyn Distribution Services

©1987 Octopus Books Limited
ISBN 0 600 553 361

Produced by Mandarin Publishers Ltd
22a Westlands Road, Quarry Bay
Hong Kong

Printed in Hong Kong

CONTENTS

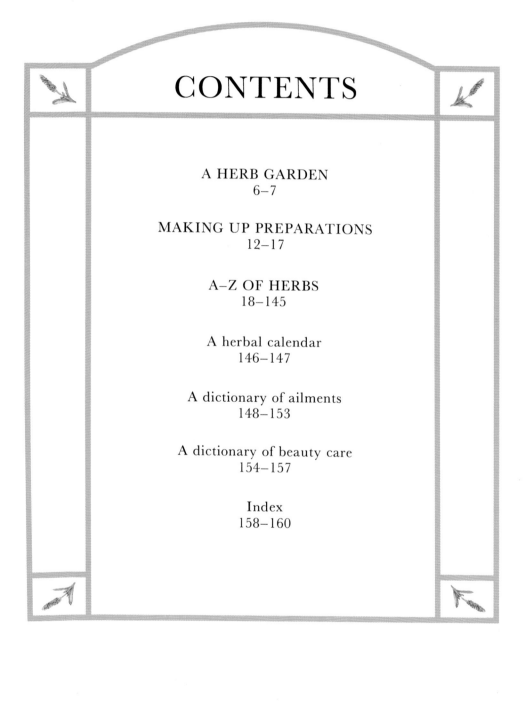

A HERB GARDEN

Nowadays many herbs and herbal preparations are readily available in supermarkets, chemists (pharmacies) and health shops, but it is infinitely more satisfying to grow and use your own. Not only do herbs make a charming and fragrant addition to the garden, but there is an elemental pleasure to be gained from harvesting and drying them and then mixing and concocting the many remedies and beauty preparations they provide. This will not require a large financial outlay or specialized skill; simply a little gardening knowledge, patience, and an interest in herbs and their properties which have proved so efficacious to the human race.

PREPARING THE GROUND

Herbs are among the easiest plants to grow and, once established in their plot, need little attention. While they will grow quite happily mixed with other plants in the garden, it is easier to have all the herbs grouped together in a separate bed.

A herb bed will last for many years, so it is worthwhile spending time and trouble in its preparation at the outset. Once the location for the herb bed has been decided upon, the dimensions should be pegged out. If it is in a lawn the turf should be carefully lifted for re-laying elsewhere or placed in a heap upside down for composting. If the planned layout includes them, paths or edging should be laid on the undisturbed soil by packing sand underneath paving slabs, stone or bricks to ensure they are firm and level.

Herb plants grow in any normal garden soil, which should ideally be a balanced mixture of clay, humus, lime and sand. The soil should have good drainage and be easy to work, so that it soon warms up in the spring; this makes it possible for the herbs to be planted much earlier in the year. Given these conditions it is only necessary to fork in some well-rotted compost and leave the soil for two or three weeks to settle before planting out the herbs.

It is unusual to find well-balanced loam soil, but the aim is to convert the soil as far as possible into a good growing medium with the vital ingredients in the right proportions. Compost can be bought ready bagged or it can be made at home. Digging is really the first stage in soil preparation, for both digging and rotavating improve the soil by breaking it down and thus allowing air to get into the soil. This helps the decomposition of humus and gives better drainage. As a general rule, add compost to the soil in the proportion of half a barrow load to 5 sq yds (4.2 sq metres).

Drainage is extremely important, because a waterlogged soil starves the herbs of air and causes a build-up of harmful bacteria, resulting in the plants dying off. A layer of small stones put down under the soil when digging may be sufficient, but otherwise the only way to ensure proper drainage is to dig a soak-away. This is a small pit about 2 ft (61 cm) square and 2 ft (61 cm) deep, sited at the lowest point in the garden and filled with brick rubble or stones to a depth of 12 in (30 cm). It is then filled up with topsoil to level off.

Lime is another important component in herb growing. Hydrated lime is the best to use, as it conditions the soil as well as breaking down the humus and releasing the ingredients which are needed to grow strong sturdy plants. It helps to break down heavy clay soil, making it more friable and easier to work, and it will bind sandy soils, thus keeping plants pest free. Lime also neutralizes acid or sour soil and encourages the beneficent bacteria and earthworms which are normally non-existent in this type of soil. Never add lime to soil when adding other plant foods but spread it evenly over the soil about two months after the digging has been completed. Allow 8 oz (225 g) to 1 sq yd (84 sq cm) and leave it for the rain to wash into the ground.

SOWING SEEDS

It is important when buying herb seed to get the correct variety and to follow the growing instructions on the packet. All annual herbs are grown from seed and many of the perennial plants also can be started in the same way.

As a general rule, annual seeds are sown under glass in the early spring or out of doors in May when there is no danger from frost. Indoors or under glass use a good organic seed compost to fill seed trays or flower pots, firm the soil and moisten with water. Leave the trays for a day or two to allow the soil to warm up, then sow the seeds as evenly as possible, pressing fine seeds lightly into the soil. Cover larger seeds with a thin layer of soil. The trays should be screened with a sheet of glass or clear plastic with newspaper on top

A pretty cottage-style herb garden which mixes its colour and fragrance with that of other garden plants and flowers. Plant tall-growing herbs such as rosemary, tarragon, mint and lovage at one end or side.

to shut out the light. Annual seeds take about a week to germinate; perennials may take three to four weeks. Remove the glass and paper as soon as the seedlings appear. The seedlings can be pricked out at the four leaf stage and should be hardened off when large enough before finally being planted out of doors in their flowering positions.

Many perennials germinate well when sown in August or September, as soon as the seeds are ripe. Collect the seeds of lovage, angelica and sweet cicely and sow them in a warm, sheltered patch, covering them with a thin layer of leaf mould. The seedlings will come up in the spring and can be transplanted into their flowering positions when large enough. Alternatively, make a small circular trench around the parent plant and when the seeds are ready to fall give the flowerhead a good shake, so that the seeds drop into the shallow trench. Cover the seeds with a little soil and leaf mould and leave undisturbed until the seedlings appear.

ROOT DIVISION

Herb plants should be divided when they become over-large and straggly. This not only increases the stock of plants but also produces vigorous new herbs.

Lemon balm, sage, costmary and calamint can all put on an enormous amount of growth in only one or two years. Divide them by digging up the whole herb and carefully pulling the clump apart by hand or slice it cleanly through with a sharp spade. The centre of the plant should then be discarded. The divided roots can be planted out in their new flowering positions in the garden and should be kept thoroughly watered until they are well established.

PROPAGATING WITH CUTTINGS

An easy and, of course, economical way to increase your stock of herbs is to take stem or root cuttings. Stem cuttings should be made only from well-established, healthy plants. Take cuttings from soft-stemmed plants during the spring and summer and from the woody-stemmed herbs like rosemary, sage and hyssop in August and September.

Cuttings of soft leafy stems should be cut 6 in (15 cm) long, just below a leaf bud. Remove all the leaves from the bottom half of the cuttings, dip them into water and then into a hormone rooting powder. Tap off the excess powder and firmly plant the cuttings to half their length into pots filled with compost. Set the pots in a shady spot and keep the compost damp until the cuttings have rooted. If you are taking a large number of cuttings they should be set into a shallow trench in sand. Again the cuttings should be in the shade, firmed well in and kept moist until rooted.

For propagating woody-stemmed herbs, a mature side shoot should be taken from low down on the stem. Pull off a 'heel' with the side shoot and remove the leaves and buds from the bottom third of the cutting. The cutting should be about 9 in (23 cm) long. Set the cuttings into a narrow trench 3 in (7.5 cm) deep. Sprinkle sand along the bottom and set the cuttings firmly into the trench. The woody-stemmed cuttings can take up to a year to root.

Root cuttings from fleshy-rooted herbs such as marsh mallow, comfrey or elecampane can be taken in the spring or autumn when the plant is being moved or divided. Cut finger-thick pieces of root into short lengths. Set the pieces of root into a deep flower pot filled with soil and cover with glass or plastic and a piece of newspaper. Set the pot in a shady spot and once the new growth has started put the plants into individual pots for planting out later.

BUYING IN

A visit to the local herb nursery or garden centre is worth while when starting a new herb garden. Container-grown herb plants, especially perennials, can be purchased and planted out at almost any time of the year, provided the ground is free of frost. It is important that bought-in plants should be small and stocky with the fibrous root formation coming through the base of the pot. This denotes a healthy, well-grown, established plant which will more quickly settle down into its new home. The herbs should be well watered and left overnight before planting. Remove each plant carefully from its pot, disturbing the root ball as little as possible. Plant the herb so that the soil comes just over the root ball and firm it down well with the handle of the trowel. Shrubby herbs should be planted to the depth of the 'soil mark' which shows on the stems. The planting hole must be large enough to allow their roots to be carefully spread out, and a handful of compost in the hole gives the herbs a good start. Once planted, the herbs should be given a thorough watering.

HERBS IN CONTAINERS

There are many herbs which can be grown in containers, both indoors and out of doors. Larger herbs with long tap roots, such as lovage or fennel, are not suitable. When growing herbs out of doors the pots, tubs or boxes should have adequate drainage, otherwise the plants will stagnate and die. They should be strong enough to hold the weight of the soil, and they must stand on bricks or stones to allow air to circulate and excess water to drain away. A layer of shingle at the bottom of a window box which has no holes will provide adequate drainage. The same rules apply to containers for indoor herbs, but as light is essential to growth, plants should stand on a sunny windowsill wherever possible. Place the pots on trays of shingle to allow air to circulate and excess water to drain away. Herbs need ventilation and will not grow well in a stuffy room, but a bowl of water will keep the air moist round the herbs (this is especially important in a centrally heated room).

MAINTENANCE

Once the herb bed is established it requires little attention. Regular hoeing between the herbs will keep the bed free of weeds and allow air and moisture to get to the plants. Moisture-loving herbs should be kept well watered in a dry spell. In spring a slow acting fertilizer should be lightly forked into the soil.

PESTS AND DISEASES

Fortunately not many diseases affect herb plants, but there are a few to watch out for.

Seedling herbs can be attacked by 'damping off' disease when the bases of the stems wither and go black. To avoid this, sow seeds thinly in sterilized compost and do not over-water when seedlings appear. A seed dressing, or a 'seed saver' preparation can be applied at the outset and seed boxes can be washed in a solution of Cheshunt compound. Affected seedlings should be removed and burnt and the remainder watered with the Cheshunt compound.

Garden mint is subject to a fungus disease known as 'mint rust' which affects plants from the inside. There is no way of treating this and all diseased plants should be removed and burnt. Mint should not be grown in the same place for at least two years. In a small garden the soil can be sterilized using a solution of Jeyes fluid.

Sweet violets are prone to attack from red spider mite, when the leaves develop yellowy patches and are covered with a fine web. This should be treated by wetting the plant with a sulphur spray every other day and spray-watering the tops and undersides of the leaves at frequent intervals until the infestation is wiped out.

Another pest which attacks herbs is the greenfly. This should be treated by frequently spraying the plants with a solution of green soft soap (or use the washing-up water). It should be done on a regular basis to keep greenfly at bay.

HARVESTING, DRYING AND STORING

The whole process of harvesting, drying and storing the herbs should be carried out as carefully and speedily as possible.

HARVESTING

Gather the leafy herbs for drying in the morning of a dry day when the dew has dried, just before the plant comes into flower. This is when the volatile oils contained in the leaves are at their highest and on this the flavour, colour and scent depend.

During the season annual herbs can be cut to within 4–5 in (10–12.5 cm) from the ground and in the autumn they can be cut right down to the ground. Perennials such as fennel, lovage and sweet cicely can be cut back to one third of their growth. Shrubby perennials like sage and hyssop can be kept neat by taking a few sprigs at a time and cutting back to half the year's growth in the autumn. Scissors or sharp shears should be used to collect the herbs, as breaking the stems or pulling at leaves will only damage the plant. Care should be taken to avoid bruising the leaves. After gathering the herbs discard any leaves that are very muddy or damaged. The herbs should then be quickly but carefully washed in tepid water.

Flowering tops such as rosemary, hyssop, thyme and mugwort should be gathered when the flowers are just beginning to open. Flowers and petals should be collected when the flowers are fully open – often on a daily basis to ensure they are picked when whole and unblemished.

Seeds of dill, fennel, caraway and sunflower are collected in the autumn. When the heads of the plant have turned brown the stems can be tapped each day to test if the seeds are ripe. If the seeds begin to fall when tapped the herb should be cut down and collected in a box on a dry day. Tie the stems together and hang them upside down in a paper bag so that all the seeds will be saved.

Berries should be gathered when the fruit is fully ripe and firm and the colour at its best. They will not

Flowering herbs, seed heads and leaves hanging up or spread out on a tray for drying. In the summer a dark, airy garden shed is ideal for slow-drying herbs and flowers. For other methods, see overleaf.

dry successfully if they are at all soft or shrivelled and they should be handled as little as possible.

Harvest roots in the autumn when the leaves have died down. If a plant such as marsh mallow is being lifted for division in spring pieces of root can be removed for drying at the same time.

HOW TO DRY

The aim in drying herbs is to remove the water content only, thus changing them as little as possible. The old idea was to hang bunches of the herbs upside down in the kitchen where there were constant changes of temperature and light. The herbs were of little value as a result. Herbs dried in the sunshine will lose colour and quality as the heat makes the volatile oils evaporate. There are a number of other ways of drying herbs successfully, as described below. Select whichever is most convenient, but for flowers and petals, read the section on these.

The first and most important rule is always to dry herbs in the dark. At the same time, ventilation and good circulation of air round the herbs should be provided. The temperature for drying can vary according to the needs of individual herbs, but during the process the temperature should be constant. Any excess moisture should be well drained before the herbs are put on to trays made by stretching pieces of nylon net tautly over the frames of old wooden seed boxes with the bottoms knocked out, the net being held in place with staples.

WHERE TO DRY

Many herbs dry quickly and successfully in a cool oven, no higher than 100°F (38°C). Leave the oven door slightly ajar to allow the moisture to escape.

Herbs can be dried on the net covered trays where a constant heat is supplied by a boiler. Stand the trays on four little pieces of wood to allow the air to circulate round them.

A warm dark room can be ideal for the slow drying of some herbs. Stand the herb trays on pieces of wood to leave space for air to circulate.

A dry, dark, airy garden shed can be used in the summer months for herbs which need to be dried slowly. Any windows should be blocked off to keep out the light and the trays can be covered with paper to keep off dust and flies which may find their way into the shed.

The airing cupboard (or heated closet) is the most suitable place for drying all parts of the herb. Leave the door slightly ajar so the moisture can evaporate and air can circulate.

Many of the more fragile parts of a herb will dry slowly and well between sheets of newspaper placed under the bed or chest of drawers in an airy room.

DRYING THE WHOLE HERB

Some low growing herbs have very small leaves and flowers and picking them separately would be an extremely laborious task. These herbs therefore are dried whole, including the stem. After cutting the herbs, and washing only if necessary, tie them in small bunches and hang them upside down in the airing cupboard (heated closet). Herbs suitable for this treatment are chickweed, centaury, heartsease, lesser celandine, separated from its roots, summer savory and woodruff. Chickweed should be dried slowly in the coolest part of the airing cupboard (heated closet), while heartsease needs to be dried as quickly as possible in the warmest part. The flowering tops of blessed thistle, hyssop, lady's bedstraw, mint, mugwort and rosemary can also be dried in the same way.

DRYING THE LEAVES

Leaves of large herbs such as lovage and sweet cicely should be stripped from the stems before drying. Thick fleshy leaves, such as those of comfrey, coltsfoot and sage, should also be dried singly. For ease of handling the leaves of other herbs can be left on the stems, though it is not necessary for the stems to be dry. Spread the herbs out evenly on the drying trays and put into a cool oven preheated to 90°–100°F (32–38°C), leaving the door slightly open. Most leaves take up to an hour to dry, but check them from time to time and when the leaves feel crisp immediately remove them from the oven. Rub the leaves off the stems and, if you like, put them through a coarse sieve before storing.

DRYING FLOWERS AND PETALS

The best method of drying small flowers and petals is to place them between sheets of newspaper in an airy room where they can be left undisturbed for several weeks. Rose petals will take much longer, but they can be crisped up quickly in a very cool oven with the door left ajar. Lime flowers and chamomile flowers are best dried in the airing cupboard (heated closet) as they are thicker and take a long time to dry. Lavender should be cut with long stems and tied in small bunches to hang upside down in a warm dark place. Dandelion flowers are dried whole and should be placed on a drying tray in the airing cupboard.

DRYING SEEDS

Seed heads which have been cut and left to hang upside down in paper bags can, when all the seeds

Bunches of lavender, tied with ribbon, make attractive and fragrant presents when dried.

have fallen, be thrown away. The seeds should then be dried for a further period of time. Spread them out on tissue over a wire cake tray in the airing cupboard (or heated closet). They are fully dry when they are hard and easy to snap.

Sunflower seeds must be properly dried before they can be stored. The flowerheads shrivel and droop as the seeds begin to ripen and the heads should not be cut until this stage is reached. Cut them on a dry day and place the flowerheads in a very cool oven until the seeds can easily be removed. When all the seeds have come away, spread them on paper and finish drying in the airing cupboard.

DRYING BERRIES
Barberries can be successfully dried for winter use. Only perfect fruit should be picked and these carefully taken off the stalks. Spread the berries between two pieces of muslin or cheesecloth and dry in a warm dark place. The berries will shrivel when dried but should remain a good colour and feel hard and crisp.

Rosehips can be dried in a very cool oven or the airing cupboard (heated closet). Slice the ripe hips with a sharp stainless steel knife and spread out on grease-proof paper or parchment on trays. When completely dry they should feel crisp and be a good red colour. Be careful, as too great a heat will turn the hips brown

and they will lose all value. After drying, rosehips should be well crushed with a rolling pin between two pieces of paper and then put through a coarse sieve to remove all the hairs. This must be done either outside or inside wearing gloves and a muslin or gauze mask over the nose and mouth as the hairs can cause irritation.

DRYING ROOTS
As soon as the roots have been lifted they should be well scrubbed and cut or sliced into small pieces. Spread the pieces on the drying trays and leave them in the airing cupboard or other warm dark place until they are hard and brittle. Valerian root, which has a strong unpleasant smell when drying, should be dried well away from other herbs.

STORING
Herbs should be stored in dark-coloured glass screw-top jars immediately they are dry, otherwise they pick up moisture from the air and will not keep. They should not be stored in tins unless they are first placed in a cotton bag because contact with the tin can damage the flavour and aroma of the herb.

Dried herbs should not be stored for longer than a winter season, or at most nine months, as they lose their colour, scent and flavour if kept for too long.

MAKING UP PREPARATIONS

There are a number of ways to make herb medicines and beauty care preparations. They are all fairly easy processes and most of the equipment required to make them is already in the home.

The first and most important rule when making any herbal remedy is that the saucepan used should be either stainless steel or enamel. Aluminium or non-stick pans should never be used as contact with their surfaces may alter the nature of the herb.

All herb medicines and cosmetics made in the home are more effective when freshly made and it is unwise to prepare a large quantity at any one time. No remedy should be kept for more than a few days.

If the recipe requires the herb to be chopped, this should be done using a stainless steel knife and wooden chopping board. Light crushing or bruising can be done in the hand, but if the leaves and flowering shoots need to be well crushed this is best done in a stone pestle and mortar. To turn herb leaves into a purée the fresh leaves can be washed and, with a little water added, pulped in an electric blender. Dried leaves will need to be reconstituted in water first. Herbs can be cooked to a mash by adding a little water to the leaves in an enamel pan. Place the pan over a low heat and stir or beat until the right consistency is obtained. Woody-stemmed herbs can be crushed in a pestle and mortar and roots, whether fresh or dried, should be grated as required and used straight away. Seeds can be lightly crushed or ground either in an electric blender or by placing between sheets of greaseproof paper or parchment and using a rolling pin. Flowers are never subjected to heavy treatment and should only be lightly crushed.

After the preparation has been made it should be strained carefully through gauze, muslin (cheesecloth) or a nylon strainer. Gauze is a loosely woven cotton cloth and is adequate for straining whole leaf infusions. Muslin or cheesecloth can be purchased in varying weaves, the very fine being the best for infusions using ground seed, verbascum flowers or rosehips. Muslin or cheesecloth and gauze can be bought at most sewing departments.

Bath sachets Adding herbs to the bath water is a most effective form of medicinal and cosmetic treatment. They are easy to prepare and the bath can be enjoyed

Relaxing and reviving a scented herbal bath sachet is a simple and soothing way of enjoying the cosmetic and medicinal benefits of the herb garden. Lovage, marigold and elderflowers combine well together as do chamomile, lavender and thyme.

PREPARING A FACIAL STEAM OR INHALATION

1 Place the appropriate crushed fresh or dried herb into a medium-sized bowl and pour boiling water over it.

2 Cover the head and bowl with a large towel and steam the face or inhale the fumes for 10 minutes.

3 After a facial steam, finish by splashing the face with cold water to refresh the skin and tighten the pores.

---

as relaxing, healing, invigorating or as an aromatic bath to perfume the body. Some medical herbalists prescribe the herb bath for a number of ailments.

To make a bath sachet, you will need a piece of muslin or cheesecloth 8 in (20 cm) square. On to this place 3 large tablespoons of chopped fresh or dried herbs. Tie the corners of the cloth square together with a piece of string and hang it from the hot water tap (faucet) while running the bath, so that the water rushes through the sachet. Once in the bath, use the bag to rub all over the skin and get the full benefit of the herbs. For added softening of the water, 1 tablespoon of oatmeal can be mixed in with the herbs.

Bath sachets can be used more than once if hung up to dry after use. The effect of the herbs will naturally become weaker with each successive bath. Two or three herbs mixed together in a bath sachet can make a refreshing and effective mixture. Herbs which go well together are chamomile and lavender flowers with thyme. Yarrow for an oily skin combines well with fennel, sage and rosemary. Lovage, which has deodorizing properties, can be mixed with marigold petals and elderflowers for a soft scented bath.

A strong infusion or a decoction of a single herb can be added directly to the bath water and is of benefit to the skin and body in a similar way to a sachet. Four cupfuls would be sufficient for an average-sized bath.

Compress This is a method of applying localized treatment using either an infusion or a decoction. It can be warm, but is usually applied cold. The infusion or decoction is left to cool then strained. A clean piece of lint or light towelling is dipped into it, the excess wrung out and the cloth immediately applied to the affected area. It should be left on for 15–20 minutes or until the heat of the body has warmed it up. Continue, using cool fresh compresses, until relief is obtained.

Cordial This is a medicine or drink which contains sugar and alcohol, so it can be kept for a period of time. There are a number of herbs which can be made into pleasant-tasting cordials and taken for digestive troubles, coughs, colds and other chest complaints. A cordial is usually made with one of the stronger-flavoured herbs such as peppermint, sage or thyme. Make a strong decoction of the herb, leave to cool then strain. Bring the decoction to the boil, remove from the heat and add sugar in the proportion of 2 tablespoons of sugar to ½ cup of cordial. The thinly-peeled rind of an orange or ½ lemon can be added if suited to the herb. Stir until the sugar has completely dissolved. Leave to cool, strain and add 2–3 tablespoons of Dutch gin. Pour the mixture into a stoppered bottle.

Decoction This method of extracting the active ingredients of the herbs is usually used for roots, stems and seeds. The root is placed in an enamel or stainless steel pan and covered with water. The water is brought to the boil and simmered for the specified time, usually about 10–15 minutes. After removing from the heat, the herb is left to steep for a further period of time or until cold. It is then strained before being used.

There are some herb leaves and flowers that can be made up as a decoction, for instance violet flowers or sage leaves. These are added to cold water, which is then brought to the boil and simmered for 3–4 minutes. The decoction is covered and left to steep for about 3 minutes before straining.

Face pack Make by mixing a strong herbal infusion with a thickening agent to form a paste. The strong infusion is made by pouring ½ cupful of boiling water on to 1–2 handfuls of herb. Leave to infuse for 15

PREPARING AN OINTMENT

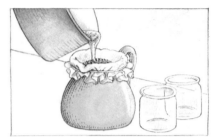

1 Melt 4 heaped tablespoons of pure lard, shortening or white petroleum jelly in an enamel pan.

2 Add the appropriate crushed herb to the lard or petroleum jelly and boil until it is crisp.

3 Strain through muslin or cheesecloth and pour it into small pots. Cover when completely cold.

minutes, strain and allow to cool. Fuller's earth, oatmeal or yoghurt can all be used to thicken the face pack. The herb can be added directly to yoghurt and left to permeate for 30 minutes before using. This may be too liquid if using an infusion and a little oatmeal mixed in will help to form a thicker paste.

To use a face pack, thoroughly cleanse the face. Spread the pack over the skin with fingers or a brush, avoiding the eyes and mouth. The eyes can be covered with cotton wool pads wrung out in cold water. Lie down and relax for 15–20 minutes. Remove the pack and wash the face with warm water, finishing by splashing the skin with cold water.

The herb used will depend upon the skin type or problem. If the skin is very oily the pack could include yarrow, parsley or elderflower. For large pores, horsetail and sage are effective and comfrey makes a soothing face pack for a dry skin. There are other ingredients which can be added: egg yolks are helpful for a dry, flaky skin, and honey in a fennel pack helps to smooth out wrinkles. Lemon juice is astringent and will help to tighten the pores in oily skins.

Fomentation This is similar to a poultice, and although less effective as a treatment it is easier to apply. It is a form of moist heat and used as a remedy to increase the flow of blood and thus relieve the affected area. As soon as the infusion or decoction has been made, strain it into a bowl standing over a pan of hot water. Have ready a piece of lint or towelling folded into the middle of a longer piece of cloth. Place the cloth containing the piece of lint in the bowl with the ends hanging over the sides. When thoroughly soaked twist the ends in opposite directions until the dripping has stopped. Quickly unfold the cloth and place the fomentation as hot as possible on to the painful spot. The fomentation can be renewed until relief is felt.

Footbath For tired, aching and swollen feet a daily footbath can bring soothing relief, help to regulate the flow of perspiration, or provide a tonic invigorating effect. A strong decoction of the appropriate herb is made by adding 2 cups of water to 2–3 handfuls of the herb. Leave to soak for a short while (the time depending on the individual herb), bring slowly to the boil and simmer gently for 15 minutes.

A strong infusion of some herbs is as effective as a decoction. Add boiling water to the herb and leave to steep for 10 minutes. Strain the decoction or infusion into a bowl and soak the feet for about 15 minutes. The effects of the footbath can be helped in some cases by putting them afterwards into a bowl of cold water. The feet should be carefully dried and rubbed with marigold oil to soothe and heal. Herbs for a footbath include horsetail, lavender and mugwort.

Herbal oil This is a simple remedy for many different ailments which will keep well over a long period of time if stored in a dark cool place. An oil can be made with fresh or dried leaves, flowers, petals, crushed stems or grated roots. Fill a wide-necked glass jar with the appropriate herb and cover the herb with almond, sunflower or olive oil (use almond oil if intending to use the preparation on your face). As a rough guide, the proportions should be 1 large handful of the herb to 1 cupful of oil. Cover the jar with a piece of muslin or cheesecloth secured with an elastic band and stand it on a sunny windowsill or in the greenhouse for 4–6 weeks, shaking the jar each day. After every 10 days, strain off the herb and pour the oil over a fresh batch of herb. Alternatively, as the herb sinks lower in the jar keep it topped up with fresh herb and shake to mix each time. Do this for 4–6 weeks. When the oil is ready strain through fine muslin or cheesecloth and pour into small screwtop bottles.

Infusion The process of making an infusion is similar to tea making. Boiling water is poured on to the fresh or dried herb and left to infuse, usually for 5–10 minutes, but it can vary according to the individual herb. The quantity most often used is 1–2 teaspoons of herb to 1 cup of boiling water. The cup should then be covered and the infusion left to stand for the required length of time. Strain through muslin or cheesecloth and use warm or cold. For a weak infusion, use half the amount stated and for a strong infusion use double the amount.

Cold infusions are used for herbs whose properties are destroyed by hot water. Pour on cold water and leave for 8, 12 or 24 hours according to the herb.

Medicinal syrup This is a solution of sugar boiled to prevent fermentation. A properly made syrup should keep for some weeks. Make a double strength infusion by pouring 2 cups of boiling water on to 4 handfuls of the herb. Leave it to infuse for 10–15 minutes according to the herb being used, or even until the infusion is cold. Strain into an enamel pan and add 8 tablespoons of sugar to 2 cups of infusion. Bring it to the boil and simmer for 20 minutes. When cold, pour into screw-top bottles and store in a cool place.

Roots or seeds should be grated or crushed and put in a pan with cold water in the ratio of 2 handfuls of herb to 4 cups of water. Leave to soak for 5–6 hours. Bring the mixture to the boil and simmer until reduced by half. Strain and add sugar as above.

When using a powdered herb, the syrup is made by adding 2 cups of sugar to 2 cups of water. Bring to the boil and simmer for 20 minutes, add 1–2 tablespoons of the powdered herb and simmer for a further few minutes before removing from the heat.

Pot pourri This is a combination of sweet-scented leaves, flowers, petals and spices which can be made either dry or moist. Dry pot pourri is placed in open bowls and the leaves and flowers should be carefully dried to preserve the brilliant colours of the flowers and the clear green of the leaves. The dried ground roots of orris or elecampane are added to act as a fixative, mingling with other scents to make them last longer. Spices can also be added and a few drops of an essential oil such as oil of bergamot. Moist pot pourri is kept in a china jar with a close-fitting lid and holes for the scents to escape. When stirred, the perfumes fill the room with fragrance.

For scented leaves, mix together the dried leaves of angelica, bergamot, costmary, lemon balm, lemon verbena, lovage, peppermint, rosemary, sage, sweet cicely, sweet marjoram and woodruff. Flowers and petals used are chamomile, cornflower, elderflower, lavender, lime flower, marigold petals, nasturtium flowers, rose petals and sweet violets.

Spices can be added to bring out further scents in the pot pourri; try aniseed, cinnamon stick, coriander seed and nutmeg. The cinnamon stick can be added in broken pieces, but all other spices should be freshly ground. Dried orange or lemon peel can also be added to the mixture.

A scented pot pourri brings the colour and fragrance of the herb garden into the home.
To make their scent last longer, pot pourri bowls and jars should be covered at night.

PREPARING A POULTICE

1 Take fresh or reconstituted dried herb, and crush or cook the chopped herb to a pulp.

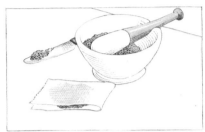

2 Spread the pulp carefully on to a piece of muslin or cheesecloth and fold over.

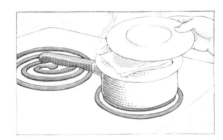

3 Put between two plates and heat over boiling water. Apply as hot as possible to the painful spot.

A dried pot pourri can be a grand mixture of any herbs, spices and oils or a simple bowl using only one or two herbs. To make a simple pot pourri take 1 handful of rosemary leaves and crush them together with 2 handfuls of lavender flowers. Add a handful of orris powder and start to fill a small bowl or jar with the mixture. Between spoonfuls add a few drops of oil of roses. Cover the container and leave in the dark for 2–3 days. Bring out and stir together with a wooden spoon to release the scents into the room.

A moist pot pourri is filled with leaves, flowers and petals, none of which needs to be fully dried, alternating with layers of kitchen salt (not iodized salt). Each layer should be pressed down and the whole process can take a period of months as the flowers and leaves are gathered at their best. Meanwhile the pot pourri is kept tightly closed. When the jar is full, the mixture is taken out and broken up into small pieces so that it can be mixed with spices and fixatives. Put back into the jar, cover closely and leave in a dark cool place to mature for up to 6 months. Pot-pourri should always be covered at night to preserve the perfume.

Tincture As these are made with alcohol in place of water they will keep for a long time. They are made using powdered herbs and the usual proportions are 2 tablespoons of herb to 1 cup of alcohol. Arnica is the exception, being made with fresh flowers. Powder the herb in a pestle and mortar or use an electric blender – it is best to use freshly ground dried herb. If medicinal or rubbing alcohol is unavailable vodka can be used. Put the alcohol and the powdered herb in an airtight jar. Leave in a warm place for 3–4 weeks, shaking the jar at least once a day. Strain through fine muslin or cheesecloth into a stoppered bottle. Dilute with water where recommended.

Toilet vinegar This provides a fragrant refreshing addition to the water when washing the face. White wine vinegar is the best to use, to which should be added highly aromatic herbs such as lavender, rose or lemon verbena. Fill a glass jar with the herb and cover it with white wine vinegar. Cover the jar with a piece of muslin or cheesecloth secured with an elastic band and stand it in a warm dark place for 2–3 weeks, shaking the jar once a day. Strain and repeat the process twice more, using the same vinegar and a fresh batch of herb. Finally, strain through fine muslin or cheesecloth and pour into a stoppered bottle. It will keep for a long time if stored in a cool place.

A bath vinegar can be made by adding 2 cups of cider vinegar to 2 cups of water in a pan and heating to very near boiling point. Remove from the heat and add 6 tablespoons of dried or chopped fresh herb. Cover and leave for a day before straining into a bottle. For an average bath, use 1 cupful.

STORAGE

The storage of herb preparations made in the home is important and varies according to the ingredients they contain. Infusions cannot be kept for longer than a few days and ideally should be stored in the refrigerator. The decoctions will keep for longer in a cool place but they lose their medicinal or cosmetic value after 7–10 days. They are stored in bottles or jars, preferably with a plastic screwtop, as herbs should not come into contact with a metal screwtop. Stoppered jars using either corks or plastic corks can be used with complete safety and are suitable for medicinal syrups, toilet vinegars, flower waters and herbal oils. Ointments and some medicinal oils which are not made in great quantity can be stored in small screwtop pots and all should be kept in a dark cool place.

A–Z

OF
HERBS

Mankind's knowledge of the culinary, cosmetic and
medicinal properties of herbs stretches back over
thousands of years. While the manner of their
usage may have altered to fit the times, many of
the herbs known today were familiar to the
Ancient Greeks. In the making of a herbal remedy,
the knowledge gained over centuries is still being
put to use today.

AGRIMONY

In ancient Greece, agrimony was believed to have magical powers, including that of healing the eyes. Later it was added to a mixture of herbs to heal wounds and treat snake bites.

Agrimonia Eupatoria
Published by Dr Woodville Oct.ᵗ 1 1791.

The common agrimony, *agrimonia eupatoria*, is a delicately scented perennial herb growing on waste land, by country lanes and in hedgerows. Common agrimony grows up to 3 ft (91 cms) high with stiff spikes of small yellow flowers. It flowers in summer and again in the autumn and as the flowers die and the petals drop there is left behind a dry woody burr which encloses the seed. This clings to clothing and animal fur to spread the seeds far and wide. The leaves consist of coarsely toothed leaflets growing thickly up the stems; soft hairs cover the whole plant. Common agrimony is not a plant for cultivation as the seeds have a poor germination, but it can readily be found growing wild.

The flowers and leaves are the parts mainly used in herbal medicine. For drying, the flowers must be gathered before the seeds have formed; the leaves can be picked at any time before the flowers bloom. They are then dried and stored in the usual way. Fresh leaves can be used for external applications.

MEDICINAL USE

Agrimony is an effective herb for coughs and chesty colds, but it has costive properties and is not a herb to be taken by those who suffer from constipation.

To make an infusion: *Pour 2 cups of boiling water over a handful of dried agrimony flowers and allow to cool. Strain and take a small glassful whenever the cough is troublesome.* It can also be used as a gargle.

To treat athlete's foot and other fungoidal attacks of the feet, plunge the feet into the bowl of agrimony infusion and sponge well between the toes. Afterwards dry the feet carefully between and underneath toes. Use a fresh infusion daily until cured.

A double strength infusion can also be used to relieve sprains or strained muscles.

To make a strong infusion: *Steep 2 handfuls of fresh or dried leaves in 2 cups of boiling water. Allow to cool, then strain and use.*

A LOE

The Greeks and Egyptians knew the value of aloe vera juice, using it in their medicines and cosmetic preparations. It is believed to have been used by Cleopatra to keep her complexion clear and soft.

L'aloe Commun.
Aloe vera X. Linn. Sp. Pl.

The aloe, *aloe vera*, is a very tall, strikingly attractive perennial plant which grows wild in the tropics, mainly of Africa and South America. Nowadays it is cultivated largely in the West Indies and in the hot climates of countries bordering the Mediterranean. In temperate climates it is cultivated as a houseplant.

An evergreen, succulent herb, the aloe has fleshy, spiny leaves which form a large rosette around the single stem. The flowers, which grow on slender spikes, are red or yellow and droop slightly when fully open; they bloom nearly all the year round in their native habitat. The leaves of the plant are filled with a yellow juice which contains the bitter-tasting drug aloes. The juice is extracted from two- or three-year-old plants and used in medicines and cosmetics.

Aloe can be grown in pots or tubs in a sunny greenhouse. It is a tough plant and in the summer can stand out of doors in a warm spot or in a sunny position indoors. Sow the seeds in a tray of sandy soil in a temperature of 70°F (21°C) and pot them on in March. Good drainage is important. Make sure the plants are moist through the summer months but do not overwater. In the winter they require very little watering. Keep at temperatures of 55–65°F (13–18°C) in the summer and between 50°F and 55°F (10°C and 13°C) in the winter.

MEDICINAL USE

For many years the aloe has been well known as a purgative, though, with its very bitter taste and tendency to cause griping, it has always been mixed with other ingredients. Painting finger nails with bitter aloes used to be a popular remedy for stopping nail-biting, as the taste is so unpleasant. The treatment was not always successful and is rarely used nowadays.

Aloe vera is a soothing and healing gel, disinfectant and astringent when used externally. It helps to keep the skin healthy by stimulating the circulation and promoting the growth of new tissue. Fresh aloe leaves can be split open and the jelly-like juice used as an instant remedy for minor cuts and burns, insect bites and sunburn. Take care when using plant leaves not to use the green part or the skin of the leaf, which may be irritant. Aloe vera medicinal preparations are available from homoeopathic chemists and stores.

BEAUTY CARE

One of the most valuable cosmetic properties of aloe vera is its ability to stimulate the circulation of the skin and remove the dead skin cells, so giving a fresher and younger appearance to the skin. It also clears away blemishes, protects the skin against infection, and reduces wrinkles. Aloe vera shampoos help to combat dry, brittle hair. Aloe vera creams, lotions and shampoos can be purchased at health food stores stocking natural beauty products.

Angelica Archangelica

ANGELICA

In the Middle Ages, when Europe was ravaged by the plague, an angel apparently came to a monk in a vision, telling him this herb would effect a cure – and ever since then, it has borne the name angelica.

Angelica, *angelica archangelica*, is a tall, sweet-scented, biennial herb, the leaves and stems carrying the fragrance and flavour. It is an attractive plant with large, deeply indented leaves and thick heavy stems. The small creamy-white flowers are clustered together at the top of short stems making large round umbels.

In the kitchen the young angelica stems, cleaned and chopped small, can be stewed with fruits such as rhubarb and gooseberries to soften their tart flavours. It improves the flavour of stewed pears, and a fresh leaf placed on the bottom of the dish of a baked custard adds a delicious flavour.

The angelica used in the home has always been a cultivated garden plant, though it does escape and can sometimes be found growing wild in damp meadows and beside streams. Angelica is an easy herb to grow in the garden, where it prefers good soil in a half shady position. In the spring buy in the initial angelica plant. Make sure the soil is deeply dug when planting out, for the roots of such a large herb grow down a long way. Water in well, and always water in dry weather as angelica is a moisture-loving plant. In the second year the herb comes into bloom, and unless the flowers are cut off before the seed is formed the plant will die, but will readily re-seed itself.

All parts of the herb except the flowerheads are used. Throughout the growing season and for so long as the plant does not flower, the leaves can be used fresh or for drying. May and June is the best time to cut the young leaf stalks, when they are soft and full of flavour. When the seed begins to form as the flower-head dies, tie a piece of muslin or cheesecloth loosely over the flower so the seeds, when ripe, will not be lost. In the autumn, after the plant has flowered, dig up the roots and dry them as rapidly as possible to retain the goodness. The roots are then stored in the usual way.

MEDICINAL USE

Angelica tea, made from the dried or fresh leaves, is a good remedy for indigestion and flatulence. It is a tonic herb, stimulating the appetite, and when taken over a number of days has a beneficial effect. It is also helpful for feverish colds.

To make angelica tea: *Use a teaspoon of the fresh or dried leaves and pour over ½ cup of boiling water. Leave to infuse for 5 minutes, strain and use. It can be sweetened with honey if desired. A small glassful of angelica tea can be taken 3 times a day and is best made fresh each time. Do not take the tea last thing at night as it may be too stimulating and cause sleeplessness.*

Angelica tea can also be made from the seeds or roots of the plant. *Crush 1 teaspoon of seeds, put them into an enamel pan and pour 1 cup of boiling water on top. Bring to the boil and simmer gently for 5 minutes. Strain at once and serve hot.* The same method is used for the grated roots.

For coughs and sore throats angelica syrup is both soothing and effective, and this can be made from the dried roots.

To make angelica syrup: *Pour 2 cups of boiling water over 2 handfuls of dried grated angelica root and add ½ cup of honey and a squeeze of lemon juice. Allow to stand, covered, until quite cold. Strain and bottle. Take 1–3 teaspoons for a sore throat or troublesome cough. Store the syrup in the refrigerator or a cold place and use within 3 days.*

An infusion (see page 15) of angelica seeds, when used as a mouthwash, will sweeten the breath and freshen the mouth.

BEAUTY CARE

To soothe the skin and to stop itching, a cold compress can be made of fresh angelica leaves, or use angelica ointment made from fresh or dried roots.

To make angelica ointment: *Slowly melt a small jar of white petroleum jelly in the top of a double boiler. Add a handful of crushed fresh angelica leaves and stir well together, using a wooden spoon. Leave to infuse over a very low heat for about 1 hour. Strain into small pots and leave. Cover when cold.*

The delicate fragrance of angelica leaves adds a soothing freshness to the skin when added to the bath water.

To make a herbal bath sachet: *Fill a square piece of muslin or cheesecloth with fresh or dried angelica leaves and tie the corners together with a long piece of string. Hang this bag from the tap (faucet) so that all the benefits of the angelica will be washed into the bath water. When in the bath, the little bag can be used to scrub the skin. Angelica roots cleaned and grated can be used in the same way, but it produces a brown liquid which does not look attractive.*

The dried leaves or dried grated roots give a fresh fragrance to a pot pourri (see page 15), though its scent is not as strong as other herbs.

CANDIED ANGELICA
Cut angelica stems into 2 inch (5 cm) lengths and soak over night in two cups of water and one tablespoon of salt. Drain, peel and wash them. Make a syrup using equal cups of sugar and water. Bring it slowly to the boil and boil gently for 10 minutes. Add the angelica and simmer until the angelica is clear. Drain the stems and when cold, store in an airtight container. Use the syrup for fruit salad or with rhubarb.

ANISE

Anise was used by the Romans both for medicinal purposes and to flavour a rich ceremonial cake, from which fruit wedding cakes are supposed to have derived. It was also known in ancient Egypt.

Anise, *pimpinella anisum*, is a dainty annual herb which is fairly short and has two sets of bright green leaves which look quite different from each other. The first, or basal, leaves are entire with saw-toothed edges; the secondary leaves are fern-like and feathery. The umbels of greeny-white flowers are small but numerous, and the little seeds begin to form in July.

Aniseed, or anise seed, is a well-known spice in the kitchen where its warm sweet biting flavour is used for cakes and pastries. It helps to reduce the tendency of vegetables such as cabbage, cucumber and onions to produce flatulence, and it adds flavour to, and helps in the digestion of, stewed fruit such as apples and pears. It is widely used in Indian curries.

Since Tudor times anise has been a cultivated spice in English gardens, but it was in the rest of Europe that anise was used much more, not only in cooking but also as a flavouring in cordials and liqueurs.

Anise grows best in dry light soil in a warm sunny position. In a cold damp summer the plant may not survive, but in a warm season anise grows well and produces plenty of seed. Sow anise seed in April in its flowering position. Thin out the seedlings when they are large enough to handle, leaving a handspan between each plant.

In August, when the green seeds begin to turn yellow, the plants are cut down, tied in bunches and hung upside down in loosely tied brown paper bags. In about a week they will be fully ripe and with a good shake of the bunch the seeds will all fall into the bag. They are then dried and stored in the usual way. When fully dry the seeds are a greyish brown. All the goodness and flavour of anise is concentrated in the

Pimpinella Anisum.

Published by D.? Woodville, Dec.? 1, 1792.

seeds and these are used medicinally and in cooking. The flavour is often used in medicines to mask an unpleasant taste.

MEDICINAL USE

Anise is an effective remedy for a hard dry cough and for chest infections. It is taken in the form of aniseed tea and this pleasant-tasting drink can also be given to children suffering from catarrh.

☛To make aniseed tea: *Pour 2 cups of boiling water over 1 rounded teaspoon of well crushed seeds, simmer gently for 5 minutes, then strain and serve immediately while still hot.*

☛Aniseed is good for the digestion, settling an upset stomach and relieving flatulence. It will also help to promote restful sleep if the aniseed tea is made using hot milk in place of water, then strained and taken warm last thing at night.

BEAUTY CARE

Crushed aniseed can be added to pot pourri, where it acts as a fixative, and the sweet spicy smell mingles with other scents.

ARNICA

Arnica grows wild in the mountains of Europe where the dried leaves used to be smoked as a kind of tobacco. Since early times it has been used in medicines for the heart.

Arnica, *arnica montana*, is for external use only. It should never be taken internally except under medical advice, as it is poisonous. It is, however, a useful herb in the home and an attractive perennial plant to grow in the garden. It is only rarely found in the wild in Great Britain, but it has long been a popular and effective remedy for minor ailments in countries where it has always grown wild. Arnica grows to medium height, the single hairy flower stem rising from a flat rosette of leaves. This stalk carries bright orange-yellow daisy-like flowers which are pleasantly aromatic. The rhizome is thick, curved and dark brown with threadlike roots on the underside.

Arnica grows well in a light acid soil with added peat. Sow the seed in early spring in a cool greenhouse and plant out in May in a shady spot in the garden. The rosette of leaves appears in the first year and the flowering stems in the second year. The flowerhead is the only part of the herb which is used; these are best when fresh, but dried flowers can be used when fresh are not available. The flowers are cut off when fully open, the green calyx is removed and the flower is then dried whole and stored in the usual way.

MEDICINAL USE

Arnica is used as a tincture to heal wounds and irritation.

To make the tincture: *Place 2 handfuls of the fresh flowers in a glass screwtop jar. Cover them with 2 cups of pure alcohol and seal. Leave the jar in the warm or on a sunny windowsill for a week or two, shaking it once a day. Filter the tincture through muslin or cheesecloth before using. If pure alcohol is unobtainable either vodka or surgical spirit can be substituted in its place.*

For phlebitis, bruises and contusions arnica is used in the form of a compress.

To make an arnica compress: *Mix together 2 cups of distilled water and I tablespoon of the tincture. Dip pieces of lint in the mixture and apply to the affected part. Renew the compress frequently.*

Arnica is also good for tired and aching feet.

To make an arnica footbath: *Put enough hot water in a bowl just to cover the feet and add half a cupful of the tincture. Immerse the feet for 10–15 minutes.*

BEAUTY CARE

In mild cases of hair loss, such as after an illness, arnica can help make the hair grow. Use a weak mixture of arnica tincture and water (*I tablespoon tincture to 2 cups distilled water*) and apply to the scalp once a day. Care should be taken by those with sensitive skins, and it is recommended that the solution is applied to a small patch of skin at first. If redness or soreness appears do not use the tincture.

B ARBERRY

Years ago barberry root bark was widely used to dye wool a lovely yellow, but the plant was mainly grown for the berries. Its country name of 'pipperidge bush', derived from 'pepon' a pip and 'rouge' red, describes the berries.

Berberis vulgaris

Barberry, *berberis vulgaris*, is a tall thorny shrub which used to grow wild in the hedgerows and on the edges of woodland. It was then discovered by farmers that barberry is a harmful plant when growing near wheatfields as it is host to wheat rust fungus which can damage the crop. Nowadays it is cultivated as an ornamental shrub in the garden. Barberry is a deciduous shrub which grows into a dense bush, with small spiny leaves growing in clusters up the stems. The golden yellow flowers have a strong, not unpleasant, smell and grow in hanging clusters from the axils of the leaves. The vivid scarlet berries which appear in the autumn are quite long and most attractive to look at, but have a rather sour taste.

In the kitchen, barberries can be used to make jams and jellies. The unusual flavour goes well with cold meats and game dishes.

Barberry can be propagated by seed, cuttings or layered root suckers, which is the most successful method. In October, bend the sucker down, cover with soil leaving only the tip showing, and use a stone or wire hook to keep it in place. It will root by the following autumn.

The berries and the bark of the root are both used medicinally, but the bark should only be used under strict medical supervision as it contains berberine which is very toxic. Gather the berries in the autumn when they are fully ripe and dry and store them in the usual way. The root can be gathered either in the spring or the autumn.

MEDICINAL USE

Barberries can be used in the home for mild disorders of the liver and the digestion. They relieve biliousness and are a mild laxative.

To make a drink using dried crushed barberries: *Soak a handful of the berries in 2 cups of water for a good hour. Bring the mixture to the boil then remove from the heat. Leave until it is just warm then strain, sweeten with a little honey and take a small glassful 2–3 times a day.*

Barberries are full of Vitamin C and a syrup or jelly made from the berries is an effective remedy for coughs and sore throats and is soothing for those suffering from tonsillitis.

To make barberry jelly using fresh berries: *Use equal quantities of washed berries and sugar. Place them in an enamel or stainless steel pan over a low heat. Stir frequently until the sugar has completely dissolved. A small bunch of sweet cicely leaves can also be added to remove some of the tartness of the fruit. Bring the mixture to the boil and boil rapidly for about 10–15 minutes until it reaches a jelly-like consistency. Strain quickly into warm sterilized jars and cover when the jelly has cooled.*

BERGAMOT

Bergamot is a native plant of North America where the wild plant, monarda fistulosa, *is also widely used. Bergamot tea was popular with the North American Indians of the Oswego area and thus came to be known as Oswego tea.*

MONARDA DIDYMA L.
Die zweyknöpfichte Monarde.

Bergamot, *monarda didyma*, has brilliant scarlet flowers which, together with its lovely fragrant scent, make it a popular plant in the garden. It is a perennial herb with creeping roots which grows to about medium height. The rough, serrated leaves smell strongly of mint when bruised and grow in pairs up the stem with the flowers blooming in whorls at the top. Bergamot flowers from July through to September; the flowers often vary in colour from the scarlet which is true *monarda didyma* through purple, lavender, pink and white. The flowers and leaves can be added fresh to salads, wines and fruit drinks. Bergamot leaves can be used in place of mint for cooking with new potatoes and in sauces. The fresh or dried leaves make a refreshing drink.

The first bergamot plant must be bought from a herb nursery, but thereafter it can be propagated by rooted cuttings taken in early summer or by division of the roots in the autumn. It is best to divide bergamot each year because the middle of the plant dies away, leaving the young strong shoots on the outside. In the spring, plant bergamot in partial shade in moist rich soil and keep it watered in dry spells.

The vivid red flowers and the leaves are the parts of the plant which are used, either fresh or dried. Both flowers and leaves are dried whole. They are then stored in the usual way.

MEDICINAL USE
Bergamot tea, made with fresh or dried flowers, is a pleasant, aromatic and relaxing drink. Its fragrant minty flavour is equally good hot or cold and it can be sweetened with honey.

To make bergamot tea: *Pour a cupful of boiling water on to a small handful of flowers. Leave to infuse for 5 minutes then strain and use.*

Bergamot milk, taken at night, is a very good sedative.
To make bergamot milk: *Pour a cup of boiling milk on to a small handful of chopped fresh or dried leaves. Leave to infuse for about 5 minutes then strain.*

A bergamot pillow has a calming effect on the nerves.

BEAUTY CARE
Dried bergamot flowers and leaves add lasting colour and fragrance to pot pourris.

BLESSED THISTLE

In the Middle Ages this handsome member of the thistle family was used in the treatment of many diseases. Holy powers were attributed to the herb and it thus came to be known as the Holly or Blessed Thistle.

Centaurea Benedicta

Published by Dr. Woodville Sept. 1. 1790.

Blessed thistle, *cnicus benedictus*, is an attractive annual herb grown as an ornamental plant in the garden, though it can be found growing in the wild as a garden escape. Blessed thistle has long, narrow, prickly leaves ending in spine; they are mostly variegated with deep white veins. The stem grows to medium height with many branches, which bear pale yellow flowers encased in a prickly calyx in July. The whole plant is covered with soft hairs.

As an annual, blessed thistle is propagated in the spring by sowing the seed in ordinary garden soil, where you wish the plant to flower. Thin the seedlings to 12 in (30 cm) apart.

The whole herb is used medicinally and can be used fresh or dried. To dry, gather the leaves and flowering tops in July when the plant is just coming into flower. Dry and store in the usual way.

MEDICINAL USE

Blessed thistle is mostly used as a tonic and is taken as a cold infusion. It stimulates the appetite and is good for indigestion and for settling mild liver disorders. A warm infusion can be given to nursing mothers to stimulate the flow of milk. A small glassful of a hot infusion of blessed thistle taken last thing at night will help to increase perspiration and so reduce a fever. Avoid using a strong infusion as it will act as an emetic and do not take the herb during pregnancy. Large doses of blessed thistle can irritate the mouth, digestive tract and kidneys and should be used with care.

To make an infusion: *Pour 2 cups of boiling water over a handful of the dried herb and allow it to stand for 10 minutes before straining and drinking warm, or leave to get completely cold.* To stimulate the appetite take a small glassful twice a day before meals. The infusion also helps to prevent giddiness.

The juice of blessed thistle leaves rubbed on to the forehead will ease a headache or migraine and if sips of cold infusion are taken at the same time it will help to prevent feelings of nausea. Care must be taken not to get the juice anywhere near the eyes.

A compress made by dipping pieces of lint into a strong decoction of the herb is helpful in soothing irritable skin.

To make the decoction: *Use 1 part dried herb to 2 parts of water, bring to the boil and simmer very gently for 10 minutes. Strain and pour into a bottle. Store in the refrigerator.*

BORAGE

A plant from the shores of the Mediterranean, borage has been known for centuries for lifting the spirits. Traditionally borage is added to drinks and salads to provide a refreshing and invigorating tonic.

Borage officinalis

Borage, *borago officinalis*, is a very attractive annual herb, with a profusion of bright blue star-shaped flowers and large wrinkled leaves. A cultivated garden plant, it is covered all over with stiff hairs, making the leaves feel quite prickly. The herb grows to medium height, with a hollow succulent stem which tends to flop over when all the leaves and flowers are out and it becomes top heavy. It may occasionally be found growing on waste ground.

The fresh leaves have a cucumber-like scent and flavour and are mostly used nowadays to decorate Pimms drinks or in wine or cider cups. You can also add them to pickles or to a pea or bean soup. The flowers can be used as a pretty addition to salads or candied to decorate ice creams.

Borage is a very easy herb to grow even though it is an annual because it self-seeds freely and will come up again year after year. Sow the seed in the spring where it is to flower and thin the seedlings to 12 in (30 cm) apart. It prefers a sunny position.

The leaves, and to a lesser extent the flowers, are the parts used medicinally and in cosmetics. Borage leaves do not dry successfully unless very young, but the flowers dry well, retaining their lovely colour.

MEDICINAL USE

Borage is a herb well known for lifting mild depression after an illness and for reducing a fever.

To make borage leaf tea: *Pour a cup of boiling water on to 1 or 2 teaspoons of chopped fresh leaves. Cover and leave to infuse for 5 minutes then strain. Add honey for sweetening and take a small glassful 3–4 times a day until relief is obtained.*

To make borage flower tea: *Add 2 teaspoons of the fresh flower to a cup of boiling water. Simmer gently for about 1–2 minutes then remove from the heat. Leave to infuse for a little while longer then strain the tea and serve.*

A hot poultice made from crushed fresh borage leaves will help to relieve the pain of gout and inflamed swellings.

To make a poultice: *Crush the leaves well and heat them by putting them between 2 plates over a pan of boiling water. For those with a sensitive skin the pulp can be placed between 2 pieces of cloth to prevent direct contact with the skin. Bandage the poultice lightly in place and keep renewing it when it gets cold until relief is felt.*

BEAUTY CARE

Borage can help to clear the skin of troublesome spots.

To make a lotion: *Mix together equal quantities of the juice of dandelion, watercress and borage. Clean the face and gently smooth the mixture over the affected parts. Allow to dry completely before washing the face again. Always prepare a fresh juice mixture for each application.*

B URDOCK

Burdock was a popular herb in folk medicine and the seeds, hung in a bag around the neck, were commonly believed to protect the wearer against rheumatism.

Arctium Lappa.
Publish'd by D.ʳ Woodville March 1, 1790.

Burdock, *arctium lappa*, is a tall, attractive, wild plant growing along country lanes, on waste ground and near populated areas. A biennial herb, it produces only the large basal leaves in the first year; during the second year thick branched stems grow from the root and the whole plant is covered with fine hairs. Loose clusters of deep maroon flowers bloom from July to September. The fruits or burrs appear soon after and these stick firmly to clothing and animal fur, so being carried quite a distance.

Burdock thrives in light well-drained soil in a sunny spot. The fast-germinating seed is sown in spring or autumn where it is to flower and the seedlings thinned to a handspan apart.

The roots from the first year's growth and the leaves both have medicinal qualities, but the leaves are used internally to a lesser extent because of their bitter taste. The roots grow quite large and in July can be lifted and dried in the usual way.

MEDICINAL USE

Burdock tea made from the root is considered in herbal medicine to be one of the best blood purifiers.
☛To make burdock tea: *Simmer a small handful of chopped root in 2 cups of water for 30 minutes.*

A decoction of burdock root is a remedy for mild stomach ailments.
☛To make a decoction of burdock root: *Soak a teaspoon of grated fresh root in a cup of water for about an hour then bring it to the boil. Immediately remove from the heat, strain and take a small glassful when needed.*

☛For painful joints, poultices of fresh leaves (see page 16) applied to the affected parts will help to bring relief. At the same time a decoction of the fresh root, mixed with milk and honey to taste, can be drunk cold a small glassful at a time. For bruises and contusions poultices of fresh burdock leaves boiled in salted water for a few minutes are effective in reducing the inflammation.

BEAUTY CARE

Burdock is a cleansing, purifying herb and a decoction of the root used as a lotion will help to clear a spotty skin.
☛To make a decoction for acne: *Bring a small handful of fresh or dried root to the boil in 3 cups of water. Boil until 2 cups remain then strain and leave to cool. Store the lotion in the refrigerator. Use the lotion on the face night and morning.* A small glassful of burdock decoction can be taken internally to assist in clearing the skin.

For dandruff and falling hair apply the lotion daily, massaging gently into the scalp. Do not use if the scalp is sore or irritated, or if there is persistent dandruff. A doctor should be consulted in these cases.

C*ALAMINT*

In the past calamint was used to calm hysterical outbursts – the sufferer was given calamint conserve to sip and a posy of the herb was tucked into the bodice so that the strong minty scent would help to clear the head.

Calamint, *calamintha officinalis*, is a delightful hardy perennial which grows along the hedgerows and country lanes in dry places. It is a bushy plant, covered with soft hairs and growing about 12 in (30 cm) high. Small rosy-purple flowers grow out of the leaf axils and these bloom in July and August. Calamint is an insignificant little plant not easily found in the wild, but it grows well in the garden and has a lovely minty smell.

Sow calamint seed out of doors in April where it is to flower, thinning the seedlings to a hand's width apart. Once established, further plants can be raised by taking root cuttings in March.

Flowering tops and leaves are the parts of the herb which are used, either fresh or dried. In July the plant is dried and stored in the usual way.

MEDICINAL USE

Calamint is a highly aromatic herb and a cordial tea is helpful in the treatment of colds and influenza as it promotes perspiration. It is also a remedy for flatulence and upset stomachs.

To make calamint cordial: *Boil fresh or dried calamint leaves with honey and a teaspoon of lemon juice. Use 2 tablespoons clear honey and crush as many leaves as possible into it in the pan, add the lemon juice and bring the mixture slowly to the boil. Simmer for 5 minutes then remove from the heat and leave to cool. Strain and store in a screwtop bottle. Dilute to taste with hot water.*

For stiff muscles, place crushed fresh calamint leaves on the affected part and secure with a bandage. Leave it in place until the muscle returns to normal.

A preserve made of the fresh young calamint tops is a remedy for nervous disorders.

Crushed fresh leaves held under the nose like old-fashioned smelling salts will clear the head and revive those who feel faint.

BEAUTY CARE

Dried calamint, both flowering tops and leaves, has a strong enduring scent and can be mixed in with other herbs in a pot pourri. It can also be used for a refreshing aromatic bath.

To make a herbal bath sachet: *Take a handful of fresh calamint leaves (half the amount if dried) and mix with an equal quantity of other herbs such as lemon balm or rosemary. Tie the herbs in a piece of muslin or cheesecloth and hang it from the bath tap (faucet) so that the water pours down through the cloth. When in the bath you can use the bag as a fragrant massage pad to rub down the skin.*

Carum Carvi.

CARAWAY

Caraway has been in medicinal use since ancient times:
Dioscorides, Greek physician of the first century AD,
wrote that caraway oil was a good tonic for girls pale of face.

Caraway, *carum carvi*, is a highly aromatic biennial herb with feathery leaves and a long thick root like a parsnip. The slender stalks grow to a medium height and the tiny white flowers are clustered in loose umbels at the top. They bloom in May and June of the second year. The flowers, which have very little scent, are followed by the brown fruits, each one of which contains two caraway seeds. It is the seeds which have the distinctive, warm, spicy caraway flavour, which is especially noticeable when the seeds are bruised.

In the kitchen, caraway is used in a wide variety of both sweet and savoury dishes, helping in the digestion of rich foods. It is a popular spice for breads and rolls and is good with rich poultry such as goose. A pinch of caraway seed added to cabbage when cooking gives a pleasant flavour and removes the harsh smell of the cabbage; it is always added when cabbage is salted down to make sauerkraut. The roots provide an unusual but wholesome vegetable. Caraway seed is perhaps most often used in cakes and buns, and particularly in apple pie; old-fashioned seed cake, which used to be a familiar sight on the tea table, is made with caraway – hence its name. Along with other flavourings, caraway is used in the making of liqueurs – especially Kümmel.

Caraway is an easy plant to grow, but the seed must be absolutely fresh and ripe to germinate successfully. Sow in the autumn and choose a sunny spot in light well-drained soil. Thin the seedlings when large enough to handle to a handspan apart and protect them through the winter with a good mulch. They will flower the following August. Seed sown in March will grow about 12 in (30 cm) high in the first year and to its full height in the second, flowering year. Caraway readily self-sows if some of the flower-heads are left to mature on the plants.

As soon as the seed has set and the fruits containing the seed have turned brown they are ready to be harvested. The seed should be gathered while the plants are still wet with the early morning dew for, when they are dry, the seeds fall from the plant and are lost. The whole seedhead should be cut off and placed upside down in a paper bag, where they will soon dry out and fall into the bag. The seeds are then dried and stored in the usual way. After flowering the whole plant dies and the roots can be dug up.

MEDICINAL USE

Caraway provides a pleasant remedy for indigestion and flatulence – for quick relief, chew caraway seeds as soon as discomfort is felt.

Caraway seeds are an important ingredient of seed tea and for this are mixed with equal quantities of aniseed and fennel seeds. It is a good remedy for flatulence.

To make the tea: *Crush the seeds finely to release the flavour. Put 1 teaspoonful of the seeds into an enamel pan and pour 1 cup of boiling water over them. Simmer gently over a low heat for 10 minutes. Strain quickly and take a small glassful after the meal until the discomfort has passed.*

Caraway is a strong spicy herb with a pleasant taste and it is used to disguise unpleasant medicines – especially for children. Caraway water can be made as a mild remedy for children with upset tummies.

To make caraway water: *Soak a handful of well-crushed caraway seed in 1 cupful of mineral water for 6 hours. Strain through a piece of muslin or cheese-cloth into stoppered bottles and store in the refrigerator. Use within a few days. Give the child 1–2 teaspoonfuls as needed.*

A decoction of caraway seed makes an effective mouthwash to sweeten the breath. It can also be used as a gargle to soothe a sore throat.

To make a decoction: *Add 2 teaspoons of crushed seed to ½ cup of water in an enamel pan. Bring to the boil and simmer for 3–4 minutes. Remove from the heat and leave to infuse for a further 10 minutes. Strain and use warm or cold.*

A caraway poultice is a soothing remedy for earache.

To make a caraway poultice: *Bruise and crush a handful of caraway seed and put in a pan with a very little water. Heat the seeds until they have absorbed the water and become a pulpy mush. Spread the pulp between 2 pieces of warm cloth and gently hold the poultice over the ear until relief is obtained. Reheat the poultice if necessary. The same poultice can be used on a painful bruise.*

BEAUTY CARE

Caraway is a disinfectant herb and is used in the making of soaps. It makes a good skin cleanser for those who prefer using soap and water on their faces.

Well-dried caraway seed ground to a powder in a pestle and mortar gives a spicy fragrance to pot pourri and herb pillows and helps to fix the scents.

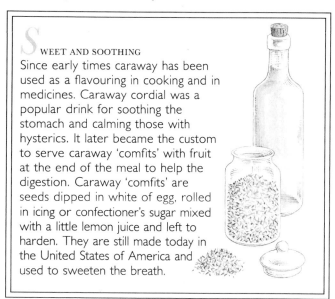

SWEET AND SOOTHING
Since early times caraway has been used as a flavouring in cooking and in medicines. Caraway cordial was a popular drink for soothing the stomach and calming those with hysterics. It later became the custom to serve caraway 'comfits' with fruit at the end of the meal to help the digestion. Caraway 'comfits' are seeds dipped in white of egg, rolled in icing or confectioner's sugar mixed with a little lemon juice and left to harden. They are still made today in the United States of America and used to sweeten the breath.

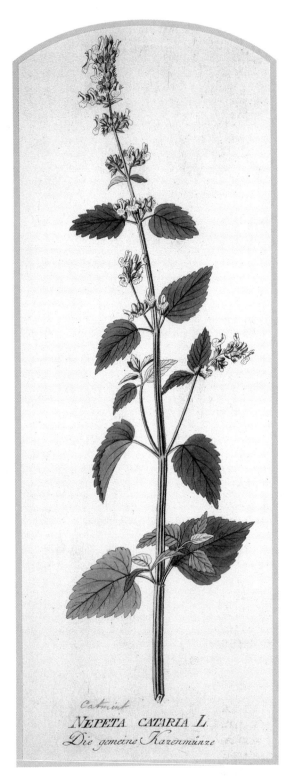

Catmint

NEPETA CATARIA L
Die gemeine Karenmünze

CATNEP

For centuries catnep has been grown in France where the young leaves and new shoots have traditionally been used as a flavouring.

Catnep, *nepeta cataria*, is a perennial wild plant growing on waste ground and along hedgerows in dry chalk or gravelly soil. It is a handsome herb which grows up to 3 ft (91 cm) tall with heartshaped crinkly leaves covered with a soft down. The little two-lipped flowers cluster thickly at the top of the stems, forming spikes; they vary in colour from pale pink with red spots to completely white. They bloom from June through to September and the whole plant has a delightful minty scent very similar to pennyroyal.

Catnep is sometimes called catmint but it must not be confused with *nepeta faassenii*, which has blue grey leaves and purple flowers. The catmint *nepeta faassenii* has a strong coarse aroma and the only similarity between the two plants is that cats love them and delight in rolling in them.

Catnep is a very easy herb to grow in any garden soil in sun or shade, though it is more fragrant if planted in the sun. In the spring catnep can be propagated either by dividing established plants or by sowing seed. Sow the seed where the herb is to flower and when the seedlings are large enough thin them out to about 12 in (30 cm) apart. The plants need little attention and will thrive for several years.

The leaves and flowering tops are the parts of the herb used in the home. The flowering tops are cut in August when the plant is in full bloom; leaves for drying can be picked at any time before the plant begins to flower. Dry and store in the usual way.

MEDICINAL USE

Catnep is full of Vitamin C and makes a pleasant-tasting healthy drink. Catnep tea is a good drink for those with feverish colds as it helps to increase perspiration and acts as a mild sedative. It will also help to settle an upset stomach and relieve flatulence.

To make catnep tea: *Pour ½ cup of boiling water on to 1 teaspoon of fresh chopped or dried catnep. Infuse for only 2–3 minutes before straining it and add honey to sweeten. Take a small glassful, either hot or warm, last thing at night.*

Chewing catnep leaves is said to be helpful in relieving toothache.

A decoction of catnep flowering tops is effective in clearing dandruff.

To make the decoction: *Add 3 tablespoons of flowering tops to 2 cups of water in an enamel saucepan. Bring to the boil and simmer for 15 minutes. Use as a lotion and rub well into the scalp. Store the lotion in a screwtop bottle in a cool place or in the refrigerator and use within a few days.*

CENTAURY

Centaury was known to the old herbalists as 'Earth Gall' because of its bitter taste. The name centaury was said to come from the Greek Centaur Chiron who, when wounded by a poisoned arrow, was cured by using the herb.

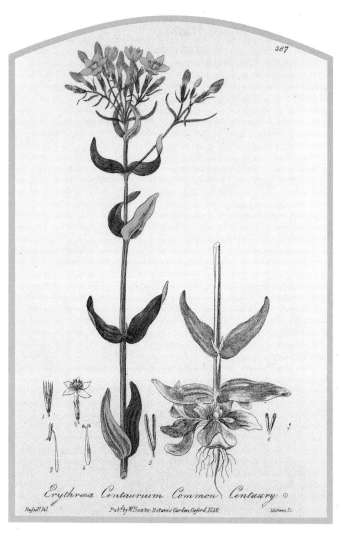

Erythræa Centaurium Common Centaury

Centaury, *centaurium umbellatum*, is an attractive annual herb with small rosy-pink flowers and sharply pointed green leaves. The sturdy, square stems grow from a rosette of leaves at the base to a height of 10–14 in (25–35 cm). It is found at the edges of dry fields and country lanes and on the slopes of chalky hills. The flowers bloom from July to October, only opening in fine weather and never after midday. Centaury can be easily found growing in the wild and is considered to be a tiresome weed in the garden so it is rarely cultivated – though it can be grown successfully.

The whole plant is cut off just above the ground immediately before the flowers bloom in July or August. It is then dried and stored in the usual way.

MEDICINAL USE

Centaury is a good tonic herb with a bitter taste. An infusion taken before meals will stimulate the appetite and help the digestion. Other herbs such as mint or angelica can be added to the infusion to counteract the bitterness. It is also a remedy for mild stomach disorders and for heartburn.

To make centaury infusion: *Pour 2 cups of boiling water over a handful of dried leaves. Leave to infuse for 5 minutes then strain.*

Centaury makes a good tonic wine, which is also slightly laxative.

To make centaury wine: *To 1 bottle of dry white wine add a large handful of fresh centaury and a few juniper berries. Leave to soak for a week, then strain the wine and sweeten it with honey. Take a small glassful before meals.*

A decoction of dried centaury is helpful for varicose veins and, applied daily to the scalp, is a remedy for falling hair.

To make the decoction: *Add 3 handfuls of herb to 2 cups of water. Bring slowly to the boil and simmer for 5 minutes. Leave the mixture until it is cold then strain. Use the decoction in the form of a compress on varicose veins.*

BEAUTY CARE

A decoction of centaury makes a good cleansing lotion for the skin. Each day the face should be washed in the lotion then left to dry naturally. This will help to clear the skin of spots and blemishes and will fade freckles. The skin will appear smoothed and softened as a result of regular use.

To make the decoction: *Use a handful of the herb to 1 cup of water. Bring to the boil and simmer for 5 minutes. Leave until cold, then strain and pour the lotion into a stoppered jar. Keep the lotion in the refrigerator. Discard any remaining and make a fresh decoction every 3 days.*

CHAMOMILE

Long ago chamomile was grown all round herb gardens in the belief that it would keep other plants growing near free from disease, and it was known as the 'Plant's Physician.'

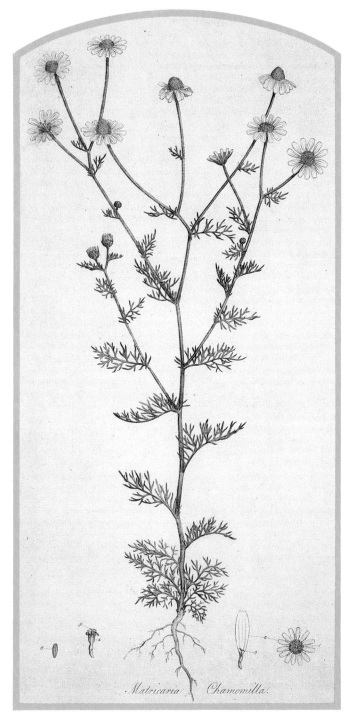

Matricaria Chamomilla.

The wild German chamomile, *matricaria chamomilla*, is a delightfully fragrant herb which grows in profusion by gravel pits and on waste lands. It will thrive anywhere if it is left undisturbed and can self-sow freely. Chamomile is an annual herb and can grow up to about 2 ft (61 cm) high. The stems are branched with delicate, fern-like leaves. The little flowers are white and rather like a daisy, but have a domed yellow centre or receptacle. This receptacle is hollow and is a distinguishing feature of the German chamomile. When the flower is in full bloom the petals grow downwards, showing the domed receptacle very clearly, so there need be no mistake when gathering wild chamomile flowers. The sweetly-scented herb blooms from June to September.

Chamomile is a very easy annual to grow and once established will readily self-seed, coming up in the same place year after year. Sow the seeds during May in their flowering position in dry sandy soil, choosing a sunny spot. When large enough, thin out the seedlings to a hand's width apart. The thinned seedlings can be planted out too, though they will suffer a check and produce their flowers towards the end of the season.

The flowers are the only part of the plant which is used in the home. Picking them is a laborious task but is well worthwhile. Not all the flowers are ready to be picked at once, so a daily cutting of those that are ready has to be done. Dry and store in the usual way.

MEDICINAL USE

Chamomile tea is a well-known herbal drink which is good for settling the stomach, especially after a heavy meal. For a sluggish digestion, flatulence and other digestive complaints chamomile tea is more effective if taken before a meal. Sachets of dried chamomile can be bought ready for tea-making from health food shops but the tea can be made equally well from home-grown chamomile and is most delicious.

To make chamomile tea: *Pour ½ cup of boiling water over 2 teaspoons of dried flowers. Leave to infuse for 5–10 minutes before straining. Add honey to sweeten and drink the tea warm.* Take last thing at night to calm the system and promote sleep.

Chamomile is a remedy for migraines, influenza and fevers, as it helps to increase perspiration. A strong cold infusion can be drunk, a small glassful at a time.

To make a stronger infusion: *Pour I cup of boiling water over 2 heaped tablespoons of fresh or dried flowers. Leave to infuse for about an hour, then strain. Add honey and lemon juice if preferred.*

For skin infections such as eczema: *Use an infusion made with 2 handfuls dried flowers and I cup of distilled water. Bring slowly to the boil, then remove from the heat and leave it to infuse for 20 minutes. Strain and add this infusion to the bath water or use as a compress over the affected part, renewing it frequently until the itching is relieved.*

Chamomile oil is a valuable remedy for attacks of cramp, for rheumaticky pains and for loss of voice.

To make chamomile oil: *Pour 2 cups of olive or sunflower oil into a wide-necked screwtop jar and add 3–4 handfuls of freshly picked chamomile flowers. Push the flowers well down into the oil, cover with a piece of muslin or cheesecloth and stand the jar on a sunny windowsill for 3 days. Remove the lid and stand the jar in a saucepan half-filled with water. Bring the water to the boil and let it simmer for 2–3 hours, stirring the oil every now and then and pressing the flowers well down. Do not let the oil boil. Strain the oil through a piece of fine muslin or cheesecloth into screwtop bottles, and store in a cool place.* Use the oil as a hot friction rub for cramp and mild rheumatic pains. For loss of voice use the warm oil as a compress; dip a piece of lint in the oil, gently squeeze out the excess and wrap it round the throat.

BEAUTY CARE

Chamomile is a cosmetic herb widely known for its soothing, softening properties.

To make a suburn lotion: *Take a small handful of flowers and simmer them gently in ½ cup of milk for 5–10 minutes. Strain and bathe the affected part until relief is obtained.*

For skin which feels rough and coarse, bathe the face night and morning with chamomile lotion.

To make chamomile lotion: *Add I large handful of the herb to I ½ cups of distilled water in an enamel saucepan. Bring to the boil and simmer gently for 10 minutes. Leave to cool, and strain into screwtop bottles. Store in a cool place or in the refrigerator.* The same lotion is good for sensitive skins and will help to keep the hands smooth and soft if the lotion is used every time the hands are washed.

For tired eyes and puffy eyelids the lotion, made as above and used in the form of a compress, will refresh the eyes and reduce the puffiness. Add chamomile lotion to the bath water to soothe the nerves and to soften the skin.

A chamomile facial steam is an effective treatment for blackheads.

To make a facial steam: *Place a handful of chamomile flowers in a bowl and cover them with boiling water. Cover both head and bowl in a towel and steam the face for about 10 minutes. Wipe down the face with clean cotton wool pads or balls and close the pores by splashing with distilled water.*

Treat tired and weary feet to a warm and fragrant chamomile footbath.

To make a chamomile footbath: *Mix together 2 parts each of chamomile and marjoram and I part each of rosemary and thyme. Make up a decoction using 2 tablespoons of the herb mixture with 5 cups of water. Bring to the boil and simmer for 5 minutes. Strain the decoction into the footbath and when cool enough immerse the feet for 15–20 minutes. Dry the feet carefully afterwards.*

Chamomile flowers add colour and fragrance to pot pourris and make a soothing herb pillow. Add a few drops of chamomile oil to dried chamomile flowers for a herb pillow to prevent the flowers crackling and to give a longer-lasting fragrance.

G OLDEN HAIR RINSE
Chamomile is a mild bleach and gives blonde hair a golden sheen. Pour 2 cups of boiling water over 2 handfuls of chamomile and leave to infuse for 30 minutes. Shampoo and rinse as normal then pour the chamomile rinse over several times. If possible use while still warm.

C HERVIL

In medieval times chervil was considered to be one of the important Lenten herbs. The leaves were eaten along with several other herbs to clear the body of winter ills and ailments.

Chervil, *anthriscus cerefolium*, is a small annual herb with a soft mild flavour. The branched flowering stem grows up to 18 in (46 cm) high with soft green fern-like leaves, which tend to turn pink at the edges if the plant is in full sun. Most of the leaves grow very close to the ground. The little white flowers are insignificant and grow in flat umbels at the top of the stem, blooming from May to July.

Chervil has such a delicate taste that it is much used in the kitchen to add flavour to salads, omelettes and many other dishes. Hot chervil soup is a warming drink in the winter or when chilled makes a refreshing summer first course to a meal.

Chervil is an easy herb to grow, though it is best to treat the plant as a biennial and sow freshly ripened seed in the autumn. Autumn-sown seed provides leaves for use very early in the year. Sow the seed in a sheltered spot in semi-shade where the plants are to flower. It will grow in ordinary garden soil in a damp position. Seed can also be sown in the spring to produce leaves in the same year. The flowers, which quickly appear, can be cut off to allow all the goodness to be concentrated in the leaves, but if some are left to go to seed chervil will freely self-sow.

Cut chervil for drying before the flowers bloom; dry and store it in the usual way. Dried chervil is useful for the winter months but in the summer it is always best to use fresh chervil.

MEDICINAL USE

Chervil is a purifying herb. It stimulates the digestive system and is a helpful remedy for mild liver and kidney disorders.

Fresh crushed chervil leaves used in the form of a poultice will relieve painful haemorrhoids, bruises and rheumatic joints.

☞To make a chervil poultice: *Mash the leaves to a pulp with a little moistened bread or put the leaves in the electric blender. Spread the pulp on to a very hot wet cloth and apply directly to the skin. Wrap another cloth around the first to retain moisture and heat.*

BEAUTY CARE

Chervil lotion keeps the skin soft and supple and helps to ward off early wrinkles. A compress can be used to soothe tired eyes and puffy eyelids.

☞To make a decoction for the lotion and compress: *Use 2 handfuls of the herb to 3 cups of distilled water. Bring the mixture to the boil slowly then remove from the heat and leave to infuse for 30 minutes. Afterwards strain into screwtop bottles. The lotion will keep for a few days stored in a cool place or in the refrigerator.*

Stellaria media.

CHICKWEED

In former times the prolific chickweed was a popular green vegetable sold by itinerant street vendors. It was eaten like spinach and said to taste just as good.

Chickweed, *stellaria media*, is a very common wild herb which grows in abundance all over England in gardens, fields, along country lanes and in waste places. Its creeping root system enables it to spread quickly and easily over the ground, especially where the soil is rich. Chickweed is a low-growing plant with small, soft, brilliant green leaves and tiny white star-shaped flowers. The flowers are in bloom for many months in the year.

Chickweed is so easily found that it can be used fresh for most of the year but it can be dried successfully for use in the winter months. The whole herb is gathered for drying between May and July. Care must be taken when drying chickweed as the soft leaves and delicate stems soon shrivel up if there is too much heat. It is then stored in the usual way.

MEDICINAL USE

Chickweed is known for its laxative properties and, taken occasionally is good for mild constipation.

To make a decoction: *Add a handful of fresh chopped chickweed to 1 cup of water. Bring to the boil and simmer for 4 minutes. Strain and drink warm.*

An infusion made with dried chickweed is an effective remedy for coughs, hoarseness and a sore throat.

To make an infusion: *Pour 1 cup of boiling water over 1 tablespoon of herb. Infuse for 10 minutes, strain and cool. Sip when the cough is troublesome.*

For bruises, chilblains, heat rash and other skin irritations a chickweed ointment is effective.

To make chickweed ointment: *Wash 2 handfuls of freshly cut chickweed. Melt 4 heaped tablespoons of lard or shortening in an enamel pan and add the chickweed, mixing well. Bring slowly to the boil. Simmer for 20 minutes, strain into pots and cover when cold.*

BEAUTY CARE

Chickweed tea is said to be helpful in a slimming programme, when a small glassful may be taken first thing in the morning. Make the infusion fresh each day and do not take it for longer than a few days.

To make chickweed tea: *Pour ½ cup of boiling water on to 1 teaspoon of dried herb and leave to stand for 10 minutes before straining it.*

Chickweed lotion helps to clear and refine the skin. Use night and morning on a cleansed face.

To make the lotion: *Pour 2 cups of boiling distilled water on a handful of herb. Cool. Strain into screwtop bottles. Keep in the refrigerator and use within 3 days.*

C HICORY

The name chicory is believed to be of Egyptian origin, but it was the Romans who relished the plant as a cooked vegetable or in salads and who took the herb with them into their conquered lands.

Cichorium Intybus

Chicory, *cichorium intybus*, is a tall, attractive, wild herb which grows on chalk or sandy soils by country lanes, in open fields, and on waste places. Chicory is a perennial herb and has a long tap root similar to a dandelion. It grows stiffly upright to a height of 2–3 ft (61–91 cm). The leaves on the branching stems are small and sparse, while the basal leaves are large and spreading. The flowers are a lovely brilliant blue, the shape and size of a dandelion, and they bloom from July until September. They open early in the morning but are always closed by midday.

In the kitchen, chicory root is sliced, dried and ground for adding to coffee blends. Young leaves are used in salads but are usually blanched before eating.

Chicory is a hardy plant and easy to grow in a sunny spot in ordinary garden soil. Sow the seed in May and, when large enough, thin the seedlings to a hand's width apart. Water the plants in a dry spell.

The root is the part that is most often used medicinally. They can be lifted at the end of the growing season, scrubbed, dried and stored in the usual way.

MEDICINAL USE

A decoction of chicory root is a helpful remedy for mild liver complaints and rheumatic twinges.

To make a decoction: *Put a handful of the dried root in an enamel pan with 2 cups of water. Leave it to stand for 30 minutes then bring slowly to the boil. Simmer for 10 minutes then strain. Take a small glassful at a time when required. The decoction is also good for the digestive system. Chicory is a tonic herb and therefore helpful to those suffering from loss of appetite.*

A poultice made of the boiled leaves and flowers is a remedy for inflammations of the skin.

To make a poultice: *Place fresh crushed leaves and flowers in a small muslin or cheesecloth bag. Tie up the top and put it into an enamel pan. Pour on sufficient water to cover the bag and bring it slowly to the boil. Remove the bag and place it, as hot as can be borne, on the skin. Secure the poultice lightly in place and use the water to bathe the skin.*

Tab. XX.

Salvia Sclarea L.
Das Muskatellerkraut.

Clary, *salvia sclarea*, is an aromatic biennial garden herb growing up to 2 ft (61 cm) high. The large wrinkled leaves are covered with soft hairs. The little flowers are pale blue or white and are set in whorls in the axils of the small upper leaves, the whole supported on reddish-coloured stems. All parts of the plant have quite a strong sweet scent. Clary belongs to the sage family of plants, but its scent is milder than that of any other sage. The taste is warm and slightly bitter. It is commercially grown in several countries for its oil, which is lavender-scented.

Clary is a pretty plant to have in the garden, and it grows easily in a light well-drained soil in a sunny position. Sow the seed in spring in a seed bed and transplant the seedlings to their flowering position in September, leaving a handspan between each plant. The plants die off in the second summer after flowering and the roots can then be dug up for drying and storing.

The leaves, roots and seeds are the parts of the plant used in the home. In the first winter and spring the young leaves are at their best. The seeds are collected for drying in August or September of the second year. Both roots and seeds are dried and stored in the usual way.

MEDICINAL USE

Cold extract of clary will help draw out thorns and splinters and reduce inflammation.

To make an extract: *Bruise or crush the seeds and soak them in water for 5–10 minutes to produce a jelly-like substance. Strain.*

An infusion can be taken in small doses on an occasional basis for mild stomach upsets.

To make an infusion: *Pour a cupful of boiling water over 2 teaspoons of fresh leaves and leave to infuse for 5 minutes before straining.*

The dried roots, crushed and powdered, can be used like snuff to clear the head and ease a headache.

An ointment made with clary leaves will help to draw out inflammation and bring boils and spots to a head.

To make clary ointment: *Fill an enamel saucepan with crushed fresh clary leaves and cover them with vinegar. Cover the pan and simmer over a low heat for about an hour. Strain off the vinegar, discard the leaves and repeat the process using a fresh lot of crushed clary leaves. Simmer gently for a further hour. When cold press all the vinegar out of the leaves and add sufficient thick honey to the vinegar to make a soft ointment.*

CLARY

Years ago clary was used as an alternative to hops in the brewing of beer. It made a much more intoxicating drink! In France, it was used in the making of perfumes.

CLEAVERS

Cleavers has always been a versatile herb; it was well known to the ancient Greeks, who used the hairy stems to strain milk and other drinks!

Galium Aparine

Cleavers, *galium aparine*, is a perennial herb which grows in profusion round fields and waste places and is a tiresome garden weed. It is more familiarly called goosegrass. A clinging, creeping plant, it has leaves and stalks covered with hooked bristles with which it grows up shrubs and hedges and spreads over other plants. The small leaves are arranged in whorls up the stem and the tiny, white, star-shaped flowers grow in the axils of the leaves. Little round seedheads follow which easily stick to clothing and animal fur so that the seeds are carried far and wide. Poultry and other animals will readily eat the herb.

The seeds can be lightly roasted, crushed or ground and used as a coffee substitute – its flavour being similar to coffee.

Cleavers is extremely easy to find growing wild and can be used fresh throughout the season but for drying, the whole plant, except the root, is collected in May and June just before the flowers appear. The herb is dried and stored in the usual way. Later in the year the seeds can be gathered for drying.

MEDICINAL USE

Cleavers tea is helpful for a head cold and is also popular for applying to skin problems.

🌱To make cleavers tea: *Pour a cupful of boiling water over 1 teaspoon of dried herb. Leave it to infuse for a few minutes and drink it hot. Sweeten with honey if needed. For external use, apply once daily and allow to dry.*

Cleavers ointment made with pure lard or shortening and using the leaves and stems of the herb is a useful remedy for minor burns and scalds.

🌱To make cleavers ointment: *Melt the lard or shortening and add cleavers to it mixing well. Bring it slowly to the boil and simmer for 20 minutes. Strain into small pots and cover when cold.*

🌱Crushed fresh leaves applied as a poultice will ease painful blisters.

BEAUTY CARE

Cleavers is a cleansing herb and can be helpful in a slimming programme, but the taste is rather dry and bitter on its own.

🌱An infusion of cleavers (see Medicinal Use) is said to be helpful in the treatment of sunburn and for fading freckles. Sponge the face in the infusion until the burning sensation is relieved.

Cleavers provides a good hair tonic to improve the texture and make the hair shine.

🌱To make a hair tonic: *Pour 6 cups of boiling water over 3 handfuls of chopped fresh herb. Shampoo and rinse the hair. Use the tonic as a final rinse.*

COLTSFOOT

The coltsfoot takes its name from the appearance of this plant's leaves. It is also variously called foal's foot, horsehoof and horsefoot, according to the region in which it is found.

Tuſsilago   Farfara.
Published by Dr. Woodville, March 1. 1790.

Coltsfoot, *tussilago farfara*, is an early-flowering perennial herb which grows wild on waste land and by the side of streams. It is a familiar wayside plant growing strongly in wet as well as dry clay soils. The leaves are not as large, but are otherwise very similar, to the butterbur (*petasites hybridus*). It is most important when gathering the leaves for use in the home that the two are not confused. Very early in the year the single flower stems appear bearing golden yellow daisy-like flowers, which grow quite low down. After the flowers have died other shoots of the plant produce the large leaves which are shaped like a horse's hoof, glossy green above, and covered with a soft down underneath. The flowerheads, when faded, turn into a downy ball like a dandelion.

Coltsfoot is so easily found growing wild it is hardly worth while growing it in the garden where, with its spreading underground roots, it can become a nuisance. However, for reasons of proper identification of the herb, it can easily be grown in the garden in an out-of-the-way spot away from other plants.

Both the flowers and the leaves are used as they contain the same active ingredients. The flowers are gathered for drying in March when at their best. The leaves can be cut at any time during May and June and used either fresh or dried. After drying, the flowers and leaves are stored separately.

MEDICINAL USE

Coltsfoot is a tonic herb and both leaves and flowers are full of Vitamin C. They have a sharp, bitter taste which can be softened by using honey as a sweetener. The plant is also full of mucilage which acts to protect the mucous membranes. Coltsfoot is an expectorant herb and is a good remedy for mild chest complaints. For bronchitis, chesty colds and chronic catarrh coltsfoot is taken in the form of a decoction. It is also helpful for laryngitis and will clear a hoarse voice.

To make a decoction: *Add 1 tablespoon of dried leaves or flowers to 2 cups of water in an enamel pan.*

Bring the water to the boil and simmer until half the amount is left. Strain and sweeten with honey. Drink a small glassful of the warm decoction once or twice a day until relief is obtained.

A cup of coltsfoot tea or infusion taken hot first thing in the morning is good for colds and obstinate coughs, especially smoker's cough.

☛To make an infusion: *Pour 1 cupful of boiling water on to 1 teaspoon of coltsfoot leaves or flowers. Leave to infuse for about 10 minutes then strain and sweeten with honey.*

☛Dried and well-crushed coltsfoot leaves are an ingredient in herbal tobacco, when they are usually combined with chamomile, thyme, woodruff and other herbs. The ground leaves can also be used on their own as a kind of snuff to relieve shortness of breath, congestion and smoker's cough.

☛Coltsfoot candy, or coltsfoot rock, is effective in soothing a sore throat and is a good remedy for a persistent cough. The candy, which is often flavoured with anise, can be bought at health food stores.

Also effective for coughs and other chest complaints is a liquorice decoction.

☛To make liquorice decoction: *Simmer 1 tablespoon of liquorice root in 3½ cups of water until reduced by half. Immediately pour over 1 tablespoon of coltsfoot leaves or flowers and a slice of lemon. Sweeten with honey and leave until cold. Strain and take as often as required.*

For insect bites, inflammations and swellings, use crushed fresh leaves in the form of a poultice.

☛To make a poultice: *Place the fresh leaves between 2 pieces of muslin or cheesecloth and crush well so the juice will run. Apply the poultice to the affected part and secure with a light bandage. Remove when relief is felt and renew when necessary.*

BEAUTY CARE

Coltsfoot has mild astringent and antiseptic properties and, while it will soften the skin, it will at the same time tighten and tone a flabby skin. A strong infusion of coltsfoot leaves or flowers can be used as a toning lotion.

☛To make a strong infusion: *Pour 1 cup of boiling distilled water over 2 handfuls of dried coltsfoot leaves. Leave to infuse for 10–15 minutes or until completely cold. Strain into screwtop bottles and store in the refrigerator. Use within 2–3 days. After cleans-*

ing the face use cotton wool pads or balls wetted with the lotion and a smooth over the skin. Leave to dry.

☛A twice-a-day treatment for dilated veins on the face is to use a lukewarm infusion of coltsfoot made as instructed above. Soak cotton wool pads or balls in the warm infusion and place on the skin. Relax and leave the pads in position until they are quite cold. Afterwards stroke evening primrose oil lightly over the skin to condition and heal.

A coltsfoot face pack is a good treatment for spots, pimples and acne.

☛To make a face pack: *Blend coltsfoot infusion with Fuller's earth or fine oatmeal until it becomes a thick paste. Clean the face, then place a hot wet cloth over the skin to open the pores. Apply the face pack while warm and relax for 15 minutes. Remove with warm water then wipe the skin over with cold coltsfoot infusion. Choose the strength of infusion according to skin type.*

☛To make an eye lotion for tired eyes: *Simmer ½ teaspoon of leaves or flowers in a cup of distilled water for 2–3 minutes. Strain and allow to cool. Bathe the eyes with the lotion or use it as a compress – soak pieces of lint in the lotion and lay them over closed eyes. Relax for 15 minutes and renew the compress if necessary.*

☛Mild cases of dandruff can also be treated with a weak infusion of coltsfoot, as above, using it as a hair rinse. Shampoo the hair, rinse through with clean water and use the coltsfoot as a final rinse, pouring it over the hair several times to be properly effective. The infusion must be made fresh each time.

A RESTFUL HERB

In olden times, coltsfoot was sometimes used for soft furnishing. Wherever it grew in profusion the country people would rub off the soft downy covering of the young leaves and use both that and the fluffy seedheads to make a soft luxurious filling for cushions and pillows.

COMFREY

Comfrey's medieval reputation for knitting broken bones is reflected in its name, which comes from the Latin conferre, *meaning to bring together.*

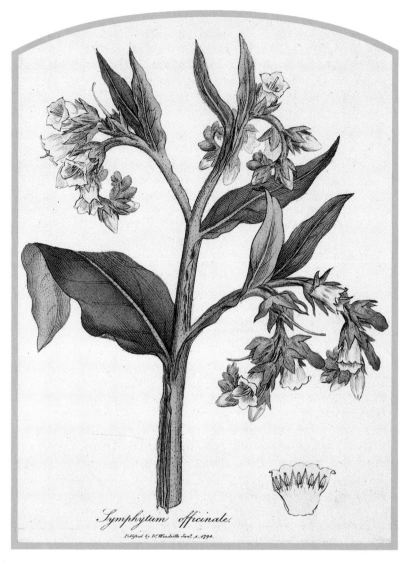

Symphytum officinale.

Published by Dr Woodville Jan. 1. 1794.

The common comfrey, *symphytum officinale*, is a perennial wild herb which grows particularly well by streams and ditches and in damp low-lying places. It is an attractive luxuriant plant, growing fairly large, with hollow stems and long pointed leaves which give out a pleasant scent when crushed. Both stems and the undersides of the leaves are covered with short stiff hairs. The flowers grow in tight clusters at the top of the stems and droop downwards. They vary in colour from creamy white to pale pink, appearing first in May and blooming throughout the summer months.

In the kitchen, young comfrey leaves can be cooked and eaten like spinach, served in a cheese sauce, or made into soup. The dried roots can be roasted and ground and drunk as coffee, although like coffee, it should not be drunk in large quantities over a long period of time.

This useful herb is so frequently found in the wild that it is seldom worth cultivating. It is sometimes grown as an ornamental plant in the garden, but once

established it is a difficult plant to contain. It can be grown in a shady spot in any ordinary garden soil. Comfrey makes a good compost plant. Cut, left to wilt then laid in the trench when planting potatoes, it will ensure healthy scab-free plants and a large crop. It is a good green mulch to spread round tomato plants and fruit bushes and is an excellent plant food when used as a liquid manure. Just cut the plants down and leave them in rainwater.

Both leaves and roots are the parts used in the home. Leaves for drying should be picked when young and the roots can be dug up when the plant has died down in the autumn or in early spring when dividing the plants. They are dried and stored in the usual way.

MEDICINAL USE

The country name for comfrey was 'knitbone' for in the past the herb was used in the treatment of broken limbs. The root was lifted in spring, grated and made into a mash that set solid, an early forerunner of the plaster or bandage used today. In the Middle Ages comfrey was highly prized by the monks who used it to heal sick and injured travellers.

This herb quickly ferments, so preparations should always be freshly made for each treatment and used or discarded the same day.

Comfrey is full of mucilage and is an ingredient in many herbal medicines as a remedy for both internal and external disorders. A decoction of the root is effective for a mild attack of diarrhoea.

To make a root decoction: *Boil 1 tablespoon of dried grated root in 3 cups of water for 5 minutes. Strain when cool and take a small glassful 3–4 times a day until relief is obtained.* The decoction can also be used as a gargle for a sore throat or hoarseness and as a mouthwash to help bleeding gums.

A decoction of the leaves is helpful for coughs and other chest complaints.

To make a decoction of the leaves: *Put a handful of fresh chopped or dried comfrey leaves in an enamel pan with 2 cups of water, bring slowly to the boil and simmer for 5 minutes. Leave to cool then strain into a screwtop jar.*

Comfrey is a tonic herb and, taken regularly, will help to lessen arthritic pain and give a feeling of general well-being.

To make comfrey tea: *Make fresh once a day by pouring 1¼ cups of boiling water on to a tablespoon of dried comfrey leaves. Leave to infuse for 10 minutes then strain and add honey to sweeten.*

Comfrey is a healing herb best known for its external use as an effective remedy for swellings, inflammations and bruises.

To make a poultice: *Use fresh leaves or the whole plant, crushed to a pulp either in a pestle and mortar or in an electric blender. Spread the pulp on a piece of muslin or cheesecloth, cover with another piece of muslin or cheesecloth and heat the poultice between 2 plates over a pan of boiling water. When using dried comfrey for a poultice, boil the leaves in a little water to form a pulp. Apply the poultice directly to the affected part and secure in place with a long cloth or bandage which will help to retain both moisture and heat. Reheat the poultice as necessary.* Use a poultice for soothing painful inflamed joints, for pulled tendons, for healing bruises, twists and sprains, and for drawing out the poison of boils and abscesses. Because of its healing mucilage, comfrey helps in reducing the painful swelling which surrounds a fractured bone, and so

enables the bones to mend more quickly.

Comfrey oil or comfrey ointment will help to soothe sprains and will take the sting out of mild burns and scalds.

To make comfrey oil: *Pour 1 cup of olive oil into a wide-necked jar and add as many leaves as can be pressed into the oil. Cover the jar with a piece of muslin or cheesecloth secured with a rubber band, and stand the jar on a sunny windowsill until the oil is a good green colour. This could take several weeks. When it is sufficiently green, strain the oil through muslin or cheesecloth into stoppered jars.*

Comfrey is a good cure for the distressing complaint of athlete's foot. First wash the feet with a good quality soap and dry, using a separate towel for each foot. Take care to dry thoroughly between the toes and in the creases underneath. Bruise or crush fresh comfrey leaves and put one in between each toe, making sure the leaf is in contact with the affected part. Secure in place with a piece of tape. Continue the treatment until all traces of the trouble have gone. A footbath using a strong decoction of comfrey will also be found to be helpful.

BEAUTY CARE

Comfrey roots, fresh grated or dried, added to the daily bath water will help to improve the texture of the skin and give a more youthful appearance.

To make a herbal bath sachet: *Place the roots in a muslin or cheesecloth bag and hang under the bath tap (faucet) to let the water pour through it. Leave it in the bath water whilst washing. Throw the comfrey root away after use.*

Comfrey ointment is good for the skin and can be used to soothe mild cases of sunburn and to soften the skin.

To make comfrey ointment: *Use 1 heaped tablespoon of dried crushed root or leaves to 4 heaped tablespoons of white petroleum jelly. Melt the jelly and add the comfrey, stirring well. Bring to the boil and simmer over a low heat for 30 minutes. Pour into small pots and cover when cold.*

CORIANDER

Coriander was introduced to the Mediterranean countries from the Middle East. It was used in Egypt and the Bible lands for both its medicinal and culinary values.

Coriandrum sativum

Coriander, *coriandrum sativum*, is a slender annual growing about 2 ft (61 cm) high with fan-shaped lower leaves and feathery leaves above. The tiny flowers, blooming in July, grow in flat-topped clusters and are a delicate shade of mauve. The fragrance is concentrated in the little round seeds which are yellowish-brown and ripen in August. Until then the whole plant has a strong and disagreeable smell about it.

Coriander is a well-known spice in the kitchen. It is one of the ingredients in mixed spice and is used as a flavouring in curries and chutneys. Whole coriander seed is often used in lamb dishes, a meat with which it goes particularly well. The seeds and leaves can also be used to add piquancy to soups and stews.

Coriander is easily obtainable from the grocer or health food shop but it is a pretty herb to grow in the garden. Seed can be sown as early as March under glass, ready to plant out in May, or sow the seed in April or May in a warm sunny spot in a fairly heavy soil. When the seedlings are large enough, thin them out to a handspan apart.

As the seeds begin to ripen in early August cover the seed heads with gauze or light muslin or cheesecloth bags to prevent the seed being lost. Later, cut off the stems, tie them together loosely, and hang them upside down in paper bags, having removed the cloth bags. When completely ripe the seeds will fall into the bags for easy collection. They are then dried and stored in the usual way.

MEDICINAL USE

Coriander is a flavouring used to disguise the unpleasant taste and griping properties of some medicines. The seeds have a sweetish flavour, strong and lemony. Coriander infusion is a stimulating drink and a good remedy for loss of appetite.

To make an infusion: *Put 2 teaspoons of crushed seed into a pan with ½ cup of water. Bring to the boil and simmer for 5 minutes. Strain immediately and serve hot, a small glassful at a time, before meals.*

A glassful of coriander water made as above is helpful in cases of upset stomach due to flatulence.

For mild rheumatic pains in the joints, coriander oil used in a compress can be helpful.

To make coriander oil: *Put coriander seed between 2 pieces of muslin or cheesecloth then crush the seed to release the essential oils. Cover the joint with the compress and secure in position.*

BEAUTY CARE

Coriander seed is used in some soaps and in toilet waters to add fragrance. Whole or ground seed is added to pot-pourri to blend the scents and act as a fixative. Coriander oil is used in perfumes.

CORNFLOWER

Cornflower was formerly much used for eye complaints. Cornflower water was said to be a remedy for weak eyes and it claimed to improve the eyesight. Taken in wine, cornflower was believed to give protection against the plague and other infectious and contagious diseases

Centaurea Cyanus

Cornflower, *centaurea cyanis*, is a colourful annual herb which grows up to 2 ft (61 cm) high. Nowadays it is rarely found in the wild, but is a well-known garden plant. The stiff, straight stem is branched and carries long narrow grey-green leaves. Both stem and leaves are covered with a soft almost silvery down. The brilliant blue single flowerheads, which bloom from June to September, grow on long stalks and are enclosed in bracts of overlapping scales; they consist of a number of tiny florets all bunched together. Other varieties have white or rose-coloured flowers and make an attractive show in the garden.

Cornflower is a very hardy annual and quite simple to grow. Sow in March or April, if the weather is suitable, or in September for flowering in the following year. Sow the seed in ordinary garden soil in sun or semi-shade where it is to flower. When large enough, thin the seedlings to a handspan apart. In the right conditions cornflowers will self-sow quite freely, but to make sure it is best to sow seed each year.

The blue flowers are the only part of the herb to be used; they are cut for drying just as they fully open. It is important to gather them when the colour is at its brightest and the flowers should be cut daily when perhaps there are only two or three that are at their best. They are carefully dried and stored in the usual way.

MEDICINAL USE

For irritation of the eyelids and mild cases of conjunctivitis cornflower is given in the form of a compress. The decoction can also be used as a mouthwash in mild cases of inflammation of the gums.

To make a weak decoction: *Put a small handful of dried flowers in a cupful of distilled water. Bring this slowly to the boil and simmer gently for 10 minutes. Leave until quite cold then strain the lotion into sterilized bottles. The lotion will keep for 2–3 days in a cool place or the refrigerator, but it is always more effective when freshly made. Dip cotton wool pads or balls in the lotion, shake off the excess and place the compresses on closed eyelids. Relax for 15 minutes, renewing the compresses until relief is obtained.*

BEAUTY CARE

Cornflower decoction (see Medicinal Use) is a refreshing facial lotion and it can be used daily for toning the skin. After cleansing the skin night and morning bathe the face in the lotion and leave to dry.

COSTMARY

In the seventeenth century costmary leaves were eaten as a salad vegetable and in soup. Country farmers who brewed their own ale used costmary as a flavouring and it was commonly known as Alecost.

Le Coq ou la Menthe Coq
Tanacetum Balsamita. L. S. P.

Costmary, *tanacetum balsamita*, is an attractive perennial herb, its leaves and flowers giving off a pleasant soft scent of balsam. It grows about 2 ft (61 cm) high, with strong stems and broadish leaves. The small yellow flowers are rather insignificant, only appearing if the plant is in full sun, and they never set seed. The flowers bloom in August.

Costmary will grow well in almost any spot in the garden but prefers dry light soil. It is propagated by root division and in autumn or early spring the whole herb can be dug up. The roots should be carefully divided and set in their new positions about 12 in (30 cm) apart. The plants gradually spread, so costmary should be lifted and divided every two or three years.

The flowers and leaves are the parts of the herb used in the home. The young leaves can be picked for drying throughout the season and the flowers should be gathered in August. They are then dried and stored in the usual way.

MEDICINAL USE

Costmary oil is a helpful remedy for mild burns where there is no blistering. It is also reported to be good for easing mild cases of gout.

To make costmary oil: *Put 1 cup of olive oil into an enamel pan with a good handful of dried costmary leaves. Bring it slowly to the boil and simmer for 5–10 minutes. Allow to cool, then strain and pour into screwtop jars. Dip pieces of lint or cotton wool pads or balls into the oil and place over the affected part.*

Costmary inhalation is a useful remedy for catarrh, helping to clear the nasal passages.

To make an inhalant: *Put a handful of costmary leaves and flowers into a bowl and pour boiling water over them, stirring well. Cover the head and bowl with a towel and inhale the fumes for 10 minutes.*

For bruises, blisters and mild irritations of the skin, an ointment using dried costmary leaves is effective.

To make costmary ointment: *Melt 4 heaped tablespoons of white petroleum jelly in a pan and add 2 handfuls of costmary. Bring the mixture to the boil and simmer for 20 minutes. Strain through fine muslin or cheesecloth into small pots. Leave to get quite cold before covering.*

BEAUTY CARE

Costmary has a strong scent of mint and when dried smells a little of lemon as well. The whole plant helps to bring out the scents of other dried flowers and leaves acting as a fixative for herb cushions, pot pourri and herb sachets.

COWSLIP

In the early herbals cowslip was known as Herb Peter or Keyflower because of the resemblance of the flowerhead to a bunch of keys hanging down – the symbol of St Peter. In former times cowslip was believed to help those suffering from rheumatic complaints and those with dropsy.

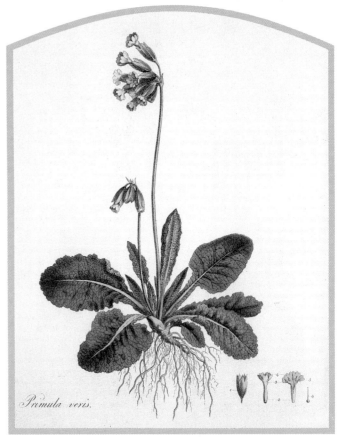

Primula veris.

The meadow cowslip, *primula veris*, is now rarely found growing in the wild. Sometimes it can be seen from afar growing in inaccessible places such as deep railway cuttings. It is a very pretty, fragrant, spring flowering herb which grows most easily on chalky soil. Cowslip is a perennial plant but is more often treated as a biennial. Flat rosettes of deeply-wrinkled leaves appear in early spring, from which grows a single stalk bearing a loose cluster of trumpet-shaped pale yellow flowers. The flowers are sweetly scented and bloom in April and May.

Cowslips can easily be grown in the garden in ordinary soil with added lime. Choose a damp, shady, undisturbed spot and sow the seed in May or June in its flowering position. When large enough, thin out the seedlings to a handspan apart. Keep the weeds down and water if necessary in a very dry spell to make sure the plants will grow strongly through the first year.

Only the yellow flower is used in the home, so a great many cowslips have to be grown to provide sufficient flowers for drying. Perfect flowers should be gathered when in full flower then carefully dried and stored in the usual way. Do not use them fresh.

MEDICINAL USE

An infusion of cowslip flowers is a soothing remedy for sleeplessness. It calms the nerves when taken hot last thing at night and will help to relieve a headache brought on by being in a stuffy atmosphere.

To make cowslip infusion: *Pour ½ cup boiling water on to a teaspoon of dried cowslip flowers. Leave to infuse for 4–5 minutes. Strain and add honey* to sweeten it. Drink the infusion, preferably when already in bed.

Cowslip flowers can be made into a syrup for calming the nerves and relieving giddiness. The syrup can be sipped a teaspoonful at a time or it can be diluted with water and taken a small glassful at a time.

To make the syrup: *Pour 1 cup of boiling water on to a handful of dried flowers. Leave to get cold then strain into a pan. Heat and add 4 heaped tablespoons of sugar. Stir until the sugar is dissolved over a low heat, bring to the boil and simmer gently until of a syrupy consistency. Pour into screwtop bottles and keep in a cool place or the refrigerator.*

BEAUTY CARE

An infusion of cowslip flowers (see Medicinal Use) is a good lotion to help prevent or reduce wrinkles. Soak cotton wool pads or balls in the cold infusion and press gently over the wrinkles.

Cowslip ointment is not only good for wrinkles and other blemishes but is said to remove spots.

To make the ointment: *Melt 4 heaped tablespoons of white petroleum jelly and add 3 handfuls of flowers. Bring to the boil and simmer gently for 20 minutes. Strain into a screwtop jar.*

DAMASK ROSE

The rose has been treasured for its lovely fragrance over many centuries; it was first cultivated in Ancient Greece. The poet Sappho called it the Queen of Flowers.

Rosa centifolia

Published by D.ʳ Woodville. May. 1. 1792.

The damask rose, *rosa damascena*, is one of the old-fashioned garden roses from which so many of our present-day hybrids have originated. It is a sweetly-scented herbaceous shrub cultivated on a large scale for its lovely perfume. In June and July it carries a profusion of white or pink fragrant flowers, each a solid mass of petals. The leaves are rather small and dull. The stems are not strong and tend to arch over, the flowers drooping down as though too heavy for the stalks.

In the kitchen, a delicious-tasting jam can be made using dried or fresh petals. Crystallized rose petals are easy to make and are a colourful decoration for cakes, puddings and icecreams.

The damask rose is a very hardy shrub and easy to cultivate. It requires good deeply dug soil and a position where it will get plenty of sunshine. Late October and November is the best time for planting a rose so it can get established before winter sets in.

The lovely velvet texture of damask rose petals and their heady perfume make it a beautiful rose whether growing in the garden or arranged in a vase. To capture this fragrance petals can be picked and, either fresh or dried, used in the home in many different ways. It is important when picking petals for drying that they are perfect, without any brown marks or withered edges. They are dried and stored in the usual way.

BEAUTY CARE

A light moisturizing lotion which is soothing for a dry skin can be made from rose petals.

☛ To make a rose petal lotion: *Crush 2 large handfuls of fresh petals in 1 cup of boiling water. Leave to infuse until it is quite cold then strain and mix with cream. Store in pots in the refrigerator. An effective and gentle hand cream can be made by mixing the infusion with glycerine.*

A rose petal aromatic bath is refreshing and relaxing.

☛To make a herbal bath sachet: *Use fresh or dried petals in a small muslin or cheesecloth bag tied to the bath tap. Let the water rush through the bag. Alternatively, a strong infusion can be made and strained before adding to the bath water.*

A cupful of rose toilet vinegar added to the bath water, or a teaspoonful in the water for washing the face, is fragrant and refreshing.

☛To make the toilet vinegar: *Use a good white wine vinegar. Fill a jar with fresh or dried rose petals and cover the petals with vinegar, pressing them well down. Cover the jar with a piece of muslin or cheesecloth secured with a rubber band. Leave the vinegar for 2–3 weeks, then filter the vinegar into stoppered bottles.* This fragrant toilet water is a good skin cleansing lotion.

Rosewater, which is used in so many beauty preparations, can so easily be purchased from the chemist that unless there is a very plentiful supply of petals available it is not worthwhile to make your own. For tired and swollen eyelids rosewater compresses are very soothing.

Concentrated rose oil cannot be made at home, but a useful rose oil can be made which will add a lovely fragrance to a pot pourri. It does require an enormous amount of rose petals.

☛To make rose oil: *Put 2 cups of olive oil into a wide-necked glass jar and add as many rose petals as possible, pressing them well down into the oil. Leave them in the sun for 3–4 days then strain through muslin or cheesecloth or a nylon strainer. Press the petals well to make sure none of the oil is left behind. Repeat the process about 8 times or as many as possible to ensure the oil will smell strongly of roses. When the oil is sufficiently perfumed, store in an airtight bottle.* Only a few drops of the oil need to be added to a pot pourri.

Rose oil can also be used to make the eyelids shine. Lightly smooth a very little oil on to closed lids.

An attractive rose pot pourri is easy to make and has a wonderful fragrance.

☛To make pot pourri: *Mix a handful of dried finely ground orris root, a ½ teaspoon each of allspice and cinnamon, and ½ teaspoon of homemade rose oil with 8 large handfuls of dried damask rose petals. Put the mixture into a polythene bag. Close the bag with a tie and shake thoroughly. Leave the bag closed and in the dark for 2–3 weeks then put the pot pourri in a pretty bowl or jar.*

Rose sachets are another way to enjoy the scent of summer through the winter months. Use the sachets amongst clothes and linen, hanging in cupboards or even tucking them into a pocket or handbag.

☛To make rose sachets: *Make up small bags of pretty muslin or organdie. Mix well together 5–6 handfuls of crushed dried rose petals, 1 handful of crushed dried lemon verbena leaves and ½ teaspoon of rose oil and fill the little bags with the mixture. Sew the tops of the bags together or tie with coloured ribbon. The same mixture would make up into a sweetly scented little cushion. A stronger smelling, spicier sachet can be made by adding some lavender flowers in place of the lemon verbena and a little orris root powder to fix the scents and make them last.*

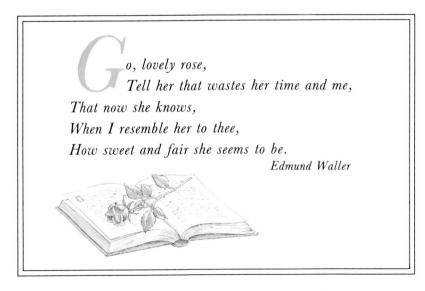

G*o, lovely rose,*
  Tell her that wastes her time and me,
That now she knows,
When I resemble her to thee,
How sweet and fair she seems to be.
                    Edmund Waller

Leontŏdon *Taraxacum*

Publifhed by Dr. Woodville Janʸ 1. 1790.

DANDELION

The leaves of the dandelion give the appearance of lion's teeth and this was emphasized in the stylized drawings in the old herbals. Hence it was named by the French 'dent de lion' and the anglicized version became dandelion.

Dandelion, *taraxacum officinale*, is an extremely well-known plant, with its brilliant yellow daisy-like flower rising on a single stem from a flat rosette of leaves. The flowers seem to appear very early in the year and to continue blooming throughout the growing season, being very noticeable along country roads and hedgerows. When the flower has withered a soft ball of white downy seeds is left for the wind to scatter. Dandelion is a troublesome and persistent weed in the garden and is difficult to eradicate, but it can be a useful herb in the home.

In the kitchen, young dandelion leaves add relish to a salad, make a tasty boiled vegetable and an unusual soup. Dandelion flowerheads make a delicious light wine for summer. The roots, carefully dried, then roasted and ground, make a delicious drink and an alternative to coffee for those who cannot tolerate caffeine. Burdock and dandelion leaves combine to make a pleasant healthy drink which helps to increase the appetite.

Dandelion is so easily available, growing as it does all over the countryside, in waste places and on fallow land, there is little need to cultivate.

Nearly all parts of the plant can be used in the home, and for winter use the flowers, leaves and roots can be dried. Leaves for drying should be picked only when young, as the older leaves will be bitter. The flowers can be picked for drying on a bright sunny day after the dew has dried. The green calyx should be removed, then flowers and leaves are dried and stored in the usual way. The roots are best when dug up either during the spring when they are young or in the late autumn, when the roots will be much larger and full of juice. They must be thoroughly scrubbed and cleaned before use. For drying the roots are chopped into small pieces then dried and stored in the usual way.

MEDICINAL USE

Dandelion can be used in quite large amounts and is often more effective in its action when combined with other herbs. It is a tonic herb, diuretic and slightly laxative when taken internally. It is helpful in the treatment of constipation, gout and for a sluggish digestion. A small glassful of dandelion tea sweetened with a little honey can be taken once or twice a day.

To make an infusion: *Pour 2 cups of boiling water over a handful of dried dandelion leaves and leave to infuse for about 10 minutes. Strain the tea and drink it while it is warm.*

Dandelion is full of vitamins and minerals and helps the liver and kidneys to function smoothly. A decoction can be made using either shredded root or a mixture of root and leaves.

To make a decoction: *Put 2 teaspoons of herb and 1 cup of cold water in an enamel pan. Bring the mixture slowly to the boil over a low heat and boil for 1 minute. Remove from the heat and leave to infuse for 15 minutes. Take a small glassful when feeling sluggish.* In the spring a concentrated course of dandelion will help to rid the body of waste matter and generally tone up the whole system.

Dandelion is recommended to be eaten by those with chronic constipation. Fresh young leaves are picked, washed, finely chopped and added to salads.

A decoction of dandelion root or herb can be taken internally in cases of eczema and other skin ailments.

To make a decoction for skin ailments: *Add 2 large handfuls of dried leaves and flowers to 4 cups of water in an enamel pan. Bring slowly to the boil then simmer gently until the liquid is reduced by half. Strain through a piece of muslin into a jug and keep in the cool. A small glassful of the decoction, sweetened with honey can be taken three or four times a day.*

While taking dandelion drink the same decoction can be used to bathe troubled areas of the skin and help to ease the intense irritation. A compress using pieces of lint can be dipped into the decoction and laid on to the affected part, pressing the lint lightly on to the skin to make sure it touches the surface. Leave on the skin for 10–15 minutes and renew as necessary. Dab the decoction on to localised spots of eczema with cotton wool as soon as the itching begins.

The strong decoction added to the nightly bath will also help to stop the itching of skin eruptions, providing a soothing and relaxing bath.

Dandelion wine is a wholesome drink which makes an excellent tonic that can be taken on a daily basis. It is made from fresh picked dandelion flowers.

To make dandelion wine: *Gather the flowers in the morning on a dry day and put 8 cups of dandelion into a bowl with an equal amount of cold water. Leave for 3 days, stirring occasionally. Strain into an enamel pan and boil for 30 minutes. Add 2½ cups of sugar and the rind and juice of a lemon and an orange. When cold add a teaspoon of yeast in warm water. Cover and leave to ferment for 2 days. Pour into a fermenting jar or cask and leave for 2 months before bottling. The wine improves with keeping.*

BEAUTY CARE

Dandelion leaves and the juice of the root are helpful in a slimming programme when plenty of exercise and a balanced diet is being followed. It helps by purifying the blood and reducing water retention. A cup of dandelion tea (see Medicinal Use) can be taken twice a day before meals. A strong infusion (see page 15, towards the end of the Infusion section) added to the bath water is also believed to be helpful and if combined with horsetail, seaweed and fennel will be more effective.

Dandelion flowers have a mild bleaching effect. A lotion made from fresh or dried dandelion flowers will help to remove freckles.

To make dandelion lotion: *Add 1 good handful of the flowers to 3½ cups of water in an enamel pan.*

Bring to the boil and simmer for 30 minutes. Strain through a piece of muslin or cheesecloth into a screw-top jar and store in the refrigerator. Wash the face night and morning with the lotion and gradually the freckles should fade.

☞For skin complaints such as spots, pimples and acne a course of dandelion tea and eating fresh young leaves in salads or sandwiches will help to clear the skin. Externally, dab fresh juice from the stems on the spots. The spots turn black overnight and the scab falls away when washing the face. The skin should be kept scrupulously clean and washed night and morning with an infusion of a disinfectant herb such as marigold or aloe vera until the skin has improved.

Dandelion face packs also help to cleanse and clear the skin. Combined with nettle, the face pack becomes more effective.
☞To make the face pack: *Pick young nettle and dandelion leaves in the early morning. Chop the leaves finely and put in an enamel pan with sufficient water to prevent them from burning. Simmer until the leaves have formed a thick mash. Remove from the heat and spread the pack on a piece of muslin. Cleanse the face and open the pores of the skin by using a warm water compress. Cover the face with the pack, avoiding eyes and lips. Lie down and relax, putting cold compresses over the eyes, for 15 minutes. Remove the pack with warm water and splash the skin with cold water or an astringent lotion to close the pores. If used every 2 or 3 days for a fortnight there will be a significant improvement in the skin.*

A warm compress, using a strong decoction of young dandelion leaves only, will improve the circulation of blood to the face and can be safely used where there are dilated veins.
☞To make a strong decoction: *Add finely chopped leaves to boiling water in a pan and allow to simmer for 5 minutes. Strain into a bowl and leave until lukewarm. Cleanse the face, then dip a piece of lint into the lotion, wring out the excess and gently cover the face with the lint. Leave for 20 minutes.*

*D*ANDELION SALAD
For a deliciously crisp salad that can be served as a starter or side dish, take 4 good handfuls washed and sliced dandelion leaves and mix with the following ingredients; 6 slices crisply cooked bacon cut into strips, 2 slices cubed bread that has been fried in butter and garlic, 3 tablespoons olive or vegetable oil, 1 tablespoon vinegar, salt and freshly ground black pepper. Place all the ingredients into a large bowl or 6 individual serving dishes, toss gently together and serve.

DILL

The name dill is said to have come from the Old Norse word 'dilla', meaning to lull, an indication as to the properties of the herb; dill water was given to babies to soothe them.

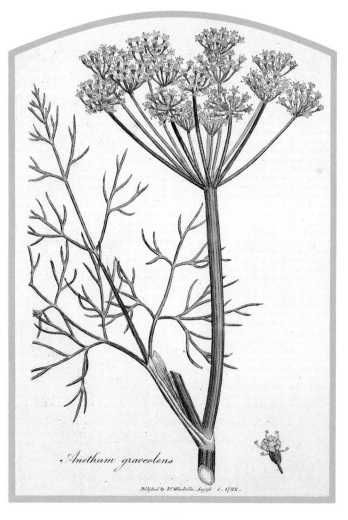

Anethum graveolens

Dill, *anethum graveolens*, is an attractive annual herb of the umbelliferae family of plants. It grows fairly tall with one strong straight stem and fine feathery leaves. The tiny yellow flowers grow in umbels at the top of the stem and bloom from June to August, when the seeds appear. Dill is a culinary and medicinal herb, the leaves and the seeds being used for cooking, while the seeds only are used for medicines.

In the kitchen, dill leaves can be added to cucumber and salads, fish and lightly flavoured vegetables. The seeds have a sharper, more aromatic flavour than the leaves. They can be added to soups and stews and to poached fish. The best-known use for dill is in pickling cucumbers.

Dill is an easy herb to grow in the garden. Sow the seed in the spring in a sunny, sheltered spot in well-drained soil and thin the seedlings to a handspan apart. Keep them well watered, especially in a dry spell. Do not plant it near fennel as cross pollination may take place and fennel will spoil the delicate flavour of the dill.

Pick the leaves for cooking and drying throughout the summer and collect the seeds for drying in the autumn, just before they are fully ripe. Cut off the stems and hang the bunches upside down in a paper bag and leave the seeds to drop into the bag. They are then dried and stored in the usual way.

MEDICINAL USE

Dill has always been a safe useful remedy for mild digestive upsets and flatulence. It is an ingredient in gripe water, which is specially made for children and young babies. Chewing dill seeds will help to sweeten the breath.

Dill is a sedative herb and a good remedy for sleeplessness, acting as a mild tranquillizer. Taken last thing at night, a small glassful of hot dill seed tea will have a calming effect. The seed tea served unsweetened will help to stop hiccups. Dill also helps to sharpen the appetite if a small cup of dill seed tea is taken about half an hour before a meal.

To make dill seed tea: *Crush 2 teaspoons of seeds and put them into an enamel pan with 1 cup of water. Bring to the boil and simmer for 10 minutes. Leave for a further 10 minutes then strain. Sweeten with honey and drink warm a small glassful at a time.*

DOG ROSE

Dog rose is the commonest of all wild roses in Britain and its name is said to derive from the Anglo-Saxon word 'dagge' which means a dagger. Whether because of its curved thorns or the stoutness of its stem, used to make the handles for the daggers, is not known.

Rosa canina

Published by D.C. Woodville April. 1.1792.

The wild dog rose, *rosa canina*, is a beautiful hedgerow climbing shrub, with its characteristic arching stems reaching out over other wayside trees and bushes. In June and July the wild profusion of the flat, pale pink flowers are a familiar sight along country lanes. The leaves are small and scentless and each is made up of two or three pairs of sharply-toothed leaflets. The strong growing stems have numerous downward curved thorns by which they cling and support themselves. The flowers are sweetly scented and open one at a time in each cluster of two or three. The lovely bright red, hard pear shaped rosehips appear as the flower dies away.

In the kitchen a purée of rosehips makes delicious desserts, icecream and jams. Rosehip tea is a good warming drink for the winter months and rosehip syrup adds an unusual flavour to a winter fruit salad and makes a delicious sauce to go with icecream or sorbet ices. Use the petals in salads or to make rose wine, Turkish delight, rose honey, rose vinegar, rose-petal jam or rose-petal jelly.

The petals can be gathered for pot pourri but it is the fruits of the dog rose which are of greatest value for they are a rich source of Vitamin C. Rosehips are said to contain up to twenty times more Vitamin C than oranges. The rosehips are gathered for drying whilst firm but fully ripe, needing to be dried with care to preserve their goodness.

MEDICINAL USES

The high content of Vitamin C in rosehips helps to prevent colds and influenza. Rosehips are diuretic, good for the kidneys and helpful in a slimming pro-

gramme. Rosehip tea can be taken everyday as a pleasant way to take extra vitamins.

☛To make the tea: *Soak 2 tablespoons of dried crushed rosehips in sufficient water to cover them in an enamel pan. Leave for about 8 hours or overnight. Pour 4 cups of boiling water on to the rosehips and simmer gently for 30 minutes. Strain the rosehips into a covered pot and store in the refrigerator. It will keep for 2 days and can be reheated, but not boiled, and sweetened with honey.*

Rosehip syrup is a refreshing healthy drink when diluted with sparkling mineral water and is made using fresh rosehips.

☛To make rosehip syrup: *Put 2 large handfuls of chopped rosehips into an enamel pan and add 2 cups of water and ½ cup of sugar. Bring slowly to the boil, stirring frequently, to make sure all the sugar is dissolved before it boils. Remove from the heat and strain through very fine muslin or cheesecloth. None of the tiny hairs which cling to the seeds inside the rosehips must be allowed to get into the syrup. Return to the pan and boil again until reduced to the right consistency. Pour into stoppered jars and cover when cold.* The syrup can be given daily to children and those who are in need of extra Vitamin C.

Sambucus nigra

Published by Dr Woodville April 1. 1791.

ELDER

An elder tree growing near the house was believed to keep witches and bad spirits away. Bad luck was said to dog the footsteps of those who cut down an elder tree or burnt its branches.

The elder, *sambucus nigra*, is a familiar small tree or shrub with large, flat-topped clusters of beautifully scented creamy-white flowers. The elder grows throughout Britain and can be found in woods and hedges, on waste lands and in gardens. It grows quickly to make a thick stout hedge and provides a good shelter in a windy garden. A very hardy perennial, it has light-coloured bark and the leaves, which have an unpleasant smell, are made up of numerous leaflets. Dried and then crushed, the leaves can be used as an insecticide in the garden. The lovely fragrant flowers bloom from May to early July and are followed by small shiny black berries; as the berries swell and ripen the stalk droops down with the weight. Birds eat the berries almost as soon as they are ripe and so scatter the seeds everywhere.

In the kitchen elderflower and elderberries can be used in many different ways. The flowers make delicious sorbet ices and syrups to add to fruit salads and summer drinks and add a delicate flavour in a soufflé or mousse. A freshly picked flower dipped in batter and quickly deep fried makes a delicious pudding. The berries are delicious in pies and tarts or made into a creamy elderberry fool. Elderberries tend to stain the teeth when eaten but the stain soon disappears. Wine can be made from both berries and flowers; elderflower wine is particularly light and refreshing, while the berries make a heavier, but good-flavoured wine. Elderberry jam or jelly is an unusual preserve but it tastes good and keeps well. Elderberries must NEVER be eaten uncooked, and nor should the raw juice be taken, as they can cause diarrhoea.

The flowers are gathered for drying just as they are opening and are stored in the usual way. The berries should be collected when fully ripe and are best bottled, frozen or used straight away. They can be used on their own or with apples and plums in pies, tarts or fruit crumbles. A puree of cooked elderberries goes well with stewed pears.

Medicinal Use

Elderflowers make a soothing, relaxing tea which is a helpful remedy for colds and for a headache. It can be tried as an alternative to aspirin, which can sometimes cause constipation. Elderflower tea, taken hot last thing at night, will help to prevent sleeplessness.

☛To make elderflower tea: *Pour a cupful of boiling water over 2 tablespoons of fresh or dried flowers. Leave to infuse for 5–10 minutes, then strain through fine muslin or cheesecloth and sweeten with honey if required.*

☛Externally, a decoction (see page 13) of dried flowers (*use 2 handfuls flowers to 2 cups water*) used as an inhalation is a good remedy for headaches, head colds and hoarseness.

Beauty Care

Elderflower is a marvellous cosmetic herb, with cleansing, soothing and healing properties. It softens, tones and whitens the skin and helps to clear away minor blemishes.

☛To make elderflower water: *Pour 2 cups of boiling water over 3 heaped tablespoons of crushed flowers in a china bowl and leave to infuse for 1–2 hours. Then strain through fine muslin or cheesecloth into jars and store in the refrigerator for up to 3–4 days. Use the lotion night and morning to cleanse and tone up the skin. It can be used on dilated veins and is good for oily skin. Elderflower water in the form of a cold compress will help to soothe and relieve sunburn* or, added to the bath water, will stimulate the circulation and soften the skin.

For deep cleansing use elderflower in a facial steam.

☛To make a facial steam: *Pour boiling water over the flowers in a wide china bowl, using either fresh or dried flowers. Put a towel over the head and the bowl and hold the face over the fragrant steam for 10 minutes. Afterwards wipe the face with a clean cotton wool pad or ball and close the pores with a splash of cold water.*

Elderflowers infused in milk can be used as a mild skin bleach and to fade freckles.

☛To make a skin lotion: *Soak a small bowlful of elderflowers in cold milk. Leave for 3–4 hours in a cool place then strain. Use cotton wool pads or balls to dab it on to the freckles and leave to dry.*

To tone and clear the skin use an elderflower face pack.

☛To make elderflower face pack: *Mix natural yoghurt and crushed elderflowers to a thick paste and leave for an hour. Cleanse the face then spread the face pack over the skin. Lie down and relax for 20 minutes, covering the eyes with cold elderflower lotion compresses. Afterwards wash the face in warm water or lotion.*

A soothing ointment for rough and itching skin also helps to relieve chilblains.

☛To make elderflower ointment: *Melt 4 heaped tablespoons of white petroleum jelly in an enamel pan and add as much crushed elderflower as possible. Bring to the boil and simmer gently for 20 minutes. Strain the ointment into small pots through fine muslin or cheesecloth and cover when cold.*

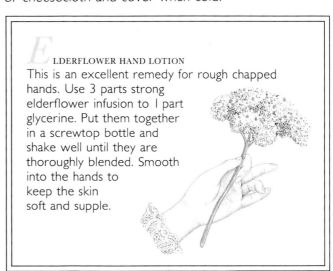

*E*LDERFLOWER HAND LOTION
This is an excellent remedy for rough chapped hands. Use 3 parts strong elderflower infusion to 1 part glycerine. Put them together in a screwtop bottle and shake well until they are thoroughly blended. Smooth into the hands to keep the skin soft and supple.

ELECAMPANE

Various legends surround the origin of the Latin name of elecampane, inula helenium. *One states that it was named after a Greek island where the largest plants grew. Another that it was called after Helen of Troy.*

Inula Helenium

Elecampane, *inula helenium*, is a very tall, scented, perennial herb which used to grow wild along hedgerows and in damp meadows. Today it is a cultivated garden plant, making a handsome show at the back of the border. The stout stems, branched at the top, grow nearly 5 ft (1.5 metres) high. The basal leaves are large and tough. The leaves on the stem are much shorter but very broad, and the whole plant is covered with a soft down. The bright yellow flowers are large and bloom from June until August.

Plant elecampane in a moist shady place in well-drained ordinary garden soil. Elecampane can be cultivated from seed sown either in the spring in its flowering position or in the autumn, using the newly ripened seed. These seeds should be sown in a cold frame and set out in the following spring.

Elecampane is grown for its roots which are large and fleshy with a tough skin, and they are highly aromatic. In the autumn, two- or three-year-old plants can be dug up and the roots can be used. Clean and chop up the roots then slowly dry them and store in the usual way.

MEDICINAL USE

Elecampane is a tonic herb which stimulates the digestion and is helpful for stomach upsets. It is also a remedy for troublesome coughs and colds.

To make elecampane tea: *Soak 1 teaspoon of crushed elecampane root in 1 cup of cold water in an enamel saucepan for 30 minutes. Bring to the boil and boil for 1 minute, then remove the pan from the heat and leave to infuse for 10 minutes. Strain, add honey to sweeten and take the mixture when cold. Drink a small glassful before meals for the digestion and sip the tea when the cough is troublesome.*

To make a strong decoction of elecampane root: *Take 2 handfuls of root to 2 cups of water. Use the same method as for tea above, but soak the roots for at least an hour before boiling them. Use this lotion as a cold or warm compress to soothe itching skin and especially for cold sores.*

BEAUTY CARE

A weak decoction is a good cleansing lotion for spots and pimples.

To make a weak decoction: *Use 1 teaspoon crushed root to 1 cup of distilled water and follow the instructions as for elecampane tea.*

The roots crushed to a powder add a pleasant scent to pot pourri and help to fix the other scents.

EVENING PRIMROSE.

The evening primrose is a native of Central America, where it was used for coughs and for healing wounds. In the 1700s the seeds found their way into the cargoes of ships travelling to Europe where the plant became naturalized.

Evening primrose, *oenothera biennis*, is totally unlike the dainty spring-flowering primrose which grows in the garden. It is a tall, attractive, wild herb standing high above other wild plants. It is fairly widespread, growing on waste land and along streams and on river banks. The brilliant yellow flowers open only in the evening between six and seven o'clock. The plant is a biennial and in the first year produces a flat rosette of long tapering leaves. The second year the single stem grows tall and straight and bears the lovely fragrant flowers all along its length. The flowers bloom from June through to September or October. The roots, which are long and tapering like a parsnip, can be eaten as a vegetable and are full of nourishment.

Evening primrose can be found growing wild but if space can be found it is an easy herb to grow in the garden. In the spring or early summer sow evening primrose seed in ordinary garden soil where it is to flower. It will readily self-seed and provide a good succession of plants. The oil is obtained from the seeds, which are gathered when ripe.

MEDICINAL USE

The oil extracted from the seeds contains valuable properties and is used in the treatment of a variety of ailments. Evening primrose oil is rich in the two fatty acids essential to the metabolism of the body. One is linoleic acid and the other is gamma linoleic acid known as GLA. This vital GLA is converted in the body to substances which help in the growth and reproduction of cells. It is helpful to those who suffer from pre-menstrual stress or the distressing symptoms of the menopause. Evening primrose oil is also effective in the treatment of eczema.

BEAUTY CARE

Evening primrose oil taken internally is believed to benefit the skin, the hair and the eyes. Externally, the oil helps the skin to retain moisture. Night and morning after cleansing the face smooth the oil over the skin. Creams and lotions containing evening primrose and the plain oil can be bought at health food shops which sell natural beauty products.

FENNEL

In ancient times fennel was a popular herb with the Greeks and Romans who ate the young shoots as a vegetable and used the seeds in cooking and for preserving foods.

Anethum Fœniculum

Published by M? Woodville, August 1, 1792.

Fennel, *foeniculum vulgare*, is a tall, graceful, aromatic plant, stout stemmed and with soft feathery bright green leaves. The yellow flowers grow in flat-topped clusters and bloom in July and August. Fennel grows wild in many coastal areas and on river banks. Nowadays it is a familiar herb cultivated in the garden.

In the kitchen, the sweet fennel is used in many fish dishes, especially with rich oily fish like mackerel and salmon. Fennel can be added to salads mixed with other herbs, and to vegetable dishes, but it is one of the stronger tasting herbs and should be used in moderation. The spicy fennel seeds are used in bread and cakes and add a special flavour to German sauerkraut and spiced beetroots.

Fennel is a hardy perennial and very easy to grow from seed sown in ordinary garden soil. In April, sow the seed directly into the flowering position in a sunny part of the border. Thin out the seedlings when they are large enough to 12 in (30 cm) apart. Once established, fennel plants need little attention and will continue to appear year after year.

The leaves and seeds are the parts used in the home. The leaves can be picked for using fresh or for drying any time before the plant flowers. The seeds are gathered in September when they are ripe – cut the whole head off and place upside down in a paper bag. The seeds will fall into the bag when they are fully ripe. Both leaves and seeds are dried and stored in the usual way. There is a variety of fennel known as Florence fennel, which is grown for its swollen edible root. Both fennels have a slight taste of aniseed, warm and pleasant.

MEDICINAL USE

Fennel is a helpful medicinal herb, well-known for its calming effect on the digestion. It is used as a flavouring and to counteract the griping effect of purgatives. Fennel tea or infusion, a small glassful of which can be taken warm after meals, is a mild effective remedy for stomach upsets, for flatulence and other digestive complaints. Fennel helps to tone up a sluggish system and stimulates the appetite and a glass of cold fennel tea should be taken half an hour before a meal. To relieve catarrh, coughs and other chest complaints hot fennel tea can be taken as required. The infusion can be made using leaves or seeds and both are equally pleasant.

To make an infusion: *Fennel leaf tea is made by*

pouring ½ cup of boiling water on to 1 teaspoon of fresh chopped leaves. Leave the drink to infuse for 5 minutes before straining. Sweeten with a little honey and serve hot or cold. The seed tea is made by pouring 1 cup of boiling water over 2 teaspoons of well-crushed fennel seeds in an enamel pan. Simmer for 5–10 minutes. Remove the pan from the heat and strain the tea.

Externally, a decoction of fennel seeds used warm or cold will sometimes help those suffering from headache and migraine.
☛To make a decoction: *Pour 2 cups of water over 2 tablespoons of crushed seeds. Bring to the boil and boil for 5 minutes. Strain, and when the right temperature bathe the temples and forehead, or use a cloth soaked in the decoction until relief is obtained. Cotton wool pads or balls dipped into the solution and laid over the eyes is soothing for inflamed eyelids. The decoction should be stored in the refrigerator and used within 3 days.*

A simple cough remedy is to mix a few drops of fennel oil with a little honey and take when the cough is troublesome. The oil can also be gently smoothed onto the skin to relieve rheumatism.
☛To make fennel oil: *Fill a small screwtop jar with crushed leaves or seeds and cover them with olive oil. Cover the jar with a piece of muslin or cheesecloth secured in place with a rubber band. Leave the jar in the warm or on a sunny windowsill for about a week. Strain and repeat the process 3–4 times until the oil is strongly impregnated with fennel. Finally strain out the oil into small screwtop jars and store in the dark.*

BEAUTY CARE
Fennel is a diuretic herb and can be helpful in a slimming programme – chewing the seeds will help to relieve hunger pangs.
☛Drinking fennel tea (see Medicinal Use) may help to rid the body of excess fluid. A glassful can be taken at night and first thing in the morning.

☛Cotton wool pads or balls wrung out in an infusion of fennel leaves and placed over the eyes for 20 minutes while relaxing will soothe and strengthen tired eyes. Always make a fresh infusion for each application.

☛Cold fennel infusion makes a pleasant toning lotion and can be kept in the refrigerator for several days. After cleansing the face night and morning use cotton wool pads or balls dipped in the lotion to smooth over the face. Leave it to dry. Fennel lotion is mildly antiseptic.

It helps to close the pores and smooth out small wrinkles as well as to protect the skin from infection.

A fennel face pack is good for the older person troubled by wrinkles and a dull looking skin.
☛To make a face pack: *Mix a strong infusion of fennel leaf or seed with honey and Fuller's earth or fine oatmeal to a thick paste. Cleanse the face thoroughly and smooth the face pack over the skin, avoiding the eye area. Cover the eyes with cold water compresses and relax lying down for 20 minutes. Remove the face pack and wash in warm water, ending with a splash of cold water to close the pores.*

Fennel can be used on its own or mixed with other herbs in a hair rinse. It helps to stimulate the scalp and strengthen the hair.
☛To make fennel hair rinse: *Take equal quantities of fennel leaves, limeflower and chamomile and add a smaller amount of any of the following herbs – nettle, burdock and horsetail, sage and rosemary. Mix the herbs of your choice together and to 3 heaped tablespoons of mixture pour on 6 cups of boiling water. Leave to infuse until the rinse is the right temperature, then strain into a jug. After shampooing the hair in the normal way rinse it well with water to remove all traces of soap. Use the herbal hair rinse last of all, pouring it over the hair several times.*

A strong infusion made from a mixture of herbs using fennel, sage, rosemary and chamomile will have a refreshing stimulating effect when added to a warm bath.
☛To make a bath infusion: *Use about 6 handfuls of the mixed dried herbs and add boiling water. Leave to infuse for about 15 minutes, then strain and add to the bath water.*

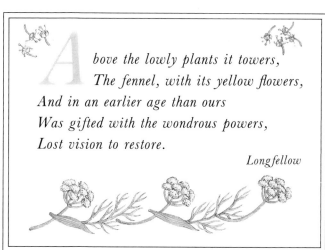

Above the lowly plants it towers,
    The fennel, with its yellow flowers,
And in an earlier age than ours
Was gifted with the wondrous powers,
Lost vision to restore.

Longfellow

F EVERFEW

In ancient times feverfew was highly valued as an effective remedy for fevers, as its name suggests. Another popular name is flirtwort, the derivation of which is more obscure!

Feverfew, *chrysanthemum parthenium*, is an attractive perennial herb with daisy-like flowers and light yellowy-green leaves. It can be found in the wild growing along hedgerows and on waste ground, but nowadays it is usually cultivated in the garden, where it is a useful border plant. Feverfew grows about 18 in (46 cm) high with branched hairy stems. The leaves resemble those of a chrysanthemum in shape but are smaller. The little white flowers have brilliant yellow centres and they bloom in June and July. The whole plant has a strong aromatic smell. There is a double variety of feverfew which is grown as an ornamental plant only.

Feverfew is a hardy plant, very easy to establish in the garden, and it flowers year after year requiring little attention. In February or March sow feverfew seed under glass. In June plant out the seedlings in ordinary garden soil in a sunny spot or in semi-shade. Feverfew self-sows freely and young plants will be found in plenty growing near the parent herb.

Feverfew can be dried for winter use but it is more effective when it is used fresh and in a mild winter the feverfew will often remain green. Both flowers and leaves can be used in the home. The dried herb has a penetrating aroma, so it should be stored separately.

MEDICINAL USE

☛Feverfew is well known for the treatment of migraine and arthritis. It is helpful to eat three or four fresh leaves a day either in a salad or between two pieces of bread and butter. Gently wash the leaves before eating them. Feverfew tablets can be purchased from some health food stores and the recommended dose should be followed.

An infusion of the herb is a good insect repellent. Sponge down the skin with the lotion and leave it to dry. It is especially effective against mosquito bites. Feverfew infusion can be used in the form of a compress to help relieve earache. Use cotton wool pads or balls wrung out in the infusion and apply to the affected part until relief is obtained. The infusion also acts as a mild sedative and is helpful in settling stomach disorders. It can be used as a mouth wash after the extraction of teeth.

☛To make an infusion: *Pour 2 cups of boiling water over 2 handfuls of fresh leaves and flowers chopped together. Leave the infusion until it is quite cold, then strain it into a stoppered jar and store in the refrigerator.*

An infusion using only the flowers is helpful for those suffering from neuralgia and rheumatism and is a good tonic.

☛To make a flower infusion: *Pour 1 cup of boiling water over a large handful of bruised fresh flowers. Leave until quite cold before straining. A small glassful can be taken 2–3 times a day.*

FLAX

Flax is one of the oldest known plants and flax seeds have been discovered in ancient Egyptian tombs. Pliny, the Roman scholar, wrote in the first century AD "What department is there to be found of active life in which flax is not employed."

Linum usitatissimum.

Published by Dr Woodville Nov 1. 1791.

Flax, *linum ustatissimum*, is a graceful plant with lovely blue flowers and is a very decorative herb to grow. It is a hardy annual growing up to 2 ft (61 cm) high, with slender upright stems and narrow, lance-shaped, blue-green leaves. The flowers bloom from June to August and are followed by the seeds which are enclosed in a capsule. Each capsule contains about ten of the smooth, shiny, light brown seeds. It is the stems and fibre of the flax plant which make the strong linen cloth and thread. As a medicinal herb, flax is grown for its seed, which is commonly known as linseed. The seeds are a source of linseed oil which has been used for varnishes, in furniture, polish and in the manufacture of linoleum.

Flax is not a difficult herb to grow, but it must be situated in full sun otherwise the plant will not produce the familiar brilliant blue flowers. Propagation is by seed sown either in April or September directly into its flowering position, in moist, fairly rich soil. The seed germinates quickly and when the seedlings are large enough should be thinned to a handspan apart.

Harvest the plants in August just before the seeds are fully ripe. Cut down the whole plant and tie the stems loosely together in bunches. Hang the bunches upside down with the heads in a paper bag for about a week or until the seeds have fallen off into the bag. Dry and store the seeds in the usual way.

MEDICINAL USE

It is most important to use only the fully ripened seed as unripe seed has little value as a remedy.

🌱Linseed contains vitamins D and E and it can be used in the treatment of mild burns and skin rashes.

For chest complaints, skin irritations and rheumaticky joints make a poultice using powdered seeds.

🌱To make a poultice: *Put the powdered seed into a bowl and pour boiling water on to it to form a thick paste. Spread this between 2 pieces of muslin or cheesecloth and secure it lightly in place. Alternatively, put the seed in a muslin or cheesecloth bag in water and boil until soft. Strain and apply the bag to affected part until relief is obtained.*

BEAUTY CARE

🌱Linseed is very good for softening the skin and when placed in a muslin or cheesecloth bag and added to the bath water will also be soothing and relaxing.

For softening and clearing the skin linseed can be used as a face pack.

🌱To make a linseed face pack: *Boil the linseed until it becomes thick and gelatinous. Use warm, spreading the pack lightly over the face. Relax by lying down for 15 minutes, then wash the face in warm water. Finish by smoothing chamomile lotion (see page 35) over the skin, it helps to keep the skin clear of infection.*

FUMITORY

Fumitory is said to have got its name from the smokelike appearance of its little grey-green leaves. Seen from a distance and growing in a mass, fumitory gives the appearance of smoke swirling off the ground.

Fumaria officinalis

Published by Dr Woodville June 1 1791.

Fumitory, *fumaria officinalis*, is a very pretty annual herb with feathery grey-green leaves and soft dusty pink flowers. It is a common wild plant, growing freely by country lanes and around fields and sometimes appearing in the garden. Fumitory is a small plant growing on rather weak straggly stems which easily get blown over. The flowers grow thinly in loose spikes and bloom throughout the summer months. Neither leaves nor flowers have any scent and insects are not attracted by it. However, the plant fertilizes itself by setting every seed and so is quite widespread.

Fumitory can easily be found in the wild but it can also be cultivated in a sunny patch in the garden where the soil is light. Sow the seed in spring or autumn where the flowers are to bloom and, when large enough, thin the seedlings to a handspan apart.

Both leaves and flowers are used in the home. In June, when the flowers are just starting to bloom, cut down the stems and dry the whole plant as quickly as possible. Store flowers and leaves separately.

MEDICINAL USE

It is important when taking fumitory internally for minor ailments not to continue treatment for longer than seven days. Fumitory is a tonic herb but over a long period it becomes strongly laxative.

To make a tonic infusion: *Using 1 teaspoon of dried leaves to ½ cup of boiling water, pour the water over the herb and leave to infuse for 5 minutes, then strain and use. Take a small glassful once or twice a day before meals. Make fresh every day.*

For mild stomach disorders an infusion of the flowers, made in the same way as above, can be taken in a small glass as a single dose.

BEAUTY CARE

Fumitory is a mild bleaching herb and when boiled in milk makes an effective lotion for fading freckles and suntan. It makes a refreshing skin toning lotion and will help to clear flaking skin and pimples.

To make a skin lotion: *Put 2 handfuls of dried fumitory into an enamel or stainless steel pan, add 1½ cups of milk, bring to the boil and simmer for 15 minutes. Leave to infuse for a further 15 minutes before straining and allowing it to cool. Pour into stoppered jars and store in the refrigerator. Use within a few days. Use the lotion night and morning on problem skins.*

Mentha viridis

GARDEN MINT

In the Middle Ages it was called 'Spere Mynte' and was used to cure all manner of ills and as a strewing herb, laid on the floors to keep the rooms sweet smelling. In France the liqueur Crème de menthe is widely drunk as a digestif.

Garden mint or spearmint, *mentha viridis*, or *mentha spica*, is a very well known perennial herb with an attractive characteristic scent and familiar flavour. The plant grows up to 2 ft (61 cm) high and the square, upright stems are thickly covered with short stiff shoots on which grow the narrow, pointed, bright green leaves. The tiny flowers, which bloom in August and September, grow densely together on tapering spikes in the axils of the leaves and are a pale mauve colour. Mint is a useful and attractive plant to grow in the garden, though once established its underground creeping stems will spread rapidly unless contained.

There are many different varieties of mint which can be grown and used in the same way as garden mint but the flavour and scent of the fresh picked garden mint is best of all.

In the kitchen mint, both fresh picked and dried, is used in many different ways. Mint jelly and mint sauce are traditionally served with lamb. It is delicious when added to vegetables, such as peas and beans, carrots and potatoes, or to pea soup and poached fish or chicken. Mint syrup is an unusual flavour in fruit salad or stewed fruit and mint ice cream has a refreshing cool taste. Garden mint is added to fruit or wine cups and adds an excellent flavour to punch; iced mint tea with a slice of lemon and sweetened with a little honey is a refreshing drink on a hot summer's day. Mint is of course used in the making of mint julep and decorates Pimms drinks.

Garden mint grows well in a rather moist spot in the garden in sun or semi-shade. It is propagated by dividing the roots of an established plant in February or March. Small jointed pieces of rootstock can be planted in trenches or boxes a hand's width apart with a good covering of soil. Water well and, when large enough, set out the mint plants in their final position in the border. Use pieces of roofing slate around the plants to keep the roots from creeping all over the bed and choking other plants.

Garden mint can be dried for winter use by picking the leaves before the flowers begin to bloom. They are dried and stored in the usual way. The flowering tops are gathered on a dry day when the flowers are fully open and at their best and they are dried for adding to pot pourris.

MEDICINAL USE

Spearmint oil is added to many medicines, especially those given to children, because of its pleasant flavour. An infusion of mint will help to relieve and prevent flatulence and assist the digestion.

☛To make the infusion: *Pour 1 cup of boiling water on to a large handful of fresh chopped mint, or 1 tablespoon dried mint. Leave to infuse for 5 minutes then strain and add honey to sweeten. A small glassful can be taken twice a day after meals. Mint infusion should not be taken last thing at night by those suffering from sleeplessness as it might make the condition worse. The infusion can be taken as a remedy for nausea and vertigo and will help to stop the hiccups.*

Fresh crushed mint leaves can be used in the form of a compress to relieve a bad headache.

☛To make a compress: *Pound the leaves to a pulp either by hand or in an electric blender, adding a little water. Spread the pulp on to a piece of muslin or cheesecloth and lay it over the forehead and temples. Leave for 15–20 minutes or until the compress is warm.*

An inhalation will help to relieve troublesome coughs and distressing bronchitis.

☛To make an inhalation: *Put 2 handfuls of fresh crushed mint leaves into a bowl and pour 2 cupfuls of boiling water over them. Cover the head and bowl with a towel, close the eyes and inhale the steam for about 10 minutes. Afterwards wipe the face dry and rest in a warm room.*

Mint can be used as a friction rub for relieving rheumatic and muscular pains. Either use the fresh crushed leaves applied directly to the affected part or make up a simple oil.

☛To make mint oil: *Fill a small glass jar with chopped fresh mint and cover with olive oil. Cover the jar with a piece of muslin or cheesecloth held in place with a rubber band and leave it on a sunny windowsill for at least 6 weeks. Finally strain the oil through fine muslin or cheesecloth and store in a screwtop bottle. Use to rub on the affected areas when required.*

BEAUTY CARE

Spearmint is good for the skin and hair. An infusion used as a lotion will help to clear the skin and improve the complexion.

☛To make the infusion: *Pour ½ cup of boiling water on to 3 teaspoons of finely chopped fresh mint leaves. Leave until cold, then strain into a stoppered bottle and store in a cool place. Use within 1–2 days. After cleaning the face night and morning use a cotton wool pad or ball soaked in the lotion to bathe the skin. It will feel cool and fresh.*

A hair tonic made with mint will help to clear dandruff when used once or twice a week.

☛To make a hair tonic: *Put 1 part chopped fresh mint leaves and 1 part white wine vinegar with 2 parts water in an enamel pan. Bring the mixture slowly to the boil and simmer for 10 minutes. Remove from the heat and strain. When cold pour into a stoppered bottle. The hair tonic is best used about an hour before shampooing the hair.*

Dried garden mint leaves and flowerheads add a lovely fragrant scent to pot pourris, herb cushions and other mixtures of dried herbs. Laid amongst clothes, cloth bags filled with mint will help to repel moths.

G ARLIC

Garlic was thought to guard the eater against the plague. In England in the Middle Ages it was also given to those suffering from leprosy in the belief it would cure them. For thousands of years it has been valued for its antiseptic qualities in the healing of wounds.

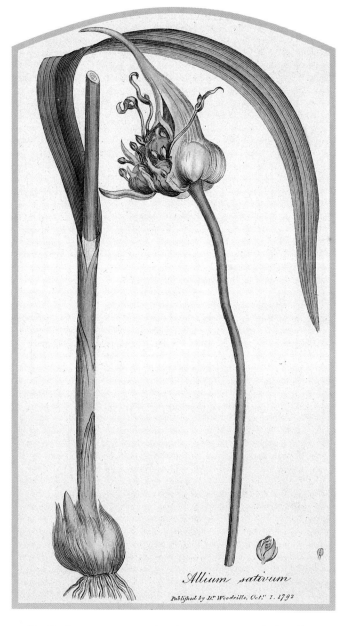

Allium sativum

Published by D.ʳ Woodville, Oct.ʳ 1. 1792

Garlic, *allium sativum*, is a pungent strong-smelling herb and a member of the onion family. It has flat, grass-like leaves, and a single stem. The flowerhead is a ball of small purplish-white flowers clustered together, blooming in August and September. The garlic bulb, which is the edible part of the plant, grows just under the ground and consists of ten or twelve bulblets or cloves. Each clove is covered in a silvery-purple skin and the whole bulb is covered in a thicker, greyish-white skin. The plant has no smell until crushed or broken, when it emits its characteristic odour.

In the kitchen, garlic is a well-known flavouring herb in meat and vegetable dishes. It is also used lightly in salads and with fish, in garlic butter and salad dressings. It is a very pungent herb and should be used with great care or it will overpower other flavours.

Garlic is a very easy herb to grow, and the flavour of fresh home-grown garlic is quite superior to the bought. In late February, set individual cloves of garlic a short way into the ground and cover them with a little soil. In August before the flowers are fully out, lift the bulbs and store them in a dry cool place. Garlic bulbs keep over a long period in this way.

MEDICINAL USE

Garlic is an effective remedy for many minor ailments, but it should be avoided by nursing mothers as it may cause colic in tiny babies. It helps the digestion and relieves flatulence. A wineglassful of a weak infusion can be taken after meals.

To make the infusion: *Pour 2 cups of boiling water over 1 crushed clove of garlic. Leave to infuse for*

5–10 minutes before straining. A little chopped parsley can be added to soften the harsh taste of garlic. The infusion can be made using milk instead of water, especially for digestive ailments. Garlic capsules are an easy way to take garlic internally and these are available at health food stores.

Externally, garlic is a useful remedy for catarrh, coughs and other chest complaints but is not recommended for those with sensitive skins or skin complaints. Smooth garlic oil on to both back and front of the chest, where it acts as a decongestant.
☞ To make the oil: *Fill a small glass jar with finely crushed cloves of garlic and cover the garlic with olive oil. Cover the jar with a piece of muslin or cheesecloth and leave to permeate for 1–2 days or until the oil is sufficiently strong. Strain the oil through a fine strainer into a screwtop jar and label.* This oil will also soothe sprains and painful joints.

For hoarseness, coughs and stubborn bronchial ailments, garlic syrup is an effective expectorant.
☞ To make the syrup: *Finely slice the cloves of a whole garlic bulb. Make a syrup using 1 cup of water and 1 cup of sugar. Bring this slowly to the boil, stirring until the sugar has dissolved. Boil hard for 5 minutes then pour over the garlic. Leave the syrup overnight before straining and bottling. To reduce the pungent smell of garlic add a few caraway seeds, crushed and boiled for a few minutes in vinegar, then strained.*

Garlic ointment is helpful for rheumatism and swollen painful joints.
☞ To make an ointment: *Crush 6 cloves of garlic to a pulp. Melt 4 heaped tablespoons of pure lard or shortening and add the garlic. Bring the mixture to the boil and simmer gently for 20 minutes. Strain through a piece of muslin or cheesecloth into small pots and leave to get cold before covering.*

Garlic vinegar, which is more usually made or bought for using in the kitchen, can be helpful in clearing the skin of spots and pimples.
☞ To make garlic vinegar: *Fill a wide-necked screwtop jar with crushed garlic cloves. Put white wine or cider vinegar into an enamel pan and bring it to the boil. Immediately pour over the garlic and cover the jar with the screwtop lid. Leave the mixture to infuse for 7–10 days in a warm place. Strain off the garlic and repeat the process with a fresh lot of crushed garlic cloves. When the vinegar is sufficiently strongly flavoured strain it through two layers of muslin or cheesecloth to make sure it is clear. Pour into screwtop bottles. Dip cotton wool pads or balls in the vinegar and dab on to spots and pimples.*
☞ Use freshly expressed garlic juice to bring painful boils to a head. Crush the garlic, dip a piece of lint into the juice and place over the boil securing it lightly, or use cotton wool pad or ball and smooth the juice directly on the boil.

Garlic is a good herb for improving the hair and stimulating its growth and the lotion will help prevent dandruff.
☞ To make garlic lotion: *Crush a clove of garlic and put it into a small jar. Add a mixture made up of equal quantities of vodka and distilled water. Leave for 3 days then strain the lotion and pour it into a screwtop bottle. Moisten a cotton wool pad or ball with the lotion and gently rub it over the head. Use the lotion once or twice a week.*

Aioli

Crush 16 peeled garlic cloves in a mortar until reduced to pulp. Add the yolks of 3 eggs and a pinch of salt. Stir with a wooden spoon. Add ½ pint (300 ml) olive oil drop by drop, stirring all the while as the aioli begins to thicken. When the oil is finished and the aioli is very thick, add the same amount of oil again, this time in a slow stream. The aioli will thicken still further. Add a little lemon juice to finish.
Serves 8.

HAWTHORN

Traditionally hawthorn was thought to have been used for the Crown of Thorns and country folk believed it to be a sacred herb. They would carry sprigs of the shrub to protect themselves against sickness and plant hawthorn trees near the houses to ward off evil and bring happiness.

CRATÆGUS OXYCANTHA. L.
Der Hehldorn.

The common hawthorn, *crataegus oxyacantha*, is a familiar hedgerow shrub or tree which in May is covered with small, white, pleasantly scented flowers. The bark is a very pale grey and the branches are covered with sharp thorns. The leaves are small and irregularly shaped. The flowers are followed in the autumn by small bright red 'haws' or berries, each of which contains two or three seeds.

In the kitchen, hawthorn flowers can be used to flavour wines and summertime drinks. Hawthorn liqueur is made using the berries steeped in brandy. The berries make a delicious jelly to serve with cold meats.

In May or June the flowers are gathered for using fresh or for drying. The 'haws' are collected in the autumn. Both are dried and stored in the usual way.

MEDICINAL USE

Both hawthorn flowers and berries are tonic, sedative and astringent. A decoction of the berries is helpful for sore throat.

To make a decoction: *Crush well I teaspoon of dried berries and cover with ½ cup of water, leaving to soak for 8 hours. Bring the decoction to the boil, remove from the heat, strain and sweeten with honey.*

Take a small glassful when required. The unsweetened decoction can be used as a gargle.

Hawthorn tea is a remedy for those who are under stress and for hot flushes resulting from the menopause.

To make the tea: *Pour a cup of boiling water over 2 tablespoons of crushed hawthorn flowers. Leave to infuse for 10 minutes, then strain and sweeten with honey.* The tea is also good for calming the nerves and helps to prevent sleeplessness.

BEAUTY CARE

A decoction of dried hawthorn flowers and berries can be used as a facial lotion for clearing the skin of acne and improving the colour.

To make hawthorn lotion: *Use 2 or more handfuls of the dried hawthorn and leave it to soak in 3 cups of water overnight. Bring to the boil and simmer for 10 minutes. Leave to cool before straining and pouring into stoppered jars. Store in the refrigerator and use within a week.*

Hawthorn can also be combined with other herbs such as rosemary and thyme to make a mild astringent lotion to pat on to the skin after cleansing.

HEARTSEASE

In ancient times heartsease was often used in love charms, for it was firmly believed to be a most potent herb. The country name given to it was Love-in-Idleness.

Viola tricolor

Heartsease, *viola tricolor*, is the wild or field pansy, a dainty low-growing annual commonly found on waste lands along hedgerows and in fields and meadows. It can often be found growing amongst weeds in the garden. The hollow branching stems carry deeply-cut leaves and the small pansy-like flowers appear on single stems. The flowers can be yellow, purple or white though they are usually a mixture of all three colours. The upper petals tend to be purple and the lower elongated petals are a deep shade of yellow with a white throat. Heartsease flowers throughout the growing season from March well into the autumn. It is an easy plant to find in the wild but if found in the garden and allowed to grow unhindered, it will soon provide plants in profusion and make an attractive patch of colour.

Heartsease is a medicinal plant and is always used in the dried state. The whole herb is cut for drying just as the plant begins to flower, then dried as quickly as possible and stored in the usual way.

MEDICINAL USE

Heartsease is a healing herb and can be used externally to soothe and relieve pain. Avoid excessive doses as they can cause allergic skin reactions and vomiting. It is an effective remedy for skin complaints, eczema, spots, pimples and acne. It is also good for urinary disorders and chest and lung inflammations. A compress using a strong infusion of the herb is helpful in the treatment of skin complaints. It is also said to relieve migraines.

To make an infusion: *Pour 1 cup of boiling water on to 4 teaspoons of dried herb in a china bowl. Cover and leave the infusion until cool, then strain. Dip pieces of cloth in the infusion, wring out the excess and place the compress over the affected part for 15–20 minutes. Renew the compress as necessary.*

The compress will help to relieve rheumatism and painful joints. Where a compress is impracticable use the infusion to bathe the affected area until some relief is felt.

HONEYSUCKLE

In years gone by, all parts of the honeysuckle plant were used in herbal medicine for many different complaints. Honeysuckle was traditionally regarded as a sign of true devotion.

Lonicera periclymenum L.

The honeysuckle, *lonicera periclymenum*, is a lovely climbing perennial shrub with strongly sweet-smelling flowers. It is a common hedgerow and woodland plant which twines itself firmly around young trees and shrubs. Its country name of woodbine aptly describes its habits. The leaves are oval in shape and grow on short stalks. The characteristic trumpet-shaped flowers are white inside, yellow or orange on the outside and bloom from June to August. As the flowers age they deepen in colour and these are followed by small clusters of brilliant red berries.

In October or April honeysuckle can be grown from rooted cuttings or seed sown in ordinary soil in a sunny spot. It is best near a fence or hedge where it can climb freely.

Nowadays honeysuckle flowers are the only part of the plant used in the home. When fully opened, the flowers can be picked for use or carefully dried and stored in the usual way.

MEDICINAL USE

Honeysuckle flowers are a helpful remedy for coughs and bronchial catarrh.

☛To make an infusion: *Add a handful of dried flowers to 3 cups of boiling water and leave to infuse for 10 minutes. A small glassful can be taken when required.*

A syrup of flowers is a popular remedy for children's coughs.

☛To make the syrup: *Pour 1 cup of boiling water on to 3 handfuls of fresh crushed honeysuckle flowers. Leave to cool, then strain into an enamel pan and place over a low heat. Stir in a cup of sugar until it has dissolved. Bring to the boil and simmer until the consistency of syrup. Pour into bottles and seal. A teaspoonful can be taken when required. Use the syrup within a week and store it in a cool place.*

BEAUTY CARE

A honeysuckle herbal bath is fragrant and will help to keep the skin soft.

☛To make a honeysuckle bath: *Put fresh or dried flowers into a muslin or cheesecloth bag to hang from the bath tap (faucet). Alternatively, make a strong infusion and add it directly to the bath water.*

Honeysuckle makes a good lotion to fade freckles on the face.

☛To make honeysuckle lotion: *Fill a small jar or bowl with fresh flowers and cover them with cold milk. Leave them to steep for 3–4 hours then strain and smooth over with cotton wool pads or balls.*

☛Carefully dried honeysuckle flowers add a delicate fragrance to pot pourri.

HOPS

Hops were not allowed to be cultivated on a large scale in Britain until the seventeenth century, but many of the country estates cultivated their own hop gardens, using the hops to flavour their home-brewed ales.

The hop plant, *humulus lupulus*, is an attractive climbing perennial and can be found growing wild over hedges and ditches and on the edges of woodland in the southern half of England. Nowadays it is mainly a cultivated plant for making into beer, for which only the female flowers are used. The stout hop stem can grow to a great height like a vine and the leaves are also very similar, having three or five lobes and saw-toothed edges. The hop flowers appear in the leaf axils in July and August, male and female flowers growing on separate plants. The male flowers form in loose hanging bunches while the female flowers look like tight leafy cones made up of yellowy-green bracts. The little cones become larger after flowering and they contain the fruits, which are full of a yellowy glandular powdery substance known as lupulin. Hops have a strong aroma and a bitter taste when fresh.

In the kitchen, the young hop shoots can be cooked as a vegetable and served with butter or french dressing.

Hops can be grown quite easily in a sheltered sunny spot and after two or three years will cover an unsightly wall or old tree stump. Hops are planted in the autumn in good soil and should be kept well watered in a dry spell.

Hops can be used when fresh but the cones are usually dried for winter use and gathered in September while they are still firm but papery to the touch and are a light brown colour.

MEDICINAL USE

The hop is a tonic herb and helps to improve the appetite and the digestion. Hops are good for curing sleeplessness without causing a headache.

☞ To make hop tea: *Pour a cupful of boiling water over a teaspoon of dried hops and leave to infuse for 5–10 minutes. Sweeten with honey and drink hot last thing at night.*

An infusion of hops is good for toning up the system.

☞ To make an infusion: *Pour 3 cups of boiling water over a handful of dried crushed hops and leave to infuse for 10 minutes. Strain and drink a small glassful of the infusion before meals.*

An infusion made using equal parts of hops and chamomile can be used to help relieve painful swellings and boils. A cloth should be dipped into the infusion, wrung out until nearly dry and applied as hot as is bearable on the affected part.

☞ For earache a small bag stuffed with warmed fresh hops is said to bring relief. Hop-filled pillows are well known to help those who suffer from sleeplessness. When making these at home, use dried hops and add a few drops of chamomile oil (see page 35) so the hops will not crackle when using the pillow.

HOREHOUND

Since early times white horehound has been widely used by country people as a remedy for lung troubles and was taken in the form of a wholesome tea or candy for winter coughs and colds.

Marrubium vulgare

White horehound, *marrubium vulgare*, is a decorative little plant with thick woolly hairs covering the whole herb. It is a hardy perennial which, although not common, can sometimes be found growing wild along country lanes and on dry sunny waste land. Nowadays it is more often cultivated in the garden as an attractive grey-leaved plant in the border. The tiny white two-lipped flowers grow in tight whorls in the axils of the leaves, somewhat resembling the white dead nettle, but horehound is a much prettier plant. When it is crushed, the whole herb gives off a pleasant, aromatic, slightly musky scent reminiscent of apples. The flowers bloom from June to October.

White horehound will grow in the poorest of soils wherever it is dry and sunny. Sow the seed in the spring and thin the seedlings when large enough to a handspan apart. The flowers do not bloom until the second year of growth. Horehound will also self-seed quite freely.

The whole herb is used in herbal medicine, either fresh or dried. For drying, the plant is gathered when in flower and the fleshy wrinkled leaves are stripped from the stems and dried separately.

MEDICINAL USE

Horehound is a safe and effective remedy for wheezing, coughs, colds and other chest complaints. It is an expectorant, tonic herb and is especially good for stubborn chesty coughs, loosening phlegm and bringing relief. Horehound is a fleshy herb which, under the right conditions, can start to ferment. All infusions, teas and decoctions to be taken internally should always be freshly made each time.

To make a strong infusion: *Pour ½ cup of boiling water over 2 teaspoons of dried herb. Leave to infuse for 10 minutes. Strain the tea, sweeten with a little honey and sip it whenever the cough is troublesome.*

Horehound is pleasant tasting and is a remedy popular with children. It is soothing and calming and is effective for coughs and stuffy colds. It is best given to children in the form of syrup.

To make horehound syrup: *Put 1 cup of brown sugar into an enamel pan with 2 cups of water. Heat slowly until the sugar has dissolved. Stir in 3 handfuls of dried horehound and bring the mixture to the boil. Simmer for 10 minutes then leave to cool. Strain the* syrup into a stoppered bottle and store in the refrigerator. Use within a few days.

Horehound tea is good for warding off a head cold. It can also be given to children with upset tummies or who are in need of a tonic after an illness.

☞To make horehound tea: *Pour a cupful of boiling water over a handful of chopped fresh herb and leave to infuse for 5–10 minutes before straining. Sweeten with a little sugar and drink the tea as hot as possible as soon as the symptoms appear.*

Horehound tea, unsweetened and drunk cold, will help to stimulate a flagging appetite. It should be taken a short time before a meal to be effective.

Horehound can be a useful herb in that it also has diuretic properties and will help to rid the body of excess fluid. For this purpose a small glassful of horehound tea can be taken cold about half an hour before a meal.

A delicious soothing horehound decoction is good for bronchial troubles and is an effective remedy for a sore throat.

☞To make a decoction: *Put a large handful of fresh horehound into an enamel pan together with 1 teaspoon of bruised crushed aniseed. Add 3–4 cups of water and bring to the boil. Simmer for 20 minutes then remove from the heat. Strain through muslin or cheesecloth, pressing the leaves to get out all the liquid. Add 2 tablespoons of sugar and stir until it has dissolved. Add the juice of a lemon and leave to cool. This can be kept in the refrigerator for up to 2 days.*

A compress prepared from a strong infusion of the herb will help to clear skin problems such as acne and will improve a dull-looking complexion.

☞To make a compress: *Make a strong infusion as directed above but omit the sweetening. Wring out pieces of lint in the cold infusion and lay them on the affected part. Renew the compress when the lint becomes warm or as necessary.*

A poultice of fresh or dried horehound will help to relieve painful rheumatism and swollen joints.

☞To make a poultice: *Use fresh leaves crushed to a pulp or puréed in an electric blender. Dried leaves can be put into an enamel pan with a little water and heated until soft, then put through an electric blender. Spread the pulp between 2 pieces of muslin or cheesecloth. Put the poultice to heat between 2 plates over a pan of boiling water. When sufficiently hot, or as hot as is comfortable, place the poultice on the affected part and secure in place with a bandage or*

long piece of cloth. As the poultice cools, moisten the cloth with hot water until some relief is obtained.

Horehound ointment is a healing remedy for minor cuts and abrasions.

☞To make the ointment: *Melt 4 heaped tablespoons of pure lard or shortening in an enamel pan. Add 2 large handfuls of well-crushed fresh leaves. Cover the pan and simmer gently for 20 minutes. Strain the ointment into small pots and cover them when cold.*

☞To help clear the head of a stuffy cold, put fresh crushed or ground dried horehound leaves into a little muslin or cheesecloth bag and hold it to the nose.

Horehound candy is pleasant to suck and will soothe a cough and relieve hoarseness.

☞To make horehound candy: *Put a handful of freshly cut horehound in an enamel pan with 1½ cupfuls of water. Bring slowly to the boil and simmer for 20 minutes. Strain and return the infusion to the pan, adding a cupful of brown sugar. When the sugar has dissolved, boil the mixture until thick. Pour into a lightly-oiled tin and leave to set. Cut the candy into small squares when cool. Store the candy in an airtight tin and suck a piece when necessary.*

Horehound pastilles and candy can also be bought at chemists or pharmacies and healthfood stores.

☞Horehound wine is a pleasant drink which can be taken to stimulate and improve a poor appetite. Pour two cupfuls of a medium sweet white wine over two large handfuls of dried horehound in a glass jar. Cover and leave to infuse for one week in a cool dark place. Strain the wine through muslin or cheese cloth into a stoppered bottle. Take a small glassful of the wine twice a day before meals for a few days when the appetite has returned.

HORSERADISH

In the Middle Ages horseradish was widely used as a medicine in Britain. Not until many years later did it become popular as a sauce or condiment to eat with meat and help the digestion.

Cochlearia Armoracia

Horseradish, *cochlearia armoracia*, is best known as a condiment mixed with vinegar or made into a pungent sauce to accompany cold beef and smoked fish. However, it is also a useful medicinal and cosmetic herb. It is a perennial plant grown for its long narrow tapering roots which, when cut, have a strong smell and a hot biting taste. It can be found growing in a semi-wild state on waste land but is usually cultivated in the garden. It grows to a medium height and has large, rather coarse, lance-shaped leaves with loosely clustered white flowers blooming in June and July.

Horseradish grows easily in rich well-dug soil. In February, plant out rooted cuttings 12 in (30 cm) apart. The roots are lifted for use during the winter in the first or second year of growth and can be preserved for months by burying them in a box of damp sand in a cool place. Horseradish is always used in the fresh state and needs careful cleaning before use.

MEDICINAL USE

Horseradish helps to prevent indigestion, especially when eaten with rich foods, by stimulating the digestion to assimilate the food. It is a remedy for coughs and bronchial catarrh and is taken as a syrup.

To make the syrup: *Pour ½ cup of boiling water on to 1 teaspoon of grated fresh horseradish root and leave for 2 hours. Strain into a pan and add 4 tablespoons of brown sugar. Bring slowly to the boil, making sure that all the sugar is dissolved before boiling hard until the mixture has a syrupy consistency. Cool and store in a stoppered bottle. Take a teaspoonful at a time on an occasional basis. Do not take large amounts of horseradish at one time.*

Externally, horseradish is used for localized treatment of rheumaticky joints and chilblains.

To make a poultice: *Grate the fresh root on to a piece of cloth, cover with another piece of cloth and place on the affected part. It will stimulate the flow of blood to the area and when a slight burning sensation is felt the poultice should be removed.*

Horseradish ointment will soothe painful joints, aching muscles and chilblains.

To make horseradish ointment: *Melt 4 heaped tablespoons of lard or shortening and add 2 tablespoons of grated root. Stir until it boils, then leave to simmer over a low heat for 20 minutes. Strain the ointment and pour into a small pot. Cover when cold.*

BEAUTY CARE

Horseradish is helpful in removing brown marks and freckles on hands and arms.

To make a lotion: *Use fresh pulped horseradish root to which is added some lemon juice. Brush this lightly on to the marks and allow to dry. Do not use this on the face as it will sting and cause redness.*

HORSETAIL

In primeval time the equisetum family of plants grew to the size of our present-day fir tree and there were huge forests full of them. The little horsetail of today is a replica of those trees

Equisetum arvense L.

Field horsetail, *equisetum arvense*, is a short, rather strange-looking little plant. It grows up to 12 in (30 cm) high and resembles a miniature pine tree. It is found in fields and waste places, along country lanes and railway embankments. It is a very common wild plant which will grow on clay soil but is more usually to be found in sandy soil, through which it can quickly spread its roots. Horsetail is a non-flowering perennial herb increasing through its spores; in the spring the fertile stems grow out of the creeping underground rhizomes. These stems are short, bare and have cone-like heads full of the spores. When these stems die down barren segmented stems appear, covered in whorls of narrow-jointed leaves like pine needles. It is the barren stems which are used in the home and they can easily be gathered from the wild. In gardens and other cultivated areas it can become a troublesome weed and it would be unwise to introduce it as it will swiftly become a nuisance.

Horsetail is used fresh or dried but is said to be more effective when fresh. For winter use, carefully cut off the barren stem just above the ground any time during the growing season. Care must be taken not to cut any plants which have brown spots, as this denotes a fungus disease. Horsetail should be carefully dried so as not to bruise or break the stems. It is then stored in the usual way.

MEDICINAL USE

The field horsetail contains a large amount of the valuable mineral silicic acid which is necessary for maintaining the body's connective tissues. It is mildly diuretic and astringent and helpful to those suffering from rheumatism and skin complaints such as acne and eczema. It is also a useful remedy in the treatment of cystitis.

☛To make a decoction: *Pour 2 cups of water over 2 large handfuls of dried or fresh horsetail. Leave to* soak for 3 hours. Slowly bring to the boil and simmer gently for 20 minutes. Remove from the heat and leave to infuse a further 10 minutes before straining. The decoction is taken cold, a small glassful at a time, 3 times a day. The treatment can be continued for 2 weeks, when an improvement should be noticeable. It is advisable to consult the doctor before embarking on a long course of treatment. The decoction should be stored in the refrigerator and used within 2 days. Horsetail is also available in pill form from most health food stores and the recommended dosage should always be followed.

Externally, a strong decoction can be used in the form of a compress for the treatment of haemorrhoids, eczema and acne.
☛To make horsetail compress: Make a strong decoction by the method described above, but use 4 handfuls of horsetail in 2 cups of water. When just warm, wring out cotton wool pads or balls or pieces of lint in the lotion and apply to the affected part until relief is obtained.

For those with tired aching feet or those suffering from excessive perspiration of the feet a daily footbath in a strong horsetail decoction will be helpful and soothing.
☛To make a horsetail footbath: Use the decoction while still warm and add a little sea-salt to the bowl. Plunge the feet into the bowl for 15 minutes. Finish by putting the feet into cold water then dry them carefully and rub the feet with a little marigold oil (see page 14).

Horsetail tea is said to be good for sleeplessness, but only on an occasional basis.
☛To make horsetail tea: Soak 1 teaspoon of the herb in a cup of water for 2 hours. Bring the mixture to the boil and simmer for 10 minutes. Leave to infuse for a further 10 minutes before straining. Sweeten to taste with honey and drink a small glassful hot last thing at night.

BEAUTY CARE

Horsetail is an important herb in beauty care, for it helps to keep the skin, hair, nails and teeth healthy. It preserves the natural elasticity in the skin and is helpful in restoring skin tone for the older person or after an illness.
☛For splitting or brittle fingernails soak the nails in warm oil for 10 minutes and then in horsetail decoction (see Medicinal Use) for a further 10 minutes. The treatment should be carried out twice a week and

horsetail tea can be taken at the same time until the nails improve. This could take a period of weeks.

☛Horsetail hair lotion is effective in mild cases of dandruff. Use a strong decoction as a final rinse after shampooing the hair in the normal way. Used on a regular basis, horsetail hair rinse will keep the hair healthy and shining.

☛A strong horsetail decoction added to the bath water will soothe skin irritations and help to heal minor abrasions. Combined with dandelion, fennel and seaweed, horsetail helps to reduce water retention in the body and this is useful in a slimming programme.

To refresh and tone up the skin and for large pores use a horsetail face pack.
☛To make a face pack: Mix together some curd, milk and honey, a little lemon juice and horsetail lotion to the consistency of a thick paste. Cleanse the face and brush the face pack thinly over the skin, avoiding eyes and lips. Lie down and relax for 10–15 minutes, covering the eyes with cold water compresses. Wash off the face pack with warm water and finish by splashing the face with cold water.

As a skin tonic, horsetail lotion can be used after cleansing the face both at night and in the morning before applying make-up.
☛To make the lotion: Soak 3 teaspoons of freshly cut horsetail in ½ cup of water for several hours. Bring the mixture to the boil and simmer for 10 minutes. Leave for a further 10 minutes, then strain the lotion into a stoppered jar. Dip cotton wool pads or balls in the lotion and smooth over the skin. Allow to dry. The lotion will keep for 2–3 days in the refrigerator.

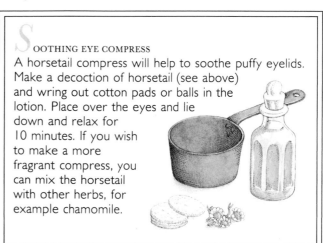

*S*OOTHING EYE COMPRESS
A horsetail compress will help to soothe puffy eyelids. Make a decoction of horsetail (see above) and wring out cotton pads or balls in the lotion. Place over the eyes and lie down and relax for 10 minutes. If you wish to make a more fragrant compress, you can mix the horsetail with other herbs, for example chamomile.

HYSSOP

In Biblical times hyssop was regarded as the herbal symbol of purification from sin and was used in the cleansing of holy places, though the hyssop that is mentioned in the Scriptures is nowadays thought to have been a species of marjoram.

Hyssopus officinalis.
Published by D.Woodville. Jan.ʸ 1. 1791.

Hyssop, *hyssopus officinalis*, is a low growing aromatic bushy shrub, cultivated in the garden as an attractive perennial border plant. Its small narrow leaves grow in great profusion on smooth stems and clusters of little blue, pink or white flowers appear on the terminal spikes. The flowers bloom from June to October and provide a long lasting patch of colours in the garden. Hyssop has a refreshing scent rather like camphor when the leaves are bruised and a slightly bitter taste of mint.

Hyssop is rarely used in cooking nowadays because of its taste, but when used sparingly it can enhance a meat stew or a rich oily fish dish. It mingles well with apricots and a little chopped young leaf sprinkled over an apricot tart will bring out the flavour of the fruit, especially if dried apricots are being used. It is one of the herbs used in making the liqueur Chartreuse.

Hyssop can be propagated by seed or by division of an established plant in spring or autumn. Sow the seed in April in boxes or pots. When the seedlings are large enough set them out a handspan apart in their flowering position. Hyssop flowers well in sun or semi-shade in a well-drained sandy soil with added lime. New plants will need watering until established, after which they require little attention.

The young leaves and flowering tops are the parts of the herb used; they can be picked at any time during the flowering period. Pick only the flowering tips for drying and gather them when the flowers are at their best. Dry and store in the usual way.

MEDICINAL USE

Hyssop is a useful remedy for complaints of the throat and lungs. It is good for coughs, colds and bronchitis and helps to ease congestion and tightness of the chest. Hyssop is taken either as an infusion or in the form of a syrup. The infusion will be found to be very effective in the treatment of influenza and feverish colds where it increases perspiration, so helping to bring down the fever.

To make a hyssop infusion: *Pour 1 cup of boiling water on to a small handful of fresh flowering tips or half the amount of the dried herb. Leave to infuse for 10 minutes before straining; add honey to sweeten. The infusion can be taken hot 2–3 times a day until the symptoms subside. A fresh infusion should be made each day and the treatment should not be continued for longer than necessary, and never longer than 2 weeks.*

To make hyssop syrup: *Heat 1 cup of water and 2 cups of sugar together in an enamel pan until the sugar is dissolved. Bring to the boil and boil hard for 5 minutes. Remove from the heat and add a small handful of hyssop; leave until cold. Strain into a stoppered jar and store in the refrigerator. Take a teaspoonful when the cough is troublesome.*

A decoction of hyssop is mainly for external use but it can be used as a gargle to treat a sore throat and chronic catarrh.

To make a decoction: *Put 1 teaspoon of the herb into 1 cup of water in an enamel pan, bring slowly to the boil then lower the heat and simmer for 5 minutes. Remove from the heat, cover and leave to infuse for a further 5 minutes.*

The decoction is said to relieve mild burns and bruises and skin irritation. Dip cotton wool pads or balls in the lotion and bathe the affected area until relieved.

The decoction can also help to relieve sprains, strains and painful muscles when used in the form of a fomentation. Wring out a piece of lint or towelling in the decoction and while as hot as comfortable place over the affected area.

A poultice is even more effective.

To make a poultice: *Mash fresh hyssop tips to a pulp, spread on to muslin or cheesecloth and heat between 2 plates over a pan of boiling water. Again, it should be used as hot as possible on the painful spot.*

Hyssop is believed to bring quick relief to the pain and bruising of a black eye.

To make an eye pad: *Fill a small muslin or cheesecloth bag full of fresh hyssop and plunge it into boiling water for 1–2 minutes. Wring out the excess water and place the bag over the eye.*

A hyssop bath is said to help those suffering from rheumatic pains.

To make a hyssop bath sachet: *Put 2–3 handfuls of the herb in a muslin or cheesecloth bag and tie to the bath tap (faucet) so that the hot water pours through the herb. Alternatively, plunge the herb bag into plenty of boiling water for 5–10 minutes and when sufficiently strong pour the decoction into the bath.*

BEAUTY CARE

Hyssop is used in the industrial manufacture of toilet waters. In the home hyssop toilet vinegar is refreshing and astringent when a little is added to the washing water. The hyssop can be combined with equal amounts of other herb flowers such as elderflowers and rose petals or used on its own.

To make hyssop toilet vinegar: *Pack a wide-necked screwtop jar with fresh hyssop flowering tops. Bring sufficient white wine vinegar or cider vinegar to the boil in an enamel pan. Pour the vinegar over the herb, filling nearly to the top, and screw on the cap. Leave the vinegar for 2 weeks in a warm place or on a sunny windowsill. Every day give the jar a shake to keep the herb and vinegar well mixed. Finally strain off the vinegar into a stoppered bottle.*

HYSSOP POT POURRI

Hyssop leaves and flowers, when carefully dried, add colour and aroma to a pot pourri bowl. To make your own mixture, gather together 6 cups dried rose petals, 2 cups dried rosebuds, 2 cups dried hyssop flowers and 2 cups dried basil or scented geranium leaves, 4 tablespoons ground coriander, 2 teaspoons ground cloves, and ½ cup orris root powder. Place in a large jar, cover and keep in a warm dark place for 4–6 weeks.

LADY'S BEDSTRAW

Lady's bedstraw was once used as a form of bedding, hence its country name. Before rennet was discovered it was widely used to curdle milk and in the making of cheese and was known as 'cheese renning'.

Galium luteum. Yellow Ladies Bedstraw.

Lady's bedstraw, *galium verum*, is a pretty little way-side herb growing about 12 in (30 cm) high which is commonly found along country lanes and hedgerows, in meadows and near woodland. The small narrow leaves grow in whorls round the straight square stem and the tiny golden yellow flowers grow in a cluster of panicles up the stem. The flowers bloom in July and August and the whole plant has a soft sweet scent, more pronounced when the sun is shining.

The leaves and flowering tips are the parts of the herb used in the home and these can be dried for winter use. Gather lady's bedstraw on a dry day and when the flowers are at their best, then dry and store them in the usual way.

MEDICINAL USE

Lady's bedstraw has a bitter, rather acid taste and nowadays is rarely taken internally. It is said to be a useful remedy for boils and acne, spots and skin irritations. It can be used externally in the form of an ointment or an infusion. For an instant treatment the juice from the fresh plant can be dabbed on to spots and pimples.

☛To make an ointment: *Melt 2 heaped tablespoons of white petroleum jelly in an enamel pan. Add a handful of fresh flowering tips, pushing well down with a wooden spoon. Bring to the boil and simmer for 15 minutes. Strain into small pots and cover when cold.*

☛To make an infusion: *Pour 2 cups of boiling water on to 2 handfuls of fresh herb, 1 handful of dried. Leave the infusion until cold before straining into stoppered bottles. Use cotton wool pads or balls*

dipped in the lotion to bathe the affected areas. For boils, use the infusion hot to draw out the infection.

When the feet perspire in hot weather a lady's bedstraw footbath will refresh and invigorate. It can also be used for swollen and walk-weary feet.

☛To make a footbath: *Make sufficient infusion to fill a large bowl. Pour in the hot infusion and as soon as possible plunge the feet in for 15 minutes. Remove the feet and plunge them into cold water to close the pores. Dry the feet carefully, smoothing lady's bedstraw ointment over sensitive areas.*

LADY'S MANTLE

In the Middle Ages the herb came to be known as lady's mantle because of the scalloped shape of its leaves, which were thought to resemble the mantle of the Virgin Mary.

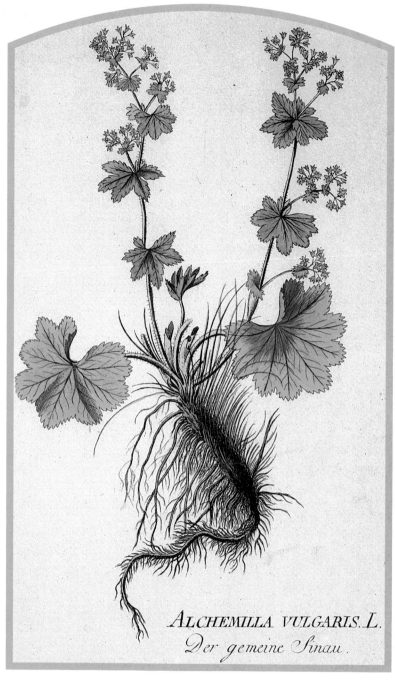

ALCHEMILLA VULGARIS. L.
Der gemeine Sinau.

Lady's mantle, *alchemilla vulgaris*, is a graceful garden plant and few realize that the popular alchemilla, so favoured by flower arrangers, is in fact a useful medicinal and cosmetic herb in the home. A perennial plant, lady's mantle appears quite early in the year, flowering up to 12 in (30 cm) high. The basal leaves grow quite large and are softly fan-shaped while the beautiful little yellowy-green flowers grow in loose clusters at the top of the short erect stems; the flowers bloom from June to August and the whole plant is covered in soft hairs. Lady's mantle can often be found growing wild in hilly districts by streams and in damp meadows.

Lady's mantle is a hardy plant. Propagation is by seed or by dividing the roots in the autumn or spring. Sow the seeds in May or June out of doors directly into their flowering position in sun or partial shade in ordinary garden soil. When the seedlings are large enough thin to a handspan apart. Keep plants well watered and free of weeds. They will flower the following year.

Both flowers and leaves are used but only in the dried state. Gather the plant for drying when the flowers are at their best, usually late June or early July. They are then dried and stored in the usual way.

MEDICINAL USE

Lady's mantle is a tonic herb with a slightly bitter taste which is not unpleasant. Internally taken in the form of a herb tea, lady's mantle helps to stimulate the appetite, can be used in the treatment of rheumatism and, best known of all, is a useful remedy for women's ailments. It helps to regularize the menstrual cycle and to protect all female organs and is recommended for those of middle age.

☛To make lady's mantle tea: *Pour a cupful of boiling water on to 2 teaspoons of dried herb. Leave to infuse for 10 minutes. A teacupful can be taken once or twice a day, sweetened with honey if preferred. Make fresh tea each time.*

The infusion can be used as a mouthwash after tooth extraction. Leave the tea until it is almost cold and thoroughly rinse out the mouth. The lady's mantle will help to stop bleeding.

Externally, a stronger infusion of lady's mantle can be used to help in the healing of cuts and abrasions.

☛To make a healing lotion: *Make the infusion as directed above, using twice as much of the dried herb. Leave the infusion until it is cold then strain. Dip cotton wool pads or balls into the lotion and bathe the cuts until the bleeding stops. A gauze swab soaked in the lotion and then laid over the cut can be held in place with a light bandage and can be equally effective.*

A strong infusion of lady's mantle added to the bath water will be soothing and also help to heal minor cuts and abrasions.

BEAUTY CARE

Lady's mantle is an astringent, healing herb and will help to restore tone and elasticity to the skin and to reduce inflammation and infection.

☛A lotion using the strong infusion of lady's mantle (see Medicinal Use) can be used night and morning after cleaning the face. Dip cotton wool pads or balls in the lotion and wipe the face. Leave the skin to dry. Make up a fresh infusion each day and between morning and evening keep it in the refrigerator. This lotion is an excellent remedy for acne and will help to clear and refine the skin.

Another effective treatment for acne is to use the juice from the fresh plant.

☛To make a remedy for acne: *Gather young leaves and flowering stems and put them in a juice extractor or electric blender. When using the blender, add sufficient water to make the herb into a pulp, then squeeze out the juice through fine muslin or cheesecloth. Dip cotton wool pads or balls into the juice and swab the infected area. Leave to dry on the skin. The juice will also help to close large pores.*

To fade unsightly freckles, use the freshly extracted juice and dab it on the skin. This treatment has to continue over a long period to be effective, but eventually will bear good results.

A pleasant fragrant way to treat acne is to have a facial steam using lady's mantle with chamomile and perhaps yarrow.

☛To make a facial steam: *Using equal quantities of the herbs, put them in a bowl and pour boiling water over them. Clean the face and then cover the head and bowl with a towel for up to 10 minutes. Wash the face with a clean cloth wrung out in cold water to remove impurities and close the pores.*

The strong infusion of lady's mantle will also help to close large pores if used on a regular basis. To help the treatment a twice-weekly face pack can be used in conjunction with this.

☛To make a face pack: *Make up a very strong infusion and while still warm mix in sufficient Fuller's earth or fine oatmeal to make a thick paste. Cleanse the skin then brush the mixture thinly over the face, avoiding the eye area and lips. Use herb or cold water compresses to cover the eyes. Lie down and relax for 10–15 minutes. Remove the face pack and wash the face with tepid water. Finish off with a splash of cold water to close the pores.*

☛A cold compress using a strong infusion of lady's mantle is a real tonic for tired and unhealthy-looking skin. It is suitable for most types of skin, but if very dry smooth a little oil over the face. Wring out a large piece of lint in the cold infusion and place it over the face pressing it lightly on to the skin. Lie down and relax for 10 minutes. The face will feel invigorated, fresh and firm as a result.

Lady's mantle can be added to other herbs such as chamomile, coltsfoot, fennel and lemon verbena in a mixture to be used in the form of a compress for tired eyes and swollen eyelids.

☛To make an eye compress: *Use a small amount of lady's mantle with marigold, fennel and chamomile and pour a cupful of boiling water over 2 teaspoons of the mixture. Leave to infuse for 5 minutes, then strain carefully through fine muslin or cheesecloth. Leave until the infusion is tepid. Cut pieces of lint, dip them into the lotion and place over closed eyes. Relax for 10 minutes. Remove the compresses and splash the lids with cold water.*

LAVENDER

Lavender has been popular for its sweet scent since the time of the Romans when it was added to the bath water for its perfume. Later it was used as a strewing herb and, as an oil, lavender cured burns and wounds.

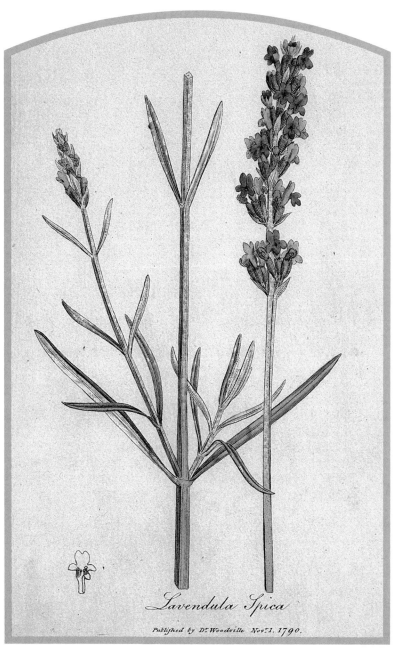

Lavendula Spica

Published by D?. Woodville Nov?1, 1790.

English lavender, *lavandula vera*, is a lovely, aromatic, evergreen shrub growing 1–3 ft (30–91 cm) high. The main stem grows in a crooked fashion with flaking bark and from this the other stems grow stiff and straight. The grey-green leaves are narrow and the fragrant flowers grow in spikes on long stems which stand out high above the plant. Other lavenders in the species have the same habit of growth, some with deep purply blue flowers, some with pink or white. The white lavender is not a very hardy plant. No other lavender has such an intensely aromatic yet delicate scent as the English lavender. Lavender is grown commercially on a large scale for the oil which is obtained from the flowers and that of the English lavender is considered far superior to the other lavenders.

In the home lavender is widely used, laid amongst clothes and linen as a perfume and moth deterrent, in pot pourris or on its own set in little bowls to fill the room with scent. It can be used for flower arrangements either fresh or dried.

Lavender will grow best in light, sandy, well-drained soil and a dry, sunny position. It can be propagated by seed or more quickly by cuttings. Cuttings can be taken in August and set into a cold frame in sandy soil or under a cloche, and planted out the following autumn. Lavender should be pruned after flowering to keep the bushes a good shape and encourage sturdy growth.

Lavender for drying is gathered when the flowers are in full bloom in late July or August. Pick them on a dry day, cutting the long stems. They are then dried and stored in the usual way.

MEDICINAL USE

Lavender is well known as a remedy for headache, migraine and nervousness. It can stimulate the circulation and is helpful in cases of nervous exhaustion. It is used to relieve neuralgia and insomnia, and will revive those who feel faint or dizzy.

Lavender is usually taken in the form of oil but lavender tea is a pleasant fragrant drink. For migraine, headache and nervous disorders a small glassful can be taken hot last thing at night and first thing in the morning. Taken at night, it is sleep inducing.

☛To make lavender tea: *Pour I cup of boiling water over I teaspoon of fresh flowers. Cover and leave to infuse for 10 minutes.*

Lavender tea can be used as a mouthwash. It will strengthen the gums and is a remedy for bad breath.

Lavender oil can usually be purchased at a chemist (pharmacy) or a simpler version made at home.

☛To make lavender oil: *Pour I cup of almond or sunflower oil into a glass jar and add a handful of fresh lavender flowers. Cover with a piece of muslin or cheesecloth and stand the jar in the sun for 3 days. Strain off the oil and repeat the process, adding a fresh lot of flowers. Continue until the oil is strongly perfumed, perhaps 2–3 weeks, then strain into screw-top bottles. For migraine and dizziness 5 drops of oil can be taken on a lump of sugar.*

Externally, the oil is a useful remedy for mild burns. It can be helpful in cases of congestion, rubbed on to the chest, and can soothe aching muscles.

BEAUTY CARE

Lavender has a lovely soft fragrance and is used in many beauty care products, soaps and talcum powders. Lavender toilet water is refreshing, cooling and slightly antiseptic. Bathing the forehead and temples with lavender water will help to overcome fatigue and exhaustion. Lavender water can be obtained from the chemist (pharmacy) or it can be made at home.

☛To make lavender water: *Put 3 handfuls of dried lavender flowers into a wide-necked screwtop jar and add I cup of white wine vinegar and ½ cup rose-water. Leave the mixture in the dark for 2–3 weeks and shake the bottle frequently.*

An infusion of fresh flowers can be used to tone the skin once a day.

☛To make lavender flower infusion: *Pour 2 cups of boiling water over 4 teaspoons of lavender. Cover and leave until cold. Strain into a screwtop bottle and use within a few days. Dip cotton wool pads or balls in the lotion and press lightly over the face.*

The infusion makes a pleasantly fragrant hair rinse. Shampoo the hair and rinse well in plain water. Finally rinse the hair several times over with warm infusion. It stimulates growth and leaves the hair shining and soft.

You can make an effective sweet-smelling hand lotion to keep the hands soft and fragrant.

☛To make a hand lotion: *Add sufficient lavender oil to scent ½ cup of glycerine in a bottle. Shake the bottle vigorously each time before using.*

For a refreshing bath, add a strong infusion of lavender flowers to the bath water.

☛To make a lavender bath: *Pour 2 cups of boiling water over 2 handfuls of dried lavender and leave until lukewarm. Strain and add to the bath water.*

Lavender flowers can be mixed with other herbs for a facial steam to improve a dull-looking complexion and tone the skin.

☛To make a facial steam: *Mix lavender with lime flowers, chamomile and sage and place 2 handfuls of this mixture in a bowl. Pour on about 4 cups of boiling water. Cover the head and bowl with a towel and steam the face for up to 10 minutes. Wipe the face thoroughly with cotton wool pads or balls and splash with cold water.*

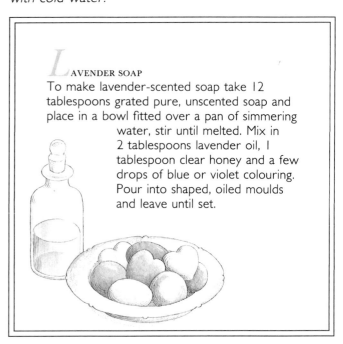

*L*AVENDER SOAP
To make lavender-scented soap take 12 tablespoons grated pure, unscented soap and place in a bowl fitted over a pan of simmering water, stir until melted. Mix in 2 tablespoons lavender oil, I tablespoon clear honey and a few drops of blue or violet colouring. Pour into shaped, oiled moulds and leave until set.

Melissa officinalis

LEMON BALM

Down the ages lemon balm has been used to cure many ailments including epilepsy and melancholia. Balm tea was also believed to ensure a long and trouble-free life.

Lemon balm, *melissa officinalis*, is an attractive herb growing to about 3 ft (91 cm) in height which was invariably to be found in old herb gardens. The straight, square stem is much branched with light green, rather coarse leaves and small white flowers growing in loose clusters in the leaf axils. The flowers bloom from July to September. The whole plant is slightly hairy and when bruised the leaves have a fragrant lemony scent which attracts the bees in great numbers. This accounts for its name 'melissa', the Greek word for bee. It is a rapid-growing perennial plant of thick and bushy growth.

85

In the kitchen, lemon balm is an important culinary herb. With its strong lemony flavour it can take the place of grated lemon peel in stuffings for poultry and game, with fish and in fruit salads, ice creams and orange mousse. It is refreshing when added to fruit drinks and wine or cider cups. Melissa tea is a well-known soothing and relaxing tea which can be taken at any time of the day.

Lemon balm grows without trouble in any garden soil in sun or semi-shade and is propagated by seed, cuttings or division of roots. Seed is slow to germinate but can be sown in the spring for planting out later in the year. Lemon balm grows best from stem cuttings which are taken in spring or autumn and planted 2 ft (61 cm) apart. It has a rampant root system, so care should be taken that it does not choke other plants; allow plenty of space or set in root tiles around it.

Lemon balm is used in the manufacture of toilet waters and perfumes. In the home the leaves and flowering tips are the parts used and these can be fresh or dried. For drying pick the leaves before the flowers appear and the flowering tips before the flowers are fully open. However, lemon balm is more effective when used fresh.

MEDICINAL USE

Lemon balm is a mild, fragrant herb that can be taken over a long period of time; it is helpful for flatulence, stomach upsets, headaches and neuralgia. It calms the nervous system, reducing tension, and melissa tea taken hot last thing at night will ensure a good night's sleep for those who suffer from insomnia. It is also a remedy for common feminine ailments.

To make melissa tea: *Pour 1 cup of boiling water on to 2 teaspoons of fresh chopped lemon balm or 1 teaspoon of dried herb. Leave to infuse for 10–15 minutes, strain and add honey to sweeten.*

Melissa tea is said to be good for the digestion when taken after a meal in place of coffee, and is a remedy for dizziness. For headaches take a cup of hot melissa tea twice a day. In cases of feverish colds and influenza lemon balm slightly increases perspiration and cooled melissa tea can be taken quite freely.

It is also one of the best herbal teas for those suffering from nausea and is good for settling the stomach. The tea can also be helpful in easing menstrual pain and can safely be drunk when required on a regular basis. Sweeten the tea with a little honey and add a slice of lemon to make a delicious lemon-scented drink.

Externally, a poultice made with fresh leaves and flowering tips is said to benefit those with rheumatism.

To make a poultice: *Crush the leaves to a pulp and spread between pieces of muslin or cheesecloth. Heat the poultice between 2 plates over a pan of boiling water and when sufficiently hot place on the affected part. Renew as necessary.*

An instant remedy for an insect bite is to rub, or to hold, well crushed leaves firmly over the spot.

Lemon balm infusion is made slightly stronger than tea. Used as a mouthwash it will help to remove bad breath and is said to relieve toothache. Cotton wool pads or balls dipped into the infusion and applied to minor cuts and abrasions will help to soothe and heal.

To make an infusion: *Pour 1 cup of boiling water over 4 teaspoons of fresh herb and leave until lukewarm before straining.*

BEAUTY CARE

Lemon balm has mild antiseptic properties and can be used as a complexion lotion to soothe irritations of the skin and protect it from infection.

To make a skin lotion: *Use 3 teaspoons of lemon balm in 1 cup of boiling water. Leave until it is cold before straining into screwtop bottles. The lotion will keep for a few days in a cool place or in the refrigerator, but freshly made lotion is always more pleasant to use. After cleansing the face, dip cotton wool pads or balls in the lotion and smooth over the skin. The lotion can be used night and morning for softening the skin and helping the complexion.*

Lemon balm can be used on its own or in a mixture of other herbs for a soothing refreshing bath.

To make a herbal bath: *Choose from rosemary, elderflower, chamomile and marjoram and make a strong infusion. Take 2 handfuls of the herbs and put in an enamel pan with 6–8 cups of water. Bring slowly to the boil and simmer for 10 minutes. Strain and add the infusion to the bath water.*

Lemon balm, with its strong lemon-scented leaves, adds a long-lasting fragrance to pot pourris and herb cushions helping to fix the scents of the other herbs.

For a sweet-smelling, soothing herb cushion which will relax those suffering from sleeplessness due to nerves: *Mix together dried crushed lemon balm, peppermint and sage in equal quantities. Add a few drops of lavender oil to soften the crackle of the dried leaves.* The cushion should be made of muslin, cheesecloth or gauze so that the full scent of the aromatic herbs can be enjoyed, and covered with a pretty flowered fabric of light cotton or lawn.

LEMON VERBENA

Originating from Chile, lemon verbena was introduced into Europe in the late eighteenth century and lemon verbena tea has been popular in France and Spain ever since.

Lemon verbena, *lippia citriodora*, is a beautiful lemon-scented deciduous shrub which, if grown in a sheltered position, can grow up to 6 ft (1.8 metres) high. The leaves are narrow, lance-shaped and deeply veined and they grow in whorls of three along the woody stems; they contain the aromatic oils and when bruised or crushed are refreshingly fragrant. The tiny pale pink flowers grow in loose spikes and are in bloom from July to September.

In the kitchen young lemon verbena leaves are added to fruit salads, fruit drinks and wine cups. Lemon verbena tea, when sweetened with honey and served iced, is deliciously cooling in hot weather.

Lemon verbena is not a hardy shrub and will need either to be protected during the winter months or to be brought indoors. It will grow in well-drained garden soil in a sheltered spot facing south. Lemon verbena is propagated from stem cuttings taken from an established plant at any time during the growing season.

The leaves for drying are at their best just before the flowers fully open. Pick only the perfect leaves and dry and store in the usual way.

MEDICINAL USE

Lemon verbena tea is very pleasant to take and is a useful remedy in mild cases of indigestion and flatulence. It is also calming and sedative and a help to those who cannot sleep due to nervous tension.

To make lemon verbena tea: *Pour 1 cup of boiling water on to 1–2 teaspoons of fresh or dried herb. Leave to infuse for 5–10 minutes, then strain and sweeten with honey. To be effective a small cup of tea can be taken hot last thing at night.*

BEAUTY CARE

Lemon verbena lotion is good for the complexion and keeps the skin clear of infection.

To make a skin lotion: *Follow the same method as described above, using 2 teaspoons of dried herb to 1 cup of boiling water. Pour into screwtop bottles, store in a cool place and use within a few days.*

The infusion makes a pleasant mouthwash and is good for bad breath. For tired eyes a compress using pieces of lint dipped in lukewarm infusion is refreshing.

To make an infusion: *Pour ½ cup of boiling water on to 1 teaspoon dried herb. Infuse for 5 minutes and strain. Place compresses on closed eyes and lie down and relax for 15 minutes.*

Lemon verbena with its fragrant lemony scent can be included in all pot pourris. Lemon verbena sachets add a lovely perfume when laid between clothes and linen. Filled cushions keep a room smelling sweet.

LESSER CELANDINE

The favourite wild flower of the poet Wordsworth, who wrote to the small celandine 'Pleasures newly found are sweet / when they lie about our feet.'

Ranunculus Ficaria

The lesser celandine, *ficaria verna*, is a pretty little herb which grows wild along ditches and at the edges of fields in damp shady places. It is a low-flowering plant with heart-shaped glossy leaves on long stalks and light golden flowers. The flowers resemble a buttercup but have more than five petals. The whole plant spreads rapidly by means of small tubes which grow from the roots, each producing a new plant. One of the earliest of the wild herbs to bloom, lesser celandine flowers in the spring from February to May; as soon as the hot summer weather arrives the whole plant dies down.

Lesser celandine can become a tiresome weed once introduced into the garden but if it can be confined to a shady spot it is worth while growing. In early summer remove the small round bulblets which grow in the axils of the leaves of an established plant and put immediately into the ground.

In March and April when lesser celandine is in flower the whole plant, including the root, is collected for drying as the flowers are at their best. This is then dried and stored in the usual way.

MEDICINAL USE

Lesser celandine is abundant in Vitamin C and for this reason was used in the treatment of scurvy. The fresh herb should never be taken internally and although its toxicity can be destroyed by drying and heating it is safer to use it externally only. The country name for this herb is pilewort and its main medicinal use is for the relief of discomfort from the distressing complaint of haemorrhoids (piles).

To make a concentrated decoction: *Use a handful of lesser celandine in 1 ½ cups of water. Leave to soak for 30 minutes. Bring the mixture gradually to the boil and simmer for 5 minutes, then strain.*

For a fomentation dip a piece of lint into the decoction, wring out the cloth and put as hot as possible on to the affected part.

A poultice may prove a more effective treatment.

To make a poultice: *Use either the fresh herb mashed to a pulp or dried herb moistened with water to the right consistency. Put the mixture between pieces of muslin or cheesecloth and heat between 2 plates over a pan of boiling water. Use as hot as possible on the affected part.*

To make an ointment: *Use a handful of grated fresh root to 4 heaped tablespoons of pure lard or shortening. Heat the lard slowly in a pan and when melted add the herb and mix well together. Bring the mixture to the boil then simmer very gently for 30 minutes. Strain into small pots and cover when cold.*

LIME FLOWER

Lime was formerly known as the linden tree, so beloved by poets. Linden tea was a popular digestive tea for many years in France; 'tilleul', made with dried lime flowers, is a well-known after dinner drink.

Lime-tree, or Line or Lind or Linden or Lynd-tree

TILIA EUROPÆA L.
Die Europäische Linde.

The lime tree, *tilia europaea*, tall and elegant with lovely fragrant blossoms, is an attractive sight in the countryside and when in flower the air round the tree is heavy with its sweet scent. The pale yellow flowers bloom in June and July, growing on short stems in clusters of five and drooping down amongst the leaves; they attract the bees in great numbers. The leaves are heart-shaped, dark green above and pale underneath, and are connected to the main stalk by a long narrow bract. Lime trees have traditionally been widely cultivated in parks and gardens and avenues of limes are a familiar sight.

Lime trees take many years to attain their full height and it is a long time before a new tree comes into flower. Lime trees are usually propagated by layering; the layered branch, once rooted, can be severed from the parent tree and planted in rich moist soil.

The flowers are the only part of the tree used in medicines and for beauty care in the home. Lime flowers have a soft sweet aromatic flavour which is distinctive and pleasant. The flowers can be used fresh or dried. For drying gather the flowers and bracts together at the end of June and beginning of July. They are then dried and stored in the usual way.

MEDICINAL USE

Lime flowers calm the nerves and digestion, help to clear catarrh, increase perspiration and bring down the temperature. Lime flower tea is good for sleeplessness when taken hot last thing at night. A cup of warm lime flower tea is also said to be helpful for migraine and can be taken once or twice a day after meals on a regular basis. This should reduce the severity of a migraine.

☛To make lime flower tea: *Pour 1 cup of boiling water over 2 teaspoons of dried flowers. Cover and leave to infuse for 5 minutes, then strain and add honey to sweeten to taste, although the tea is already pleasant to drink without extra sweetening. For a feverish cold or influenza the infusion should be taken as hot as possible.*

For a head cold accompanied by a headache lime flower tea acts like an aspirin, relieving the symptoms and soothing the head. It will help to ease a harsh cough, loosening the mucus and is, at the same time, a soothing and pleasant drink to take. For digestive troubles a cup of hot lime flower tea will be helpful taken after meals.

To clear a head cold or chronic catarrh an inhalation can be an effective treatment.

☛To make an inhalation: *Use a handful of each of the following flowering herbs: lime flowers, sage, elder-flowers and peppermints. Place the herbs in a china bowl. Pour 6 cups of boiling water over the herbs and immediately cover both head and bowl with a large towel to stop any steam escaping. If the heat and steam become overpowering the towel can be partially lifted. Inhale the steam for 10–15 minutes or until all the steam has disappeared. Afterwards wipe the face and neck with cold water. It is important after this treatment not to go outside but to rest and relax in bed in the warmth. An inhalation can be used once a day until relief is felt.*

In the spring when the leaves first appear, lime leaf tea can be made to help relieve those who are suffering from nerves.

☛To make lime leaf tea: *Pick only the round, tender leaves and chop them finely. Pour ½ cup of hot water over the leaves and leave to infuse for 15 minutes. Strain carefully and drink while still hot.*

BEAUTY CARE
Lime flower is one of the most helpful cosmetic herbs. It has slight bleaching properties and can therefore help to fade freckles.

☛To make a skin lotion: *Pour ½ cup of boiling water on to a small handful of lime flowers. Leave until cold before straining into a screwtop bottle. Dab the lotion on to the freckles night and morning. Make fresh lotion each day.*

Lime flower lotion is good for the skin, stimulating

the circulation. Used as a compress it can also help to smooth out tiny wrinkles. Dip a large piece of lint into the lotion and cover the face, pressing the lint gently down on to the skin. Relax for 10–15 minutes. Alternatively pat the lotion on to the wrinkles.

A facial steam is an effective way to cope with blackheads by cleaning the pores.

☛To make a lime flower facial steam: *Pour boiling water on to lime flowers in a bowl and cover head and bowl with a towel. Steam the face for 10 minutes. Clean the face with a cotton wool pad or ball and close the pores using cold water.*

A strong infusion of lime flowers added to the bath water is delightfully fragrant and relaxing to those who are weary after a long day.

☛To make a strong infusion: *Pour 4 cups of boiling water on to 3 large handfuls of lime flowers and leave to infuse for 10 minutes. Strain the infusion and add directly to the bath water.*

For tired, swollen and aching feet and ankles a lime flower footbath is very helpful.

☛To make a footbath: *Prepare 2 bowls each large and deep enough to hold the feet comfortably. Fill 1 bowl with tepid water and pour a strong hot infusion of lime flower into the other. Plunge feet and ankles into the hot lime flower infusion for 5–10 minutes. Then dip them quickly into the tepid water bowl. Repeat the treatment then dry the feet carefully. Relax lying down for a short while with the feet propped up higher than the head.*

Lime water hair rinse used regularly will help to keep the hair soft and in good condition.

☛To make a hair rinse: *Make a strong infusion of lime flowers, leaving it to infuse for 5–10 minutes before straining into a jug. Shampoo the hair and rinse well in water. Finally pour the lime flower rinse over the hair 2–3 times. This will leave the hair shining and improve its texture.*

Ligusticum Levisticum

L OVAGE

In former times, lovage cordial was a popular drink with country people, who took it for sore throats and quinsy. John Gerarde, who wrote his Herball *in 1597, considered lovage to be one of the wonder drugs at that time.*

Lovage, *levisticum officinale*, is a stout-stemmed hardy perennial herb which has always been a cultivated plant and looks attractive at the back of the herbaceous border. In the winter lovage dies right back, but as soon as spring comes it grows quickly to reach its full height of 5–6 ft (1.5–1.8 metres). The large leaves are deeply divided into three or more leaflets, looking very like celery or angelica leaves. The greeny-yellow flowers, which first appear in June, are in umbels and these are followed by oval-shaped pale brown fruits.

The whole plant, when bruised, is strongly aromatic and it has a warm, savoury taste.

In the kitchen lovage makes a delicious soup on its own, or it can be added to other vegetable soups, meat stews and casseroles. It adds an unusual flavour to green salads and savoury egg dishes and, added to oatmeal, lovage makes tasty oatcakes to eat with cheese.

Lovage is an easy herb to grow and once established will self-sow in a good season. It is propagated by seed or division of roots in spring. For best results sow the seed as soon as it is ripe and when the seedlings are large enough to handle transfer them to their flowering position 18 in (46 cm) apart. Lovage produces luxuriant growth if planted in rich well-drained soil in a sunny spot.

All parts of the plant can be used in the home but nowadays only the leaves are used to any extent. Lovage leaves should be gathered for drying before the flowers come out and, for a good season's picking, the first flowers to appear should be cut off. The leaves should be picked first thing in the morning. Because they are large and fleshy, they need careful drying. They are then stored in the usual way.

Medicinal Use

It is important that lovage should never be taken by anyone suffering from a kidney complaint or during pregnancy. Lovage stimulates the digestion and can be a useful remedy for an upset stomach, mild cases of diarrhoea, and for getting rid of flatulence. It is well known for the cleansing effect it has on the whole system. Lovage is taken as an infusion made with the dried leaves which tastes more like a broth than a tea.
To make an infusion: *Pour 1 cup of boiling water on to 1–2 teaspoons of dried herb and leave to infuse for 10 minutes, then strain. Take a small glassful as required and make a fresh infusion each time.* Lovage broth is also good for nursing mothers as it helps to stimulate the production of milk.

Lovage is an antiseptic herb and a weak infusion can be made for soothing and healing sore feet. Gently bathe the feet in the infusion until relief is obtained. Lovage infusion made with distilled water is an effective lotion and can be used as an antiseptic for bathing cuts and abrasions.

A poultice made with lovage leaves is said to bring boils and virulent spots to a head.
To make a poultice: *Use well-crushed fresh or dried leaves. Melt sufficient lard or shortening in a pan for the herb to take up without burning. Add the leaves and press down well. Heat until the lovage is crisp. Spread the hot mixture between 2 pieces of muslin or cheesecloth and place as soon as can be borne on to the affected part. Continue with the poultice until the boil has burst or relief is felt.*

Beauty Care

Lovage is a deodorant herb and is useful for keeping the skin free from impurities. To increase the effect on the skin, lovage can be taken internally at the same time. A strong infusion of lovage can be used regularly as a complexion lotion. This will keep the skin free from spots and will also fade freckles.
To make a strong infusion: *Pour 2 cups of boiling water on to a large handful of lovage leaves and leave to infuse for 15 minutes. Strain and pour into stoppered bottles. The lotion will keep for a few days in a cool place or in the refrigerator but whenever possible use freshly made lotion, as it is far more effective. Dab cold lotion on to the blemishes or freckles daily.*

The strong infusion can be added to the bath water for a relaxing cleansing bath, while an infusion made with a mixture of herbs will soothe and soften the skin as well as adding a lovely mingling of scents.
To make an instant herbal bath: *Fill a square of muslin or cheesecloth with fresh chopped or dried lovage leaves and hang it underneath the hot tap (faucet) so that the water flows through the herb.*

Lovage can be used in a mixture of herbs in the form of compresses to soothe tired eyes and puffy eyelids.
To make an eye compress: *Add only a small amount of lovage to chamomile and fennel, marigold and summer savory. Mix the herbs together and pour a cupful of boiling distilled water on to a heaped teaspoon of the herbs. Leave to infuse for 5 minutes then strain and leave until lukewarm. Cut pieces of lint and dip them into the infusion. Place the compresses over closed eyes and lie down and relax for 10 minutes. After removing the compresses splash the eyelids with cold water to tighten up the skin.*

*L*OVAGE SOUP
Place 1 large, chopped onion and 1 tablespoon oil in a pan, cook until transparent. Add 2 chopped potatoes, 2 tablespoons fresh or green dried lovage and 2½ cups chicken stock. Simmer for 10–15 minutes. Leave to cool, then blend in a food processor. Return to the heat adding milk to taste. Serve hot.

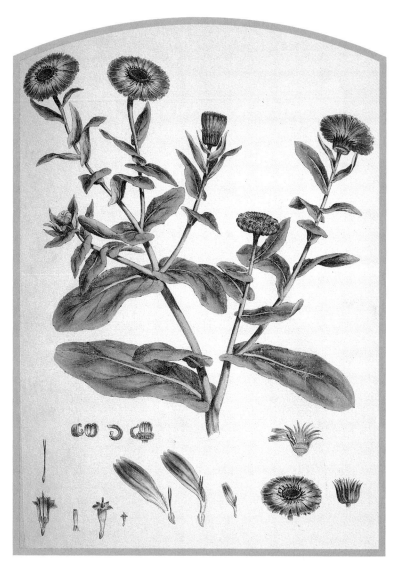

MARIGOLD

In the sixteenth century marigold was a common garden plant valued by herbalists for comforting the heart and soothing the spirit. The dried flowers went into the making of broths and teas, and were used to add colour to cheese.

Marigold, *calendula officinalis*, with its brilliant orange daisy-like flowers, makes a vivid splash of colour in the flower garden. The light green lance-shaped leaves are soft and velvety. The flowers will bloom throughout the summer months and often until the first frosts of autumn if the dead heads are immediately cut off. Neither flowers nor leaves have any marked scent.

In the kitchen young leaves and petals, with their slightly sharp taste, add a tang to salads. The fresh petals can be added to cheese and egg dishes and to rice in place of saffron.

Marigold is a hardy annual and very easy to grow but there are many varieties and it is important to purchase *calendula officinalis*, the flowers of which have so many uses in the home. Marigolds grow in any type of soil in a sunny place. In March or April sow the seeds directly into their flowering position; they germinate quickly. When the seedlings are large enough, thin the plants to a hand's width apart. Marigold readily self-sows all over the garden and the small seedlings which come up in the spring can be transplanted to their flowering position.

Marigold leaves and flower petals are the parts of the herb used in the home. Young leaves can be picked for drying before the flowers open and the petals gathered when the flowers are fully open. Leaves and petals are dried and stored separately.

MEDICINAL USE

Marigold is a gentle remedy when taken internally for mild digestive ailments. The tea will help to increase perspiration and so reduce a fever and is said to be good for bringing out the spots in cases of measles.

☞To make marigold tea: *Pour 1 cup of boiling water over 4 teaspoons of fresh petals or 2 of dried and leave to infuse for 5 minutes. Strain and add honey to sweeten it. Take a small glassful as required.* The tea is also helpful to those suffering from bad circulation and varicose veins.

Marigold is best known for its healing properties of all kinds of skin complaints. In the form of an ointment marigold is a remedy for eczema, acne, pimples and spots. It can be used in the treatment of boils to prevent the formation of scar tissue, and also helps to heal minor cuts and abrasions.

☞To make marigold ointment: *Use equal quantities of crushed dried petals and white petroleum jelly. Melt the jelly in an enamel pan and add the marigold petals, pressing them well down. Bring the jelly to the boil and simmer gently for 20 minutes or until the marigold petals are crisp. Strain immediately into small pots and cover when cold.*

Marigold lotion used in the form of a compress will help to soothe painful burns, sprains, bruises and strained muscles.

☞To make the lotion: *Pour 1 cup of boiling water on to a good handful of petals. Leave until cold then strain into screwtop bottles. Soak pieces of lint in the lotion and place on the affected part, renewing the compress as necessary until relief is obtained.*

☞The freshly expressed juice of the plant is said to be a remedy for warts, corns and calluses and should be dabbed on the affected area morning and evening until the problem is cured.

A decoction of marigold petals can be used to bathe scratches, cuts and grazes and will also help to relieve painful chilblains.

☞To make a decoction: *Soak a handful of petals in a cupful of cold water in an enamel pan. Bring the water slowly to the boil and simmer for 3–4 minutes. Remove from the heat, cover and leave to infuse for a*

further 3 minutes; strain and leave to cool. To prevent chilblains forming bathe the hands or feet in the decoction to which a small handful of sea salt has been added. The treatment should be carried out both morning and evening to be really effective.

For painful chilblains a poultice made from dried petals is also said to bring relief.

☞To make a poultice: *Crush the petals into a pulp with a little milk or water. Spread the pulp on to a piece of cloth and heat the poultice between 2 plates over a pan of boiling water. Using the poultice as hot as possible, place it directly on the chilblains.*

BEAUTY CARE

Marigold petal lotion is slightly astringent and is good for oily skins.

☞To make a lotion: *Pour 1 cup of boiling distilled water on to a handful of dried petals. Leave until cold, then pour the lotion into screwtop bottles. Store in a cool place and use within a few days.*

The lotion can be used as a compress for reducing large pores. Dip pieces of lint in the lotion and gently press on to the face avoiding the eyes and mouth. Lie down and relax for 15 minutes.

Use marigold ointment (see Medicinal Use) to soothe and soften chapped hands and rough skin. Marigold oil is also effective for this and can be used for sunburn and in the treatment of acne.

☞To make marigold oil: *Fill a small glass jar with a large handful of fresh crushed marigold petals and add a cup of almond oil. Cover the jar with a piece of muslin or cheesecloth and leave on a sunny windowsill or in the greenhouse for 3–4 weeks. As the petals sink to the bottom of the jar add more freshly picked ones. When the oil is sufficiently strong strain through fine muslin or cheesecloth, pressing all the oil out of the petals. Smooth the oil over the affected part.*

☞Adding a decoction of marigold petals to the bath water is soothing for tired and aching limbs. Equally effective is to fill a muslin or cheesecloth bag full of petals and hang it beneath the hot water tap (faucet).

For tired, aching and swollen feet a footbath can be very comforting and beneficial.

☞To make a marigold footbath: *Make an infusion by pouring 4 cups of boiling water on to 2 large handfuls of fresh chopped or dried young marigold leaves. Cover and leave to infuse for 10 minutes, then strain into a bowl. Plunge the feet into the bowl for 10 minutes or until relief is felt.*

Althæa officinalis

Published by Dr Woodville Nov.r 1. 1790.

MARSH MALLOW

The sweet of this name was once made from the root of this herb. The plants were gathered by fishermen's wives in the marshes of the East coast.

Marsh mallow, *althaea officinalis*, is a tall attractive herb growing wild by river estuaries, along salt marshes and by ditches. It is also cultivated as a garden plant and is attractive at the back of the herbaceous border. Marsh mallow is a perennial and dies right down in the winter. The fan-shaped leaves are soft and velvety with bluntly serrated edges. The flowering stems rise from the axils of the leaves and single pale pink flowers grow in clusters at the top. Fine hairs cover the whole plant, giving it a soft appearance amongst harsher greens in the garden. The flowers are in bloom during August when some of the other summer flowers are over.

Marsh mallow can be grown from seed sown in any ordinary garden soil and in any position. When grown in moist ground the leaves and roots will grow larger. Sow the ripe seeds in early autumn directly into their flowering spot and thin out the seedlings when large enough. Marsh mallow can be propagated by root division. In spring or autumn, before the plant is in leaf or after it has died down, lift the roots, put aside those needed for drying, divide the remainder and replant 2 ft (61 cm) apart.

The flowers, leaves and root are the parts of the herb used in the home. The leaves are picked off the stems for drying just before the flowers come out. The flowers can be gathered when fully open and the roots dug up in the autumn. All are dried and stored separately.

MEDICINAL USE

Marsh mallow roots contain, amongst other properties, a mucilage which thickens into a jelly-like substance when mixed with water. It is effective in the treatment of coughs, bronchitis and sore throat and helps to relieve indigestion.

☛To make an extract of the root: *Soak 3 teaspoons of grated dried marsh mallow root in 1 cup of cold water for about 8 hours; strain and heat by standing the container in a pan of hot water until lukewarm. Take a spoonful as required. For sore throats and tonsillitis, gargle with the extract as frequently as possible to bring quick relief. Keep in the cool or in the refrigerator and use within a few days.*

An extract of marsh mallow leaves is said to be a useful remedy for chesty colds and coughs.

☛To make an extract of the leaves: *Soak 2 teaspoons of chopped leaves in 1 cup of water for 6 hours. Strain and reheat as described above and sweeten with honey if preferred. A spoonful can be taken as required. Keep in the cool or in the refrigerator and use within a few days.*

For stuffy head colds and sinusitis use marsh mallow in the form of an inhalation.

☛To make an inhalation: *Into a bowl pour 2 cups of boiling water on to a handful of dried crushed leaves. Cover the head and bowl with a towel and breathe in the warm fumes for up to 10 minutes. Afterwards dry the face and remain indoors in a warm room.*

Use the same mixture in the form of a fomentation for congestion. Wring out pieces of lint in the lotion and apply as hot as possible to the chest.

Externally, a strong extract of marsh mallow will help to alleviate bruises, sprains and aching muscles.

☛To make an extract for external use: *Soak 2 handfuls of dried grated root in 1 cup of water for 6 hours and then strain. Use warm or cold and smooth over the affected part.*

For mild burns use an extract in the form of a compress.

☛To make a compress: *Soak 2 tablespoons of dried leaves in 2 cups of water for 30 minutes. Strain and dip a piece of lint into the solution. Place over the affected part. Renew the compress as necessary.*

Marsh mallow ointment is also a remedy for mild burns and bruises and will help reduce inflammation and swellings caused by bee and wasp stings.

☛To make an ointment: *Melt 4 heaped tablespoons of white petroleum jelly in an enamel pan. Remove from the heat and add 4 tablespoons of extract a little at a time while stirring. Pour into small pots and cover when cold.*

A marsh mallow poultice will reduce inflammation and bring boils and persistent spots to a head.

☛To make a poultice: *Use fresh root crushed to a pulp with a little water, or mixed with a little honey to a thick paste. Spread the pulp between 2 pieces of muslin or cheesecloth. Heat the poultice between 2 plates over a pan of boiling water. Place on the affected part as hot as is bearable and reheat the poultice if necessary to reduce inflammations.*

☛A freshly crushed or well-bruised leaf is an instant remedy for insect bites and stings.

BEAUTY CARE

Marsh mallow is one of the most effective herbs for moisturizing and softening the skin.

☛To make a skin lotion: *Soak 3 teaspoons of dried grated roots or leaves in 1 cup of distilled water for 8 hours. Strain into a stoppered jar and use morning and evening after cleansing the face. Use within a few days and keep the lotion in a cool place.*

☛The jelly-like extract (see Medicinal Use) can be added to plain cold creams available from the chemist (pharmacy) for using as a moisturizer under make up.

☛Add the extract to glycerine and use a little every night to soften rough skin and relieve painful chapped hands. It will also help to soothe skin irritations.

A marsh mallow face pack helps to combat dry flaky skin.

☛To make a face pack: *Use the extract of the root, made with distilled water, and mix into a paste with Fuller's earth or fine oatmeal. Cleanse the face and brush the pack over the skin, avoiding eyes and mouth. Use cold water compresses on the eyes. Relax for 15–20 minutes. Remove face pack with warm water and smooth on marsh mallow complexion lotion.*

M EADOWSWEET

In former times meadowsweet was often used to flavour beers and wine and was known as the honey-wine herb. It was a popular strewing herb laid upon floors and in cupboards to keep rooms sweetly scented.

La Reine des Prés.
Spiræa ulmaria. Linn. Sp. Pl.
Angl. Meadow Sweet. Allem Geiss-bart.

Meadowsweet, *spiraea ulmaria* (or *filipendula ulmaria*), is often called Queen of the Meadows. It is a lovely herb with masses of creamy white blossom in July and August. It grows in damp meadows and by the side of rivers and streams but is mainly found in ditches along country lanes. The square, reddish stems grow tall and straight with deeply divided serrated leaves which are silvery white on the underside. Both leaves and flowers have a delightful sweet scent but each has a quite different fragrance to the other.

If a sufficiently damp spot can be found for meadowsweet in the garden it will readily become established. It is propagated by root division in the spring or autumn.

Meadowsweet is easily found growing in the wild and can be gathered for drying or for using fresh in the home. Choose plants growing in ditches which are well away from busy roads and arable fields so there will be no danger from pollution from petrol fumes or chemical spraying.

Gather leaves and flowers for drying in July when the flowers are first coming out. Strip them off the stems and dry them separately; they are then stored in the usual way.

MEDICINAL USE

Meadowsweet is a form of natural aspirin as it contains salicylic acid, so it is helpful in cases of headache, colds, influenza and rheumatism. For these ailments an infusion of the flowers is used.

To make an infusion: *Pour a cup of hot – not boiling – water on to 2 teaspoons of meadowsweet flowers. Leave to infuse for 10 minutes before strain-ing and sweetening with honey. Drink 1 cup of meadowsweet tea per day and make a fresh infusion each time you take it.*

A stronger infusion can be used to bathe cuts, scratches and abrasions. It will be effective in helping them to heal more quickly.

To make a strong infusion: *Use 1½ cups of warm water poured on to 2 handfuls of flowers and leave until cold. Strain into a screwtop bottle and use within a few days.*

A poultice of fresh flowers can be used on rheumatic joints to help relieve the pain.

To make a poultice: *Mash sufficient flowers to a pulp, using a little water to get the right consistency. Spread the pulp carefully between 2 pieces of muslin or cheesecloth and heat it between 2 plates over a pan of boiling water. When it is hot, place the poultice as soon as is possible over the affected part until relief is obtained.*

MELILOT

Melilot was widely cultivated as animal fodder; horses, cattle and even deer would feed on it, giving it its country name of harts clover.

Melilotus officinalis. Common Melilot ♂

Melilot, *melilotus officinalis*, is a tall, fragrant, perennial herb which can be found growing along country lanes, railway cuttings, on chalky banks and in waste places. The leaves are divided into three leaflets which are bright green and oval-shaped. The smooth straight stem is branched, and each stem carries a long spike of attractive little yellow flowers, which bloom from June to September. The whole herb has a sweet smell much like new-mown hay which is very noticeable when the plant is dried and which is similar to woodruff. Both herbs contain a substance known as coumarin which attracts bees and accounts for the characteristic scent. The seed pods are ribbed and hairy and each pod contains two seeds.

Melilot herb or seeds can be collected from the wild, but it is a graceful plant in the garden when grown at the back of the flowerbed. Collect fresh seed from the wild plants in the autumn and immediately sow them in ordinary garden soil directly into their flowering position. Thin out the plants if required to a handspan apart. Melilot is a hardy plant and self-sows readily. It needs little care or attention.

In the home melilot is a good moth deterrent laid among clothes and linen or hanging in a cupboard (closet). Leaves and flowering tips gathered early in the season are the parts of the herb used medicinally and these are dried separately and stored in the usual way. The dried herb is lightly scented but has a sharp, slightly bitter flavour.

MEDICINAL USE

Melilot tea relieves flatulence and other digestive troubles. It is also a remedy for sleeplessness and a cup of hot tea taken occasionally last thing at night will help to promote restful sleep.

☛ To make melilot tea: *Pour a cup of boiling water on to 1 teaspoon of dried flowering tips and leave to infuse for 5–10 minutes. Strain and add honey to sweeten and remove some of the bitterness. For mild digestive upsets, take a small glassful after a meal on an occasional basis only and make the tea fresh for each treatment.*

Use a lotion as a compress for relieving painful and swollen joints.

☛ To make a compress: *Pour 2 cups of boiling water on to 3 teaspoons of dried herb and leave to infuse for 15 minutes. Strain carefully into stoppered bottles and store either in the cool or in the refrigerator. Use within a few days while still fresh. Dip a piece of lint into the lotion and secure lightly over the affected part, or use the lotion on cotton wool pads or balls to bathe the area whenever possible.*

MOTHERWORT

In medieval times motherwort was widely cultivated as a medicinal plant as it was considered to be of value for female complaints – hence the name.

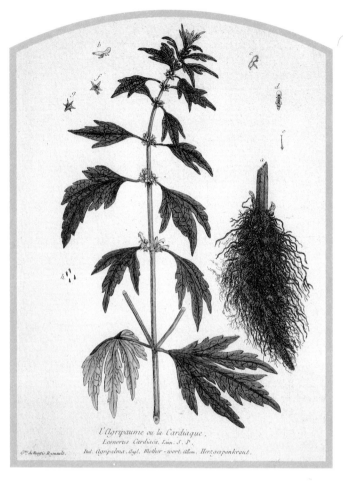

L'Agripaume ou la Cardiaque.
Leonurus Cardiaca, Linn. S. P.
Ital. Agripalma, Angl. Mother-wort, Allem. Herzgespankraut.

Motherwort, *leonurus cardiaca*, is a sturdy square-stemmed perennial herb, growing 2–3 ft (61–91 cm) tall. It was once a familiar plant in country gardens, where it was grown simply as a medicinal plant. It is rarely found in the wild and then only as a garden escape. Motherwort is easy to distinguish amongst others of the same species by its leaves, which are deeply divided into three or five lobes. The straight simple stems are covered with short bristly hairs. The flowers are a dull pink and grow in the axils of the upper leaves. They bloom from July to September. The whole plant has a strong pungent smell and a very bitter taste.

Motherwort is a hardy plant and once established will readily self-seed, appearing in odd spots all over the garden. Sow the seeds in spring directly into their flowering position in a sunny place in ordinary garden soil. When large enough thin out the seedlings to 12 in (30 cm) apart.

The flowering tips of motherwort are used in the home and these are gathered for drying in August when the plant is in full flower. Gloves should be worn by those with sensitive skins as direct contact with the plant can cause skin problems. The herb is dried and stored in the usual way.

MEDICINAL USE

Motherwort is considered to be a helpful remedy for nervous tension, migraine, neuralgia and menstrual problems. It is also very beneficial for stomach cramps. It is one of the best tonic herbs, and is most effective if the bitter-tasting tea is taken.

To make the tea: *Pour 1 cup of boiling water on to 1 teaspoon of dried herb. Leave it to infuse for 10 minutes before straining. Honey can be added to taste to soften the bitter flavour. A small glassful should be taken after meals once or twice a day. The tea is also a good remedy for the discomfort of flatulence and can act as a mild sedative.*

A more palatable way to take motherwort as a tonic is in the form of a syrup.

To make the syrup: *Pour a cupful of boiling water on to 1 tablespoon of dried motherwort. Leave it to infuse for 10 minutes, then strain the infusion into an enamel pan and add 1 cup of water and 4 tablespoons of honey. Heat the mixture slowly to boiling point and then simmer gently until a syrup consistency has been reached. When it has cooled, pour it into screwtop bottles and take a teaspoonful of the syrup after meals once or twice a day.*

MUGWORT

Mugwort was always considered to be a good country cure for fatigue and mugwort leaves were put into the shoes when walking to save the feet from getting weary.

Artemisia vulgaris

Published by Dr Woodville Jan 1 1792.

Mugwort, *artemisia vulgaris*, is a stiff-stemmed aromatic perennial herb, commonly found growing wild along country lanes and hedgerows. It is easy to recognize from its reddish stems and deeply cut leaves which are dark green above and covered with a silvery down on the underside. The insignificant little flowers are a dull yellow and grow in long spikes at the top of the stem. They flower from July to September and have a lovely strong scent. The leaves have no scent. From a distance mugwort looks very like common wormwood but on closer inspection the leaves of mugwort are sharply pointed and only downy on the underside, whereas the wormwood leaf is blunt ended and covered all over in down.

In the kitchen, mugwort is a savoury herb which can be used to bring out the flavours of rich meats, poultry and game and make them easier to digest. Mugwort is a strong-flavoured herb and needs to be used with care. It is also a useful moth repellent and small bags of mugwort mixed with other herbs can be laid amongst clothes or hung in cupboards (closets).

Mugwort can be grown in ordinary garden soil and is propagated by cuttings taken in the spring or root division of an established plant in autumn or spring.

The leaves and flowering tips are the parts used. The leaves are gathered for drying before the flowers appear, and the flowering tips while in bud. They are dried and stored separately in the usual way.

MEDICINAL USE

Mugwort is said to assist in the digestion of rich foods and in stimulating a poor appetite. It can be taken as tea twice a day before meals. It should not, be drunk over a long period of time. Mugwort tea is made using dried or fresh flowering buds only.

To make mugwort tea: *Pour a cup of boiling water over 1 teaspoon of mugwort and leave to infuse for 10 minutes. Strain and sweeten with honey.*

Mugwort oil is effective on rheumaticky joints.

To make mugwort oil: *Put a cup of sunflower oil in an enamel pan and add a handful of fresh or dried mugwort leaves. Bring slowly to the boil and simmer until the leaves are crisp. Strain into stoppered bottles and store in the cool. Smooth the oil on the joints.*

Mugwort infusion is good for tired and swollen feet.

To make the infusion: *Pour 4 cups of boiling water over 4 handfuls of mugwort buds. Leave to infuse for 10 minutes. Strain into a bowl. Plunge the feet into the infusion for at least 15 minutes. Afterwards dry the feet well and dust with dried and powdered mugwort. For painful blistered feet, apply the lotion with a cotton wool pad or ball.*

M ULLEIN

One of mullein's country names was 'the candlewick plant', so called because the thick down was rubbed off the plant and used to make the wicks in lamps and candles.

Verbascum Thapsus

Mullein, *verbascum thapsus*, is a tall, attractive biennial herb and a lovely plant to grow at the back of the border. In the first year a flat rosette of large, thick, downy, green leaves appears. Mullein grows wild on waste ground, along country lanes and by hedgerows. In the second year each plant produces one stout stem which grows up to 5 ft (1.5 metres) high. The brilliant yellow flowers, blooming from June to August, grow in dense profusion on the long spikes at the top of the stems and the whole plant, including the flower, is covered with fine hairs. The seedpods, when ripe, are hard and full of seeds which eventually fall round the plant so that it self-sows quite freely.

To grow mullein in the garden, sow the seed in October when it is ripe in well-drained ordinary soil in a sunny spot well sheltered from the wind. Mullein seeds can also be sown in a frame in April, pricked out when large enough, and set into their flowering positions in September. The plants may need protection from slugs, which have a particular liking for mullein.

It is the flowers of the mullein which are used in the home for internal use, but young leaves can be used for external treatments. The leaves carry too many hairs for them to be taken internally. The flowers for drying are gathered on a dry day when fully open and the blooms are perfect. The young leaves can be picked at any time during the season. They are dried and stored separately in the usual way. It is important when drying the flowers that they retain their bright yellow colour otherwise they lose their medicinal value. They have a sweetish pleasant taste.

MEDICINAL USE

Mullein is one of the most useful herbs for chest complaints and mullein tea can be taken two or three times a day for persistent coughs and chesty colds. Mullein is also slightly sedative and a glass of hot tea taken last thing at night will usually help those who cannot sleep.

☞To make the tea: *Pour I cupful of boiling water on to I heaped teaspoon of dried or fresh flowers. Leave to infuse until the tea is a strong yellow colour, which will take about 10 minutes, then strain and drink warm. It is important to strain the tea most carefully through very fine muslin or cheesecloth to make sure none of the hairs are left in the infusion. Make the tea fresh each time.*

Mullein tea can be used as a lotion to bathe cuts and abrasions, for mild burns and for skin rashes. The lotion is more effective as a compress. Dip pieces of lint into the lotion and spread it over the affected part, pressing it lightly on to the skin. Renew the compress as necessary or until relief for the condition is obtained.

A poultice made from fresh leaves can be applied to the chest to relieve congestion and also to loosen a stubborn cough.

☞To make a poultice: *Pound a quantity of leaves to a pulp either by hand or in an electric blender. Spread the pulp carefully between 2 large pieces of muslin or cheesecloth and heat it over a pan of boiling water. When it is sufficiently hot, place it over the chest and cover it with a further cloth to keep the heat in. Leave in place until the poultice loses its heat and keep renewing as needed.*

A decoction of flowers, dried or fresh, can be effective when used as a gargle for throat complaints, tonsillitis and laryngitis and it is good for easing hoarseness and soreness of the throat.

☞To make the decoction: *Add a cupful of water to a handful of dried. or fresh flowers in an enamel pan. Bring it slowly to the boil and simmer for 3–5 minutes. Remove from the heat and strain carefully through fine muslin or cheesecloth. As a warm gargle the decoction can be used freely until relief from irritation and soreness is obtained.*

A poultice made from fresh mullein leaves with milk is an effective remedy for boils, whitlows and virulent spots. The action of the poultice brings them to a head and with the pus removed the pain and swelling is considerably eased.

☞To make a poultice for skin complaints: *Place a handful of fresh or dried leaves in a pan with sufficient milk to cover. Bring slowly to the boil and simmer for 5 minutes. Strain, reserving the milk, and either place the leaves directly on the infected spot or spread them on to a piece of muslin or cheesecloth. Renew the poultice and apply until relief is felt. The poultice is also helpful to those suffering from chilblains and the milk in which the leaves have been boiled can be used to bathe painful haemorrhoids (piles).*

Mullein oil can be used to stop irritation and relieve chilblains and haemorrhoids (piles). It is soothing and softening and will help to heal painful bruises.

☞To make the oil: *Put as many mullein flowers as possible into a small glass jar. Fill the jar with olive or almond oil, covering the flowers completely. Cover the jar with a piece of muslin or cheesecloth held in place with a rubber band. Stand the jar on a sunny windowsill or in the greenhouse for 3–4 weeks until it is a strong yellow colour. Shake the jar occasionally. Finally strain the oil carefully through several layers of fine muslin or cheesecloth into a stoppered bottle. Use to bathe the piles or the chilblains whenever they are painful.*

Sufferers from a stuffy head cold and congestion will find that an inhalation of mullein flowers can provide effective and immediate relief.

☞To make an inhalation: *Pour a cupful of boiling water over a handful of flowers in a bowl. Place a towel over the head and bowl and inhale the fumes for 10 minutes or until relief is felt. Afterwards wipe down the face with a towel and stay indoors in the warm for at least I hour.*

☞Fresh crushed mullein flowers applied directly to warts have been used to help in curing this unsightly problem.

N ASTURTIUM

Nasturtium is a native of South America and was brought to Europe by the Spaniards. Until the eighteenth century nasturtium was used as a salad vegetable and the flowers were used for tea.

Tropaeolum majus

Nasturtium, *tropaeolum majus*, is a climbing annual plant with brightly coloured flowers of orange and yellow which make a colourful show in the garden. The leaves are almost round with deep veins radiating from the centre. The trumpet-shaped flowers, often larger than the leaves, bloom from June into the autumn.

Nasturtium is grown from seed sown in ordinary garden soil in a sunny spot. Sow the seeds in early spring directly into their flowering position in light well-drained soil. It is a useful plant in the garden, helping to protect plants growing nearby from troublesome pests, especially aphids.

Nasturtium leaves have a rather biting peppery flavour and can be used dried and powdered in place of pepper as a seasoning. Fresh nasturtium leaves and flowers can be added to salads and used in sandwich spreads. It is a strong herb, so needs to be used with care and only small amounts should be eaten on any one day. The larger seeds, which appear in the autumn, can be pickled and eaten with cold meats in place of capers.

The leaves dry well for use in the winter and these should ideally be gathered while young and before the flowers appear, though this can sometimes be difficult in practice. They are then dried and stored in the usual way.

MEDICINAL USE

Nasturtium is a herb full of Vitamin C, which helps to prevent infection, and eating nasturtium leaves at the onset of a cold or influenza may help to clear up the symptoms.

The juice extracted from the stems and fresh leaves can be applied directly to the skin as a remedy for itching.

A poultice made of crushed nasturtium seeds is helpful in bringing persistent spots and boils to a head.

To make a poultice: *Crush the seeds to a pulp and spread it on to a piece of muslin or cheesecloth. Cover with another piece and put to heat between 2 plates over a pan of boiling water. Once it is hot enough, lay the poultice over the affected part.*

BEAUTY CARE

Nasturtium contains a high concentration of sulphur which is good for the hair and scalp.

To make a simple hair lotion: *Put 1 large handful of fresh chopped nasturtium leaves into a wide-necked screwtop bottle and add 1 cup of vodka. Cover and keep in a warm place for 2 weeks, shaking the bottle once a day. Carefully strain the lotion until it is absolutely clear. Apply to the scalp once or twice a week, using a cotton wool pad or ball moistened in the lotion. Take care not to get any of the lotion anywhere near the eye area.*

NETTLE, LESSER

Before flax was known and cultivated, nettle fibre was used to weave both coarse and fine cloth. Nettle leaves were used to dye yarn as a good green colour was produced, while the root mixed with alum yielded a soft yellow dye.

Urtica urens.

The lesser nettle, *urtica urens*, is an annual, and a shorter version of the perennial common nettle *urtica dioica*. The sharp-pointed, jagged-edge leaves are smaller and the creamy-green flowers grow in little clusters, each containing both male and female. They bloom from June to September and are rather insignificant. Except for the stinging hairs, the small nettle is smooth and it only grows about 12 in (30 cm) high. It is a troublesome weed everywhere and seems to appear in the garden in great profusion as soon as winter is over.

In the kitchen, fresh picked young nettle tops can be boiled and eaten as a green vegetable. They look and taste like spinach and make a healthy addition to the diet. Nettles lose their sting in the cooking and also when they are dried. Never eat uncooked old nettle leaves as they can cause kidney damage.

The whole herb is cut down for drying in May or

June just before the plant begins to flower. It is best to wear gloves and long sleeves when gathering the nettles, and to use scissors for cutting them. The herb should be gathered on a dry day and only perfect leaves used. They are then dried and stored in the usual way.

MEDICINAL USE

Nettle is considered to be a good all-round tonic, stimulating the digestion, improving the appetite and generally producing a feeling of well-being.

Nettle contains Vitamin C and a cup of tea taken last thing at night and in the morning will help to ward off colds and coughs. The tea used as a gargle is an effective remedy for a sore throat. A course of nettle tea, especially in the spring, will tone up the whole system, cleansing the blood of impurities and generally improving the health. To eat young nettle tops at the same time will make the treatment more effective.

To make nettle tea: *Pour a cup of boiling water on to a teaspoon of dried leaves. Leave to infuse for 10 minutes then strain. The nettles have a rather salty taste. The addition of a sweetener may not be required but honey can be added if preferred.*

To relieve coughs, stuffy colds and other bronchial ailments, use nettles in the form of an inhalation.

To make an inhalation: *Pour boiling water on to 2 handfuls of dried nettles in a bowl. Cover the head and bowl with a towel and breathe in the fumes for 5–10 minutes. Dry the face with cotton wool or a clean towel.*

An alternative way to clear a chesty cold is to burn dried nettle leaves and inhale the fumes.

BEAUTY CARE

Nettle has tonic and astringent properties and is an excellent herb for improving the skin and the hair. For the skin, nettle can be used in the form of a face pack.

To make a face pack: *Put finely chopped fresh young nettle leaves and tops into an enamel pan with a little water added. Bring to the boil and leave to simmer until the nettles form a thick paste. Clean the face in the usual way, spread the nettle pack on to a piece of muslin or cheesecloth and place over the face, avoiding the eyes and mouth. The eyes can be covered with cotton wool pads or balls soaked in cold water. Lie down and relax for 15 minutes. Remove the pack and wash the face in tepid water. In the spring a face pack used regularly over two or three weeks will clear the skin and improve the texture after the damaging effects of winter weather and* central heating. Nettle and dandelion together also provide an effective face pack.

Nettle or nettle and dandelion together used in the bath will be refreshing and good for the skin.

To make a herbal bath: *Use dried herbs and make a strong infusion using 5–6 cups of boiling water poured on to about 8 handfuls of herb. Leave to infuse for 15–20 minutes. Strain the infusion and add directly to the bath water.*

Nettle is good for the hair, stimulating the circulation to the scalp and improving growth. It will condition the hair and will also help to prevent excessive loss.

To make nettle hair lotion: *Finely chop a good handful of fresh young nettle tops and put in an enamel pan with 4 cups of water. Bring them to the boil, cover and simmer over a low heat for 1 hour. Strain and when cold pour into a stoppered bottle. Use the lotion freely twice or four times a week, massaging it into the scalp. Keep the lotion in a cool place and use within a few days. Fresh lotion is always more effective.*

To make nettle hair tonic: *Use 2 handfuls of chopped herb with 2 cups of water and 2 cups of wine vinegar. Put all into an enamel pan, bring to the boil and simmer for 30 minutes. Strain carefully and pour into a screwtop bottle. Massage a little of the tonic into the scalp each day.*

In conjunction with the hair lotion and tonic, use a nettle shampoo (see below) once a week to make the treatment more effective.

NETTLE SHAMPOO

Add 2 handfuls of soapwort to 1½ cups water, simmer for 10 minutes. Cover and cool. Strain the mixture into a screwtop bottle. Take a handful of young nettle leaves, add to 1 cup of boiling water and leave to infuse for 10 minutes. Cool and strain into the screwtop bottle. Shake vigorously to blend.

O RRIS

Orris root was originally used as a medicinal herb in the treatment of dropsy and bronchial ailments. Always considered to be a noble herb, the iris, from which the root comes, symbolized power and majesty.

Iris florentina

Publijhed by Dr Woodville August 1. 1790.

Iris florentina is slightly fragrant, with large beautiful white flowers. It is mainly cultivated as an ornamental plant in the border. The flowers, which bloom in May, have only a short flowering season but it is a handsome plant to grow in the herb garden. The spear-shaped leaves are flat and pale green and the whole plant grows about 2 ft (61 cm) high. *Iris florentina* is a perennial herb with fleshy creeping rhizomes; it is the rhizomes which, when dried, produce the orris root known as *rhizoma iridis*. There are two other iris which produce orris root: *iris germanica*, which has large deep blue flowers, and *iris pallida*, with scented pale blue flowers, but *iris florentina* produces the best orris root.

Iris florentina, once established in the garden, needs little attention. It will grow in ordinary garden soil in a sunny position with the roots buried and the crown of the rhizomes facing towards the sun. Plant the orris in April for flowering the following year. Division of the plant is best done in the spring.

When the plants are two or three years old the rhizomes are gathered for drying. They are scrubbed and cut into small pieces then dried and stored in the usual way. The orris has very little smell when it is first dried and it has to be stored for some time before the full well-known violet scent begins to be released. As the years go by the fragrance becomes stronger and stronger.

BEAUTY CARE

Orris powder adds its lovely fragrant scent of violets to many commercially-made cosmetics and perfumes, dry shampoos, herb sachets and pot pourri and is easy to use in preparations made in the home.

To make a dry shampoo: *Grind to a fine powder some dried orris root and mix it with a little powdered starch. Sprinkle the shampoo on to the head and brush it well through the hair to banish a greasy and lanky appearance.*

Those who suffer from the embarrassing complaint of bad breath will find that chewing a piece of orris root will help to disguise it.

Powdered orris root provides a very good fixative in herb sachets, herb pillows and pot pourris, strengthening the scents of other herbs and helping to preserve those perfumes over a long period of time. Herb sachets and pillows are made of a material through which scents can easily permeate such as muslin, cotton lawn, organdy or voile. There are many herbs and spices suitable for using in pot pourris and other sweet-smelling mixtures and these can be varied according to their use. There are sleep-inducing herbs, herbs for clearing the head, invigorating or calming. But for most of the mixtures a fixative will be needed and orris root is one of the most effective dried fixatives available.

Apium Petroselinum
Published by D.r Woodville March 1. 1791.

73

PARSLEY

In Ancient Greece parsley was a ceremonial plant dedicated to the dead and tombs were festooned with wreaths of parsley. Gradually it was used more both medicinally and in cooking and by the Middle Ages was a popular herb.

Parsley, *carum petroselinum* (or *petroselinum crispum*), is probably the best known of all the herbs and the one most widely used. It is a biennial plant mostly grown as a hardy annual since the leaves have a more delicate flavour in the first year. Parsley has an abundance of crisp, very curly, bright green leaves. In the second year the main stem grows quite tall and branched, each branch carrying a flat-topped umbel of tiny yellow flowers. If the flowering stems are cut as soon as they appear the parsley plant will continue for another year. There is a plain-leaved variety which is not attractive to look at but has all the same properties as curly-leaved parsley. Yet another variety is known as Hamburg parsley, grown entirely for its edible root. The roots are either round like a turnip or long and fleshy, resembling a parsnip and they have a sweet flavour similar to that of parsnip.

In the kitchen parsley has many uses, in soups and stuffings, with fish and finely chopped in salads, with vegetables or simply used as a garnish. Parsley is rich in Vitamins A, B and C and should be part of a healthy everyday diet. The round root of the Hamburg parsley can be used to flavour soups and casseroles while the long roots are eaten as a vegetable on their own and cooked like parsnips. Parsley has a mild deliciously savoury taste and has the ability to soften or disguise other harsher flavours. It is particularly useful in banishing the flavour of garlic – either mixed with it or eaten later on its own.

Parsley can be sown two or three times a year so that it is available throughout the year. It grows in good garden soil and in sun or semi-shade. Sow seed in February, May and again in early August. The first sowing will take time to germinate – perhaps up to six weeks. When the seedlings are large enough thin them to a handspan apart, and to keep the leaves tender and sweet water well in a dry spell. The seed sown in August should be sown in a sunny sheltered position for picking fresh parsley throughout the winter.

For cooking parsley is mostly used when fresh picked but it can be successfuly dried for winter use. It is always used dried for parsley tea. Gather young leaves for drying in their first year of growth then dry and store in the usual way.

MEDICINAL USE

Parsley is full of iron and calcium as well as vitamins and it stimulates the circulation and the digestive system. It is a good tonic herb and is a remedy for troublesome flatulence. Parsley is also mildly diuretic and said to be helpful in cases of rheumatism, as it removes excess fluid from the body. It is believed to be an internal remedy for painful haemorrhoids when a short course of parsley tea should be tried. At the same time use parsley lotion to bathe the affected part. Parsley tea taken hot last thing at night can be effective in loosening a stubborn cough. For medicinal purposes parsley tea is most usually made from the dried leaves.

To make parsley tea: *Pour 1 cup of boiling water over 2 teaspoons chopped parsley and leave to infuse for 5 minutes then strain. A cup of hot parsley tea once a day is recommended.*

Fresh crushed parsley leaves can be used externally for relieving insect bites and stings. As an instant remedy take fresh or pulped leaves and place on minor cuts and abrasions to soothe and heal.

BEAUTY CARE

Parsley contains slight bleaching properties and can be used on a regular base to fade freckles. The juice freshly expressed each day can be dabbed on to the freckles and allowed to dry.

Parsley lotion will help to clear a muddy complexion and stimulate the circulation of blood to the skin.

To make parsley lotion: *Soak a handful of crushed fresh parsley leaves in water and cover for 12 hours or overnight. Strain into stoppered jars. Cleanse the face night and morning before using the lotion then leave it to dry. Keep the lotion in a cool place or in a refrigerator and use twice daily. The lotion can also be made by pouring 2 cups of water on to 2 large handfuls of parsley in an enamel pan. Bring slowly to the boil and simmer for 15 minutes. Cool, strain and pour into a bottle. This lotion will keep longer than the unheated infusion.* To make the treatment more effective a cup of parsley tea (see Medicinal Use) taken daily will be found helpful.

Parsley helps to combat oily skin, especially if mixed with yoghurt and used as a face pack.

To make a face pack: *Make a strong infusion of parsley by pouring a cupful of boiling water on to 2 handfuls of parsley. Strain and leave to cool a little before mixing it with the yoghurt. The mixture must not be too liquid. Cleanse the face and thinly brush the pack over the skin, avoiding eyes and neck. Cover the eyes with cotton wool pads or balls soaked in cold water. Relax for 15 minutes. Remove the face pack with warm water and pat parsley lotion over the skin.*

PARSLEY BUTTER

To make a flavoured butter that adds zest and flavour to grilled fish and meat or makes a crispy hot herb loaf, take 6 tablespoons butter and beat in a bowl until soft. Add 1 tablespoon lemon juice, 2½ tablespoons chopped fresh parsley, salt and freshly ground black pepper. Beat thoroughly until all the ingredients are well combined. Chill in the refrigerator until firm.

Mentha piperita

Published by D.ʳ Woodville Oct.ʳ 1. 1792.

PEPPERMINT

The Greeks and Romans used peppermint as a flavouring in cooking. It was not until the eighteenth century that peppermint began to be widely used as a medicinal plant.

Peppermint, *mentha piperita*, has perhaps the strongest scent of all the different mints and is certainly one of the most attractive with its dark red stems and greeny-red leaves. It is a fragrant plant to grow in the herb garden but it needs to be contained by setting in pieces of roofing slate around the herb, otherwise the creeping roots will grow into other plants. The herb grows up to 2 ft (61 cm) high and the soft violet-coloured flowers grow in whorls in the axils of the leaves. The flowers bloom in July and August. The whole plant has a strong aromatic scent and the delicious flavour characteristic of peppermint.

Peppermint is well known in the kitchen as a flavouring in fruit cups, sweets and confectionery. Dried peppermint is delicious sprinkled on to hot split pea soup which makes a warming start to a meal. It can be added to potato salads and other vegetables, but only in small amounts as peppermint is a strong herb and is best used in moderation.

Peppermint will grow in any garden soil, but the flavour is more pronounced if it is grown in moist rich soil in a sunny position. It is propagated by cutting off rooted pieces of the rootstock – even the smallest piece will grow. Set out new plants a handspan apart and keep them well watered. Cut the roots back regularly so that the herb does not spread into other plants' root systems.

The long-lasting scent makes peppermint a rewarding plant to dry. Gather the leaves just before flowering and dry and store in the usual way.

Medicinal Use

Peppermint is much used to disguise the unpleasant tastes of other medicines. It is a good remedy for digestive upsets, for flatulence and colic and for relieving stomach ache. It has a calming and relaxing effect on those who suffer from tension and stress. A cup of tea after a meal will help to relieve indigestion.

To make the tea: *Pour a cup of boiling water on to 1–2 teaspoons of dried peppermint. Leave to infuse for 10 minutes then strain and add honey to sweeten.*

Peppermint is also helpful for stomach ache when taken with milk.

To make peppermint milk: *Put a tablespoon of dried peppermint and a cup of milk together in an enamel pan. Bring slowly to the boil, simmer for 1 minute then remove from the heat and strain. It should be taken hot.*

Peppermint infusion will help to ward off a cold if taken as soon as the symptoms appear. It increases perspiration and reduces fever and is a useful remedy for chesty colds and mild cases of influenza.

To make an infusion: *Use equal quantities of peppermint and elderflower and mix in a little dried yarrow. Pour a cup of boiling water on to a handful of the mixture and leave to infuse for 20 minutes. Add sugar or honey to taste. Drink the tea as hot as possible and preferably when in bed.*

An effective way to clear a stuffy head cold and relieve chest complaints is to use peppermint in the form of an inhalation. Mixed with other herbs it is a helpful treatment.

To make an inhalation: *Use equal parts of the following herbs mixed in a bowl: peppermint, lime flowers and chamomile. Pour boiling water over the herbs. Cover the head and bowl with a towel and inhale the steam for about 10 minutes. Remove the towel and wipe the face with cotton wool.*

Peppermint contains the valuable substance menthol which is so important in medicine. It is used externally in the form of an oil to relieve neuralgia, rheumatism and lumbago pains. Oil of peppermint can be purchased from the chemist (pharmacy) and is a useful remedy to have in the home. Gently smooth oil on to the temples and forehead for neuralgic headaches. For rheumatism and lumbago it is brushed on to the affected part. Peppermint is also antiseptic and acts as a mild pain killer; oil of peppermint can help to relieve toothache. A herb cushion filled with peppermint with a drop of peppermint oil added is helpful for headaches and is refreshing after a tiring day.

Rubbing crushed fresh peppermint leaves on to the forehead and temples will help to cure a headache.

Beauty Care

Peppermint is both disinfectant and antiseptic and is helpful to those suffering from skin problems. It stimulates the circulation, so helping to throw out the impurities. Used in the form of a compress peppermint acts as a skin tonic and will reduce large pores.

To make a compress: *Make an infusion of peppermint by pouring a cupful of boiling distilled water on to a heaped tablespoon of dried leaves. Leave to infuse for 20 minutes, strain and stand until cold. Cleanse the face thoroughly and if the skin is very dry smooth a little oil on to the face. Dip pieces of lint into the cold infusion and lay on the face, pressing lightly on to the skin. Leave it for 10–15 minutes and renew the compress when it becomes warm.*

For tired and aching feet a footbath using a decoction of herbs can be soothing and invigorating.

To make a footbath: *Mix together dried peppermint, thyme, chamomile and mugwort. Make the decoction using 2 handfuls of the mixed herbs in an enamel pan with 4 cups of water. Bring to the boil and simmer for 5 minutes. Strain and pour into the footbath. When it has cooled sufficiently plunge the feet into the bath for 10 minutes.*

Both the leaves and flowers, dried and crushed, can be mixed in when making pot pourri. Use other strong-scented herbs in the mixture; choose from rosemary, marjoram, lemon verbena and sage, and add flowers and colourful leaves to make it attractive.

Plantago major

Publish'd by Dr. Woodville March 1.1790.

PLANTAIN

In an old Anglo-Saxon manual of medicinal preparations called the Lacaunga *there is a song known as the 'lay of the nine herbs'. One of the nine magic herbs is given as waybread, the old country name for plantain.*

Plantain, *plantago major*, is a very common perennial wild plant. It can be found flowering everywhere and is considered to be a troublesome weed in the garden, especially in the lawn. The long pointed oval shaped leaves are deeply ribbed and grow in a flat rosette on the ground. The flowers, which bloom from June to August, grow on single stems standing out above the foliage. The flowerheads are short spikes of tiny greeny-white flowers. Plantain is so easily found in the wild it would be unwise to introduce it into the garden.

When gathering the herb for use in the home it is best to pick those plantain growing well away from busy roads and other areas which might be polluted. The leaves and flowerheads are the parts of the herb used and these have a bitterish, rather salty flavour.

The herb can be used both fresh or dried; for drying the leaves are picked before the flowers appear. The flowers can be gathered when fully open. They are both dried and stored in the usual way.

MEDICINAL USE

Plantain is astringent and an expectorant helpful for bronchial ailments. It is taken as an infusion.

☛To make an infusion: *Pour a cupful of boiling water on to a handful of plantain. Leave it in a warm place to infuse for 20 minutes then strain through a piece of fine muslin or cheesecloth. Pour into a screwtop bottle and leave until cold. It can be taken a small glassful at a time 2–3 times a day. Sweeten with honey if the drink is found to be too bitter.*

Plantain ointment is a remedy for haemorrhoids (piles).

☛To make plantain ointment: *Melt 2 heaped tablespoons of pure lard or shortening and add 2 tablespoons of dried plantain. Bring to the boil and simmer for 15 minutes. Strain into small pots and cover when cold. Smooth on to the affected part when necessary.* The ointment will also soothe insect bites and is a remedy for mild burns and scalds.

A poultice can also be made to relieve the pain and discomfort of haemorrhoids (piles).

☛To make a poultice: *Gather a sufficient quantity of fresh leaves and mash them to a pulp, either by hand or using an electric blender. When dried leaves are being used they should be reconstituted in a little water before being made into a pulp. Spread the pulp on to a piece of muslin or cheesecloth and heat between 2 plates over a pan of boiling water. Apply the poultice as hot as possible on the affected part and leave in place for 10–15 minutes until relief is felt.*

☛A quick and effective remedy for wasp and bee stings is to rub the area with a freshly crushed leaf, which is said to remove the irritation and pain. This treatment will also bring immediate relief to nettle stings, mosquito and other insect bites. It is said to stop bleeding from minor cuts and abrasions, but the leaf should be well washed before being crushed.

A strong infusion of plantain leaves and flowers is a useful remedy for shingles and other skin problems. It can be used as a lotion to bathe itching irritated areas until relief is obtained.

☛To make a strong infusion: *Pour a cupful of boiling water on to 2 handfuls of plantain and leave to infuse for 15 minutes. Strain through muslin or cheesecloth and when cold pour into a screwtop bottle.*

The infusion can be used as a compress. Dip pieces of lint into the lotion and press lightly over the affected areas, leaving in place for 10–15 minutes.

☛The decoction (see page 13) can be made with an equal quantity of plantain and comfrey and when cold it can be used to bathe painful haemorrhoids (piles).

A weak infusion can be used as a gargle for a sore throat and mouth.

☛To make a gargle: *Pour 2 cupfuls of boiling water on to a small handful of plantain leaves and flowers. Leave to infuse for 20–30 minutes before straining. Pour into a stoppered bottle and keep in a cool place. Use within a few days.*

When freshly made and while just warm the infusion can be used as a compress for inflamed eyelids. Dip pieces of cotton wool into the infusion and place over closed eyes. Lie down and relax for 10 minutes.

BEAUTY CARE

Plantain is a useful cleansing herb and will help towards a clear healthy skin.

☛To make a skin lotion: *Pour 2 cups of boiling water on to 1 tablespoon of dried leaves and flowers. Leave it for an hour then strain into a screwtop jar. Keep in the refrigerator and use within a few days.* The lotion helps to heal and soothe chapped skin and thread veins on the face.

☛Freshly expressed juice extracted from the fresh plant is excellent for closing the pores and refining a coarse skin and the juice can be added to a plain, soft proprietary skin cream. It can also be mixed with milk and dabbed on to the area.

Plantain can be incorporated in a simple face pack to help close the pores of the skin.

☛To make a face pack: *Cook fresh or dried leaves to a mash in a little water to prevent burning. Mix the herb with a little yoghurt or Fuller's earth to make a thick paste. Cleanse the face thoroughly and spread the paste directly on to the skin, avoiding the eyes and mouth. Cover the eyes with cold water compresses and relax lying down for 15 minutes. Remove the face pack with warm water and splash the skin with cold water to leave it feeling fresh and clean.*

PRIMROSE

In former times the primrose grew wild in great profusion and the flowers were used in cooking. It was also believed to be a good remedy for rheumatism and for muscular complaints. The tea was taken for hysterics.

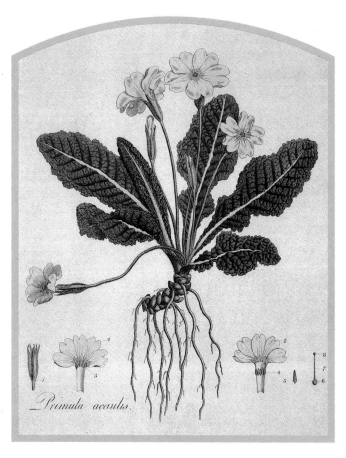

Primula acaulis.

The primrose, *primula vulgaris*, with its pale yellow flowers is a very pretty little spring flowering plant. It grows along hedge banks and railway cuttings and can sometimes be found growing in woodland. Primrose is no longer a common wild flower. Nowadays it is grown in the flower garden where it is one of the earliest plants to bloom. The wrinkled, deeply-veined leaves grow in a flat rosette and the flowers on single stems growing 4–9 in (10–23 cm) high appear in March and April, their yellow petals becoming darker towards the centre. Both the flowers and the root are refreshingly fragrant.

In the kitchen, primroses can be used to make a refreshing and delicate-flavoured wine. They can be used in salads or candied as a decoration for cakes and desserts.

Primrose is a perennial plant and if left undisturbed will gradually spread. Set out primrose plants a hand-span apart either in the autumn or the spring for flowering the following year.

All parts of the primrose are used in the home. The roots of two- or three-year-old plants should be dug up in the autumn. The root is the only part of the plant to be dried and after scrubbing and chopping into small pieces it is then dried and stored in the usual way.

MEDICINAL USE

An infusion made from the flowers is said to be calming for those suffering from nervous tension. It is also effective for headaches and migraines and general debility. Taken hot last thing at night it will be helpful for those who cannot sleep.

To make an infusion: *Pour a cup of boiling water over 1 teaspoon of fresh crushed flowers and leave to infuse for 5 minutes before straining.*

An ointment made from primrose leaves is believed to heal cuts and abrasions.

To make the ointment: *Melt 4 heaped tablespoons of white petroleum jelly in an enamel pan and add a handful of fresh chopped primrose leaves, pressing them down with a wooden spoon. Bring to the boil and simmer for 20 minutes. Strain immediately into small pots and cover when cold.*

BEAUTY CARE

Primrose is an astringent herb and an infusion of the fresh flowers is slightly bleaching. It will help to fade freckles when used on a regular basis.

To make a skin lotion: *Pour 4 cups of boiling water on to a handful of flowers. Leave to infuse for 5 minutes then strain. Pour the infusion into screwtop jars and store in the cool or in the refrigerator. Use the lotion to dab on to the skin night and morning and leave it to dry. Use the lotion also against premature wrinkles on the face.*

Use the ground and powdered dried herb to add fragrance to pot pourris.

PURSLANE

For centuries purslane has been used in cooking as a flavouring herb. Purslane tea was considered to be good for all pains in the head which resulted from lack of sleep.

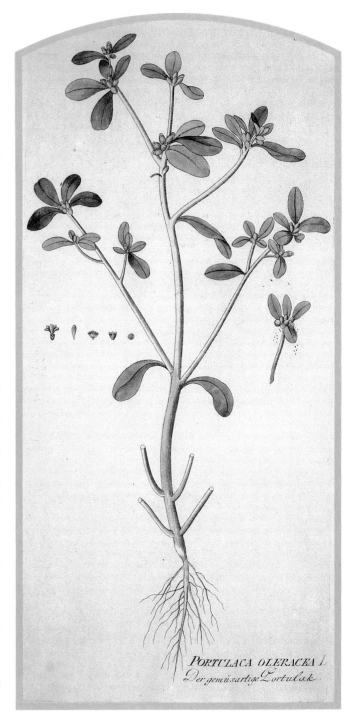

PORTULACA OLERACEA L
Der gemüsartige Portulak.

Purslane, *portulaca oleracea*, is an attractive succulent little hardy annual with smooth wedge-shaped leaves and a much branched reddish stem. The tiny yellow flowers appear in June and July, growing singly or in clusters at the top of the stems.

In the kitchen, small amounts of purslane can be chopped and added to salads. Purslane is one of the ingredients in the traditional French *soupe bonne femme*. For winter use, the thick succulent stems can be pickled in vinegar as an accompaniment to cold meats. It is a summer herb full of Vitamin C and a healthy addition to a salad, and it stimulates the appetite.

Purslane can be grown from seed sown in the spring from May onwards into its flowering position. Sow in a sunny spot in ordinary garden soil and when the seedlings are large enough thin them out to a handspan apart. The seeds germinate quickly and the plants are ready for eating in six weeks, so a succession of sowings can be made throughout the summer.

Purslane is always used fresh, because of the difficulty in drying such a thick fleshy leaf. Leave some of the early sown plant for seed.

MEDICINAL USE

Purslane is a tonic herb and is slightly laxative. An infusion will help to stimulate the appetite and is also a remedy for digestive ailments.

To make the infusion: *Pour 1 cup of boiling water on to 2 teaspoons of finely chopped leaves. Leave to infuse for 5 minutes. Strain and sweeten with honey if preferred. Purslane has a sharp slightly peppery flavour so it is probably nicer without sweetening. Make the infusion fresh every time and drink a small glassful or as required once or twice a day.* It can also be taken for coughs and chest ailments.

For a stubborn cough the expressed juice of the herb can be taken with a little honey a teaspoonful at a time when the cough is troublesome.

For instant relief from the heat, well-bruised or crushed leaves can be placed on the temples and forehead to cool and soothe the head.

ROSEMARY

Rosemary was believed to stimulate the brain and help the memory and so it came to be associated with remembrance. The old custom of leaving rosemary at the graveside and for handing a bunch of it to those bereaved is carried on to this day. Rosemary also stood for fidelity and was included in bridal bouquets.

Rosmarinus officinalis

Published by Dr Woodville June 1. 1791.

Rosemary, *rosmarinus officinalis*, is a lovely sweet-scented evergreen shrub with small pale blue flowers growing in twos or threes in the axils of the leaves. There is a trailing rosemary which is rather a tender plant and another variety known as Mrs Jessup's Up-right, *rosmarinus pyramidalis*, which is suitable for growing as a hedge. The flowers are in bloom in April and May and make a lovely show in the border. The short, stiff, narrow leaves are deeply cut, dark green above and pale grey underneath and they grow in dense profusion up the stems. It is a tall hardy shrub and a well-known garden herb. Rosemary is one of the herbs which are intensely fragrant fresh or green dried, and has many uses in the home.

Rosemary is a herb very well known in the kitchen for both sweet and savoury dishes. It is most commonly used with lamb, but it adds a delicious flavour to other roast meats and to poultry and game. Rosemary is added to chicken soup and vegetable broths and gives a subtle taste to omelettes and scrambled eggs. It imparts an unusual fresh flavour when added to fruit salads, wine or fruit cups and other summer drinks. Rosemary is a strong herb and should be used lightly in cooking. It is one of the herbs used in the making of vermouth.

Rosemary grows well in light, well-drained, sandy soil in a sunny sheltered spot. Propagation is by seed, cuttings or layering; the best plants are those grown from seed, although it is a slow process for the seed takes about three weeks to germinate. If taken in August cuttings will root quite easily. Cuttings 6 in (15 cm) long are taken from a woody shoot — soft stem cuttings will wither and die. Remove the lower leaves and set the cuttings two-thirds of their length in the soil. Choose a shady, sheltered, undisturbed spot in which to grow the cuttings. They will be ready to plant into their final positions the following year, or while still small they can be potted up and brought indoors for the winter. Young plants outside may need protection in a harsh winter.

The leaves and flowering tips are the parts of the shrub used in the home. The leaves for drying are taken from the stems before the flowers appear. The flowering tips are cut when the flowers are fully open. They are dried and stored in the usual way.

MEDICINAL USE

Rosemary is an effective remedy for digestive upsets and flatulence when taken with food. It stimulates the circulation and rosemary tea can be taken for a nervous headache while a compress of rosemary is applied to the forehead and temples.

To make rosemary tea: *Pour ½ cupful of boiling water on to 1 teaspoon of dried herb, leaves or flowering tops. Leave to infuse for 5–10 minutes, then strain and add honey to sweeten. Drink it warm and make fresh each time. Do not take over long periods.*

Rosemary tea, allowed to cool, makes an effective mouth wash for those suffering from bad breath.

Oil of rosemary, which can be purchased from some chemists (pharmacies), makes a good ointment for relieving painful gout and rheumatism, and for soothing eczema and other skin irritations. The oil should never be taken internally.

To make the ointment: *Add 1 tablespoon of rosemary oil to 4 tablespoons of white petroleum jelly melted in an enamel pan. Stir well together then pour into small pots and cover when cold.*

A few drops of oil of rosemary on cotton wool held under the nose will help to revive those who feel tired and faint. Rosemary oil rubbed on to cold hands and feet will stimulate the circulation and they will quickly warm up. A milder form of rosemary oil can be made at home.

To make rosemary oil: *Put 2 handfuls of rosemary into a glass jar and add a cupful of olive or almond oil. Cover the jar with a piece of muslin or cheesecloth held on with a rubber band and stand the jar on a sunny windowsill for 2–3 weeks until the oil is well impregnated. Strain the oil into small screwtop jars and store in the dark. Use to massage gently on to painful joints and bruises.*

Rosemary conserve is an old-fashioned recipe which is said to lift the spirits and relieve depression.

To make a conserve: *Add 1½ cups of sugar to ½ cup of fresh soft flowering tips. Grind in a pestle and mortar, or the electric blender, with a little rosemary infusion added to stop the mixture from sticking. Add more infusion if necessary to make it the consistency of thick honey. Pour into a stoppered jar and keep in a cool place or in the refrigerator. Take 1 teaspoonful for a headache, cold or when feeling depressed.*

To relieve a stuffy cold and a feeling of congestion a small muslin or cheesecloth bag can be made containing a mixture of fresh finely crushed rosemary and coltsfoot leaves. Held under the nose it helps to clear the head.

BEAUTY CARE

Rosemary is used in many beauty care products, in soaps and perfumes, toilet waters and hair preparations, all of which can be purchased from health stores or chemists. It is an excellent herb for the hair, stimulating the circulation of the scalp and thus helping to get rid of dandruff and to improve the growth and condition of the hair. Rosemary hair lotion can be applied to the scalp four times a week.

To make the lotion: *Pour 1 cupful of boiling water on to 1½ tablespoons of fresh or dried rosemary. Leave the infusion to stand for 20 minutes. Strain into a stoppered jar and store in a cool place. Use within a few days. Dip cotton wool into the lotion and rub into the scalp. This is a good lotion for all types of hair.*

Rosemary shampoo made at home uses a strong decoction of rosemary added to soapwort shampoo (see page 125).

To make the decoction: *Pour 1 cupful of water on to 1 heaped tablespoon of dried rosemary in an enamel pan. Bring it slowly to the boil and simmer gently for 20–30 minutes. Strain and leave to cool before mixing it with soapwort shampoo.*

As a hair rinse for dark hair, make double the amount of decoction and after shampooing the hair and rinsing it in the usual manner use rosemary decoction to rinse through the hair several times. It will leave the hair soft, shining and easy to manage, and it improves the colour of dark hair.

✒Rosemary makes a good skin tonic, stimulating and clearing a dull complexion. It will help to reduce puffiness under the eyes. The lotion is made as rosemary tea (see Medicinal Use) and left to cool before straining into a stoppered jar. In the morning use cotton wool soaked in lotion to smooth over the face, pressing lightly on to the puffiness. Do not use on the skin under the eyes at night. Use up the lotion within a few days.

A rosemary skin lotion, which can be kept for longer than rosemary tea lotion, can be made using distilled water and a little brandy.

✒To make skin lotion: *Into an enamel pan put a handful of fresh or dried rosemary leaves. Add 1 cup of distilled water and 1 tablespoon of brandy. Bring the mixture to the boil, cover and simmer for 20 minutes. Strain and when cold pour into a screwtop bottle. Keep in a cool place.*

A decoction of rosemary is good for fading freckles and reducing wrinkles.

✒To make a skin tonic: *Add 2 handfuls of the herb to 2 cups of water in an enamel pan. Bring to the boil and boil for 2 minutes. Leave to infuse for 20 minutes, then strain into a stoppered bottle. Keep in the cool and dab on the skin night and morning.*

A rosemary footbath is a refreshing remedy for tired, swollen, sweaty feet and, used two or three times a week, will help to reduce excessive perspiration.

✒To make a footbath: *Make sufficient rosemary decoction to cover the feet when placed in a bowl. Allow it to cool until lukewarm, then strain into the bowl. Soak the feet for 10 minutes and dry well afterwards. Make a fresh decoction for each application.*

For a stimulating, fragrant and refreshing bath add rosemary infusion to the bath water.

✒To make a herbal bath: *Make a strong infusion, using a cup of boiling water poured on to 2 handfuls of rosemary, and leave it to stand for 15 minutes. Strain the infusion and add to the bath water.*

✒Dried rosemary leaves and flowering tips can both be added to a pot pourri containing many other herbs. Its strong aromatic scent mingles well with any herb mixture and helps to provide a long-lasting fragrance. Rosemary on its own, arranged in a vase or dried and put into a bowl, will cleanse the air in a stuffy room and help to keep it fresh and sweet. Small muslin or cheesecloth bags filled with dried rosemary can be laid between clothes and linen or hung in the wardrobe (closet). It will act as a moth deterrent and impart a sweet fragrance to the clothes.

A herb cushion with its clean clear scent can be filled with a mixture of finely crushed rosemary, woodruff, lemon verbena and angelica. Use a fine muslin or cheesecloth for the inside cushion and make a pretty flowered cotton cover. The herb filling will need to be renewed after six or nine months when it begins to lose its fragrance and strength.

MEMORABLE ROSEMARY
Rosemary is associated with fidelity, love and remembrance. In the Middle Ages, in Europe, rosemary was said to possess magical qualities. In England, if a rosemary plant grew outside a house it was a sign that the wife ruled the household. Some husbands would remove the root of the plant so it withered and died, therefore dispelling rumours from prying neighbours.

Salvia officinalis

Published by D.r Woodville August 1.1790.

SAGE

The botanical name given to sage comes from the Latin 'salvere' meaning to be well and refers to the healing properties of the herb. Sage was widely used to steady the nerves and was said to sharpen the wit and the brain.

Common sage, *salvia officinalis*, is a well-known, strong-smelling evergreen shrub which grows 1–2 ft (30–61 cm) high. The narrow pointed leaves are a dull greyish-green and have a rough wrinkled texture. The attractive pale violet-coloured flowers bloom in August, growing on long spikes which stand out above the foliage. It makes an attractive small shrub in the border and if kept cut back can be used as an edging

plant. Other varieties of sage are the broad-leaved and the purple- or red-leaved sage. Less familiar are the golden-leaved sage and the pretty tricolour with leaves of white, purple and green, but all the varieties have the same properties and can be used in the home in similar ways.

In the kitchen, sage is perhaps best known in sage and onion stuffing, used with pork and rich poultry such as duck and goose. Sage can be added to soups and meat casseroles and put in the water when poaching fish. It is also used for flavouring cheese and bread. Sage jelly makes a delicious accompaniment when served with cold meats. A fresh leaf gives a good flavour when added to apple juice and other fruit cups and summer drinks. Sage has a warm, strong taste, so needs to be used lightly in any dish, otherwise it will dominate other flavours.

Sage, grown in ordinary garden soil, likes a dry sunny spot in the border, preferably in light soil in a sheltered position. Plant sage in the spring and, once established, remove the tops of the shoots to encourage bushy growth. It should be pruned back in October after flowering. Sage is propagated mainly by cuttings taken in the spring; they should be kept well watered in a dry spell during the first season. It can also be grown from seeds sown in March under glass and transplanted in May into their flowering position, setting the plants 12 in (30 cm) apart. After four or five years sage plants should be renewed.

Sage leaves for drying can be picked at any time during the growing season but always before the plant begins to flower. They are then dried and stored in the usual way.

MEDICINAL USE
Sage helps in the digestion of rich foods and heavy meals and can be taken in the form of sage tea after a meal. It should not be taken internally on a regular basis for longer than two or three weeks as the stimulating effect may prove to be too strong and produce giddiness or sickness. Sage tea is helpful for those going through the menopause who are subject to hot flushes (flashes) and night sweats. It reduces and prevents excessive perspiration. A small glassful can be taken two hours before going to bed.
To make sage tea: *Pour 1 cupful of boiling water on to a small handful of chopped sage leaves. Leave it to infuse for 5 minutes then strain and sweeten with honey to taste.*

You can make another, delicious, sage tea: *Pour 4 cups of boiling water on to a large handful of chopped sage, 3 tablespoons of sugar and the grated rind of a lemon. Leave to stand for 30 minutes before straining.* A small glassful of warm sage tea will help to soothe a nervous headache.

A cup of sage milk can be very effective in helping to ward off a cold.
To make sage milk: *Pour a teacupful of boiling milk on to 2–3 whole sage leaves and leave to stand for 5 minutes. Strain and drink hot at the first symptoms.*

Sage is used in the form of an infusion as a mouthwash for infections and inflammations of the mouth, bleeding gums and to regulate the flow of saliva. As a gargle it is an effective remedy for a sore and inflamed throat, tonsillitis and laryngitis.
To make the gargle: *Pour ½ cup of malt vinegar and ½ cup of water on to a handful of fresh chopped sage leaves in an enamel pan with 2 teaspoons of honey. Bring the mixture slowly to the boil and simmer for 5–10 minutes. Remove from the heat and strain carefully into a jug. Gargle with the warm mixture when required.*

A decoction of sage can equally well be used as a gargle for throat infections.
To make a decoction: *Pour 2 cups of water on to a handful of chopped sage leaves in an enamel pan. Bring to the boil and simmer for 10 minutes. Remove from the heat and leave to stand for a further 10 minutes. Strain and use the hot decoction to gargle until relief is obtained.*

A strong decoction of sage leaves used in the form of a compress, or used to bathe the affected part, will help to heal cuts, scratches and abrasions, eczema and virulent spots.

An instant remedy for insect bites is to apply well crushed fresh sage leaves to the bite to reduce the pain and irritation.

Sage embrocation is helpful for easing muscular pain, for rheumatism, sciatica and for loosening stiff and painful joints.
To make an embrocation: *Melt 2 heaped tablespoons of pure lard or shortening in an enamel pan. Add 1 heaped tablespoon of chopped herb and bring slowly to the boil. Simmer gently for 15 minutes. Remove from the heat and strain carefully through muslin or cheesecloth into small stoppered pots. Cover when cold.*

Dried ground sage leaves can be put in a muslin or cheesecloth bag and held under the nose to clear a stuffy cold in the head.

BEAUTY CARE
Sage is used in many beauty care products, in creams and toothpastes, in hair lotions and shampoos. Oil of sage can be purchased from some chemists (pharmacies) and specialist herb shops.

Sage is a good hair tonic and the infusion, used as a hair lotion, can be rubbed on to the scalp every other day to ensure healthy shining hair. It is particularly good for dark hair, strengthening the hair and deepening the natural colour.

☛To make the infusion: *Pour a cupful of boiling water on to 1½ tablespoons of fresh crushed leaves. Leave to stand for 15 minutes then strain into screw-top bottles. Keep in a cool place and use within a few days. After shampooing the hair and rinsing in plenty of plain water, use warm sage infusion and rinse through the hair several times to leave the hair soft and shining.*

For large pores, use the cooled infusion as a face lotion and compress. Dip pieces of lint into the lotion and place over the skin, pressing lightly. Relax for 10 minutes then remove the compress and wipe the face with cold water. The lotion can be used daily dabbed on to the large pores with a piece of cotton wool, and left to dry.

A face pack using sage will also help to shrink large pores and can be used on younger and oily skin.

☛To make a face pack: *Add a little strong infusion to a mixture of yoghurt and honey and mix to a thick paste with some Fuller's earth or fine oatmeal. Cleanse the face thoroughly and smooth the pack over the skin, avoiding eyes and mouth. Use cold water compresses over the eyes. Lie down and relax for 10–15 minutes. Wash the face pack off with warm water and finish by splashing the skin with cold water.*

For the older or very fair skin a warm sunflower or almond oil face compress will help against a tendency to dryness.

☛To make a compress: *Use lint soaked in the warm oil and cover the face, avoiding the eyes and mouth. After 10 minutes remove the lint and carefully wipe the face. Finish with a compress of warm sage infusion. Remove the compress when it is cold and finally splash the face with cold water. The sage compress will help to refresh the skin and shrink large pores without making the skin too dry.*

Sage cream is a useful remedy for distressing cold sores which occur on or near the mouth.

☛To make sage cream: *Melt together 3 tablespoons of almond oil and 3 teaspoons of beeswax. Stir in 1½ tablespoons of oil of sage and beat together until the mixture is cold. Pour into small screwtop pots and store in a cool place. This cream will also help to soothe chapped lips.*

SAGE TALES

Apart from its culinary value in flavouring strong meats and game the medicinal properties of sage cover a wide range of ailments. As a drink sage tea and ale were popular during the Middle Ages and sage leaves were eaten with bread and butter.

S T JOHN'S WORT

St John's wort has been used to cure many ailments for hundreds of years. 'Wort' is an Anglo-Saxon word meaning a medicinal herb. The name St John's wort came about because it was used by the Knights of the Order of St John to heal the deep wounds sustained during the battles of the Crusades.

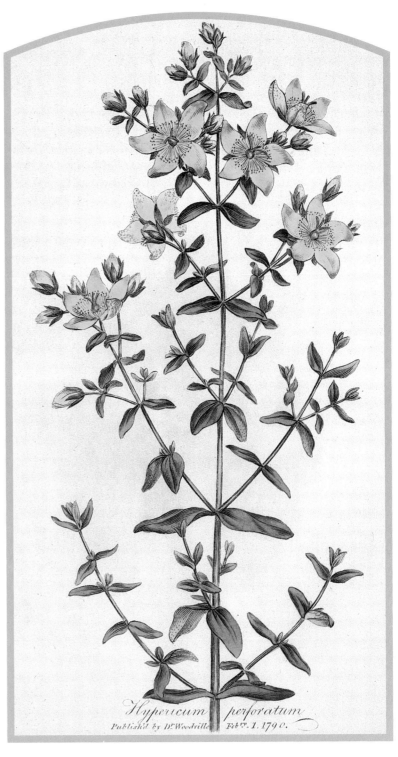

Hypericum perforatum
Publish'd by D.ʳ Woodville Feb.ʳʸ. 1. 1790.

St John's wort, *hypericum perforatum*, is an attractive medicinal herb which grows about 1–2 ft (30–61 cm) high. Its upright, reddish stems are square and branched. The small thin leaves have veins radiating from the base of the leaf and growing thickly along the branches. Each leaf has numerous small perforations which can be clearly seen if a leaf is held up to the light. They are transparent oil glands, containing the same valuable oil as the flowers. This feature of the leaves is an easy way to distinguish the St John's wort from other hypericums. The flowers, which bloom in June and July, are bright yellow star-shaped blossoms clustered together at the top of the stems. When in full flower the stamens stand up above the petals. The herb can be found growing along country lanes, on dry banks and waste lands, in hedges and meadows.

St John's wort is a neat growing herb to have in the garden and it can easily be grown from seed sown in May directly into its flowering position. Sow the seed in light rich soil in sun or semi-shade and, when large enough, thin the seedlings a handspan apart. In March it can be propagated by careful division of an established plant. St John's wort has little fragrance when in flower, but when crushed the plant has an aromatic smell of balsam. The ripe seeds have a strong smell and the leaves and flowers have a bitter dry flavour.

MEDICINAL USE

St John's wort is a useful remedy for many minor ailments and is usually used in the form of an oil. The oil can be purchased from homeopathic chemists (pharmacists) or it can be made in the home. St John's wort oil is helpful in relieving bruises and contusions, sciatica and other cases of nerve injury; it is a remedy for skin irritations, shingles and burns, cuts and abrasions. The oil is used in the form of a compress which is most effective or, where the skin is unbroken, it can be lightly smoothed on to the affected part. It will also soothe and heal a heat rash.

To make the oil: *Fill a small glass jar with freshly picked flowers and pour on sufficient olive oil to cover the flowers. Cover the jar with a piece of muslin or cheesecloth held in place with a rubber band and leave on a sunny windowsill or in the greenhouse for 3–4 weeks depending on the amount of sunshine. When ready for use, the oil should be a strong red colour. Strain into dark glass screwtop bottles and store in a cool place. The oil can also be made using almond in place of olive oil – this will make a more penetrating oil.* It is important that preparations containing St John's wort made for external use should only be used at night-time because its use can make the skin sensitive in susceptible persons and cause discoloration.

St John's wort tea, made from the dried flowers or leaves, can be taken as a remedy for bronchial catarrh and headache. It is soothing and calming and can be helpful to those who cannot sleep. It is also said to be a remedy for depression.

To make the tea: *Pour ½ cup of boiling water on to a teaspoon of the herb. Cover and leave to stand for 5 minutes. Sweeten it with honey and drink warm or cool as wished.*

BEAUTY CARE

St John's wort helps to keep the skin soft and supple and the infusion can be added to creams and lotions for using at night. St John's wort oil (see Medicinal Use) can be rubbed over the hands at night to prevent age spots and to keep the skin smooth. The infusion used as a lotion is an effective moisturizer, again only for applying at night. The lotion is gentle and can be used on dry, delicate skins.

To make an infusion: *Pour 1 cupful of boiling water on to 3 teaspoons of dried flowers. Cover and leave to infuse for 10 minutes before straining into a stoppered bottle. Store in a cool place and use within a few days.*

As a moisturizer, use in the form of a compress. Cleanse the face thoroughly, then dip pieces of lint in the lotion and cover the face, pressing the lint lightly on to the skin. Do not cover the eyes or mouth. Relax with the compress in place for 15–20 minutes. Afterwards rinse the skin with soft water or milk.

St John's wort tincture can be bought at some chemists or specialist herb shops but a simple preparation can be made at home.

To make a tincture: *Use powdered dried herb, both flowers and leafy tops. Put 2 tablespoons of the herb in a screwtop bottle and add 1 cup of rubbing alcohol or vodka. Cover and keep the jar in a warm place for 2–3 weeks, shaking the bottle once a day. Strain the tincture through a fine cloth.*

The tincture can be used to make a hair lotion which stimulates the growth and keeps the hair shining and in good condition.

To make a hair lotion for blonde hair: *Add 1 part of the tincture to 2 parts tincture of chamomile flowers and add an equal amount of rosewater. Put all into a stoppered bottle and shake thoroughly. Use the lotion not more than twice a week, rubbing it into the scalp with a pad or ball of cotton wool.*

SALAD BURNET

In Tudor times, salad burnet was planted in knot gardens in Britain. Originally a native of the Mediterranean countries, it was later taken to America by the Pilgrim Fathers.

SANGUISORBA OFFICINALIS. L.
Der offizinelle Wiesenknopf.

Salad burnet, *pimpinella saxifraga*, is a small, slender perennial herb with dainty leaves consisting of seven to fifteen leaflets. The flowering stems stand out above the foliage and the whole plant grows about 12 in (30 cm) high. The stems and the little round flowers are reddish in colour and the flowers bloom in June and July. The leaves, when crushed, smell of cucumber. It is also known as burnet saxifrage.

The taste of cucumber in the leaves makes salad burnet a useful herb in the kitchen. It gives a delicious flavour to salads and salad dressings; it can be added to soups and home-made cream cheeses, and the pretty leaves add a refreshing flavour to fruit drinks and wine cups. Salad burnet tea is pleasant-tasting and good for digestive problems and loss of appetite.

Salad burnet is a hardy plant and can be propagated from seed or division of roots in spring or autumn. Sow the seeds when they are ripe in autumn in ordinary garden soil, and when large enough thin the seedlings to a handspan apart. Plants will thrive year after year if they are kept free of surrounding weeds.

The leaves are gathered for drying in June before the flowers start to bloom and are dried and stored in the usual way. For winter flower arrangements, dry the flowerheads on long stems.

BEAUTY CARE

Salad burnet is an excellent herb for improving the texture of the skin and is used in the form of a compress or complexion lotion.

To make the infusion: *Pour 1 cup of boiling water on to 2 tablespoons of fresh chopped leaves. Leave to infuse for 10–15 minutes. Strain and pour into stop-pered bottles when cold. For a skin treatment, cleanse the face then dip pieces of lint into the lotion and lay them on the face for 15 minutes. Lie down and relax, covering the eyes with cold water compresses. Remove the compresses and leave the skin to dry.*

After washing the face night and morning dip a cotton wool pad or ball in the lotion and smooth over the skin.

For a facial steam, dried or fresh salad burnet can be added to a mixture of herbs to help the skin.

To make a facial steam: *Mix together any of the following herbs: chamomile flowers, lime flowers, marigold petals, nasturtium flowers, nettle, fennel and yarrow. All have a beneficial effect on the skin. Put 2 handfuls of the mixture into a bowl and pour 4 cups of boiling water on top. Use a towel to cover both head and bowl so that no steam escapes. Steam the face for up to 10 minutes, then wipe the face with cotton wool and pat cold distilled water over the skin to close the pores.*

SELFHEAL

Selfheal was once traditionally considered a great healer of wounds, hence the name and variants such as allheal, hockheal and woundwort.

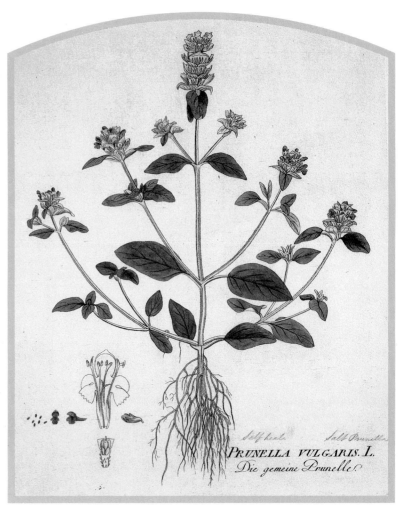

PRUNELLA VULGARIS. L.
Die gemeine Prunelle

Selfheal, *prunella vulgaris*, is a low-growing attractive little perennial plant used as a medicinal herb. It grows wild in fields and woods and on waste lands. The leaves are small, oblong and blunt-ended, and they grow closely in pairs up the stem, forming a rather dense spike. The lower parts of the stem have a reddish tinge. The attractive violet-coloured flowers stand out above the foliage, growing directly from the creeping roots; they bloom all summer long. The whole plant grows about 6 in (15 cm) high.

Selfheal can be propagated either by seed or by removing the rooted side shoots and planting them immediately. It will grow in any garden soil in sun or semi-shade. Sow the seed in April directly in the flowering position and thin out the seedlings, when large enough to handle, to a handspan apart. The little plants soon spread and selfheal is a good ground cover plant.

The leaves, stems and flowers are used in herbal medicine and for drying, the plant is cut down when the flowers are open. The leaves and flowers can be stripped off the stems and are dried separately but they can be stored together in the usual way.

MEDICINAL USE

Selfheal is used as a good tonic herb, stimulating the appetite and generally toning and strengthening the whole system.

To make an infusion: *Pour 2 cups of boiling water on to 2 handfuls of the herb and leave to infuse for 10 minutes. Strain carefully and take a small glassful about 30 minutes before meals. Make a fresh infusion each time.*

Selfheal infusion sweetened with honey can be taken warm for a relaxed throat and a sore mouth. At the same time the infusion should be used as a gargle for greater effect until relief is felt.

Selfheal can be combined with agrimony and wood betany in the infusion.

To make a mixed herb infusion: *Use equal quantities of the herbs with 5 cups of water and make as described above. The infusion can be sweetened with honey.*

The juice expressed from the fresh plant and mixed with a little lavender oil is a useful remedy for a headache when dabbed on the forehead and temples or used in the form of a compress.

S OAPWORT

Soapwort has been used for its cleansing properties since the time of the Ancient Greeks. It is still occasionally used for washing delicate antique fabrics and tapestries – and also for producing a head on beer!

Saponaria Officinalis.

Published by Dᵣ Woodville, August 1ˢᵗ 1794.

Soapwort, *saponaria officinalis*, is an attractive perennial garden herb. The oval-shaped pale green leaves grow in pairs on the red-tinged branching stem. The clear pink flowers appear in July and August, growing in loose clusters, and when grouped closely together the plants make a lovely patch of colour. The creeping rootstock grows quickly through moist light soils and needs to be kept in check or it can become too invasive.

As its name implies, soapwort is a cleansing plant containing a soapy substance called saporina. When the plant is boiled in water it produces a lather like soapsuds or detergent. This can be used to wash delicate fabrics, such as silk, cashmere and woollen knitwear. If a pinch of dried orris root is added to the rinsing water the clothes will be fresh and fragrant as well as clean.

Soapwort grows best in damp places in sun or semi-shade and should be planted in spring or autumn. It can be grown from seed, but the results are poor. Once a soapwort plant is established it can readily be propagated by root division at any time during the growing season.

Soapwort is used in homeopathic medicine but it is not recommended for use in home-made medicine. At no time should it be eaten or swallowed. If eaten the pungent bitter-sweet taste is followed by numbness in the mouth. Soapwort is a cosmetic herb and it can be used for external application. The leaves and roots are dried for winter use, the leaves being picked before the flowers bloom and the root at any time during the season. The roots are thick and need careful drying. The leaves are dried and stored in the usual way.

BEAUTY CARE

Soapwort shampoo leaves all types of hair soft, shining and easy to manage. A decoction can be made using fresh or dried soapwort and distilled water, or still mineral water.

To make a decoction: *Take 2 handfuls of soapwort and add 1½ cups distilled water. Bring the water slowly to the boil and then simmer gently for 5–10 minutes. Remove the decoction from the heat, cover and leave to cool. Strain carefully through muslin or cheesecloth. When it is cold, add a concentrated infusion (see page 15) of another herb such as nettle or southernwood for greater effect.*

An infusion of soapwort makes a good cleansing lotion and is suitable for most types of skin, leaving it refreshed and softened.

To make an infusion: *Use a handful of chopped leaves and pour on a cupful of boiling water. Leave to infuse for 5 minutes then strain carefully into a stoppered jar. Label it and keep in a cool place. Use for cleansing both hands and face and make a fresh infusion every few days.*

SOLIDAGO

The generic name solidago *is from the Latin* solidare, *meaning to join together or make whole – a reference to the healing properties of the plant, which was once carried by soldiers as they went into battle.*

La Verge d'Or
Solidago virga aurea — Linn. Sp. Pl.
Ital. Virga aurea. Angl. Golden Rod. Allem. Heydnisches Wund-Kraut.
(Genevieve de Naggis Regnault f.)

Solidago, *solidago virgaurea*, also known as goldenrod, is a tall attractive perennial, with its daisy-like flowers forming spikes of brilliant yellow from July until the autumn. The narrow pointed leaves have a pleasant scent when bruised but the flowers have a strong musty smell. Solidago can be found growing wild on the edges of woodland and on dry undisturbed land.

Solidago is a hardy plant and, once established in the garden, will need little attention. It is propagated by seed or by division of roots in the autumn. Sow the seeds in early spring, directly in their flowering position. Choose a sunny dry spot in the garden in ordinary soil. When the seedlings are large enough to handle thin them to a handspan apart.

Solidago is a medicinal herb and the flowering spikes are the parts used in the home. They should be gathered for drying at the height of the flowering period and carefully dried to retain their goodness. They are then stored in the usual way.

MEDICINAL USE

Solidago is a mild diuretic herb and can be taken to help the kidneys and bladder to function properly. It is also said to be good for arthritis and rheumatism. It is a gentle and effective remedy for cystitis. Solidago is taken in the form of a tea or a syrup.

To make solidago tea: *Add 2 teaspoons of the chopped herb to 1 cup of cold water. Bring to the boil and immediately remove from the heat. Leave to infuse for 10–15 minutes before straining; add honey to sweeten. A small glassful 2–3 times a day is the recommended dose. Take between meals and do not continue the treatment for longer than a week.*

To make solidago syrup: *Add 2 handfuls of chopped herb to 2 cups of water. Boil for 10 minutes. Leave to infuse overnight, then strain into a pan. Add 8 tablespoons of sugar and simmer for 20 minutes until syrupy. Take one teaspoon a day for not more than a week.*

Solidago is a mild disinfectant and the infusion (see recipe for tea, above) can be used as a lotion for cleaning cuts and abrasions. Used in the form of a compress and laid on to the affected part, the lotion will help in healing and stop infection spreading.

As an instant remedy for minor cuts, grazes and insect bites use crushed fresh leaves which will help to cleanse, heal and relieve the pain.

Solidago ointment is soothing for bruises and swellings and useful to have in store.

To make an ointment: *Melt 4 heaped tablespoons of white petroleum jelly and add a good handful of dried solidago. Bring to the boil. Simmer for 15–20 minutes. Strain. Pour into small jars. Cover when cold.*

SOUTHERNWOOD

Years ago bunches of the strong-smelling southernwood were carried through evil-smelling streets before the days of proper drainage. It was believed to be a protection against infection for the bearer.

Artemisia Abrotanum

Published by D.ʳ Woodville Dec.ᵗ 1 1791

Southernwood, *artemisia abrotanum*, is an attractive, ornamental garden shrub with soft, feathery, greyish-green leaves and a refreshing lemony scent. The yellowy-white flowers are small and inconspicuous and only bloom in warm climates. The shrub grows quite tall but becomes rather ragged and needs to be trimmed to keep a good shape. It is a very popular background plant to have in the border.

In the home southernwood is a useful herb as a moth deterrent. Small bags filled with dried southernwood can be hung in cupboards (closets) and drawers amongst linen and woollens. The little bags should be refilled every year. The herb loses its fresh lemony scent and it is not so effective.

Grow southernwood in ordinary garden soil in a sunny position. It is propagated by long cuttings taken in April. All the leaves from the lower half of the cutting should be removed and the cuttings set into sandy soil, burying half the stem. They will be ready for planting in their permanent position the following spring.

Southernwood will dry easily and retain its strong scent. Cut down the stems in July and August for drying and remove the lower part of the stems. Tie the stems together in loose bunches and hang them upside down in a warm cupboard. As soon as the leaves crackle when touched strip them off the stems and store the leaves in the usual way.

BEAUTY CARE

Southernwood, with its strong but refreshing scent, can be added to the bath water for a relaxing soothing bath after a tiring day.

To make a herbal bath: *Fill a muslin or cheesecloth bag full of southernwood and tie it to the hot water tap (faucet) so that the water passes through it.*

Southernwood makes a good dry shampoo for oily hair where continuous washing does not help.
To make a dry shampoo: *Mix finely-powdered dried southernwood with an equal quantity of arrow-root powder. Sprinkle lightly over the hair, and mass-age it into the scalp. Leave it for 5–10 minutes then brush the hair well to remove all the shampoo.*

A concentrated infusion (see page 15) of southernwood can be added to a strong soapwort solution (see page 125) and used as a wet shampoo.

A hair rinse made with a mixture of southernwood, rosemary, parsley and yarrow will prevent oily hair.
To make a hair rinse: *Mix equal quantities of the herbs together. Pour 2 cupfuls of boiling water over 2 tablespoons of dried herbs. Leave for about an hour, then strain into a screwtop bottle. Use regularly.*

SUMMER SAVORY

The name savory is derived from its old name of satureia, *which is believed to have meant 'satyr' – a reference to the plant's supposedly aphrodisiacal qualities.*

La Sariete.
Satureia hortensis. L. S. P.
Ital. Coniella. Angl. Savory. Allem. Saturey.

Summer savory, *satureia hortensis*, is a dainty aromatic herb which grows about 12 in (30 cm) high. The stems are reddish and the narrow oblong leaves are a soft greyish-green. The tiny flowers are white or pale mauve and grow in the axils of the leaves, sometimes three together. They bloom in July and August and the whole plant is strongly but sweetly scented.

Summer savory has an unusual taste, somewhat like thyme but not so strong, and it is slightly peppery. It has a definite place in the kitchen where whole fresh sprigs, dropped into the water when cooking broad beans and peas, bring out their flavours so that they are particularly delicious. It can be added to pea soup, meat stews and poached fish, stuffings for poultry and to a savoury butter. It is quite a strong herb and should be used in moderation.

Summer savory is a bushy annual and grows from seed sown in early April. Choose a sunny position in light soil to which some good compost has been added. The seeds are slow to germinate but make sturdy plants once they start to grow. Thin out the seedlings to a handspan apart.

Summer savory leaves can be used fresh up until the time the flowers appear. Just before the flowers bloom the plants can be cut down for drying for use in the winter months. They are then dried and stored in the usual way.

MEDICINAL USE

Summer savory is an excellent herb for the digestive system and for flatulence and colic.

To make savory tea: *Pour 1 cup of boiling water on to 1–2 teaspoons of herb. Leave to infuse for 10–* 15 minutes. Strain and sweeten with honey if necessary. The tea can be taken after meals but should be freshly made each time. For flatulence a small glassful taken first thing in the morning on an empty stomach may be helpful.

Summer savory provides an instant remedy for bee and wasp stings. Rub fresh crushed leaves on to the affected part to relieve the pain.

BEAUTY CARE

Summer savory can be added to the bath water. The sweet intense perfume makes a heady and invigorating bath.

To make a herbal bath: *Put a large bunch of the herb in a muslin or cheesecloth bag and tie it to the hot tap (faucet) so that the water rushes through.*

The strong aromatic scent of the herb makes it a suitable one to add to a pot pourri mixture or to pack into small muslin or cheesecloth bags and place in drawers or cupboards (closets).

SUNFLOWER

The sunflower originally came from Peru in the sixteenth century where, as in Mexico, a number of different varieties grow in the wild. It was a plant highly prized by the people, who adorned their temples with sunflowers made of pure gold.

Helianthus añuus L.

The sunflower, *helianthus annuus*, is a well-known tall, handsome plant which makes an attractive show at the back of the border and is a familiar sight in many cottage gardens. The stout hairy stems can grow up to 12 ft (3.6 metres) high and on these grow big broad rough-textured leaves. Each stem carries one large bright yellow flower. The flowerheads are flat and totally round, often growing 12 in (30 cm) in diameter. The seeds, which start to ripen in September, are a greyish white, flat and wedge-shaped. As the seed ripens the flowerhead droops downwards.

Sunflower seeds when just ripe are rather oily but have a delicious nutty taste. In the kitchen, seeds can be added to salads and soups or lightly roasted in oil and dipped in crushed sea salt and eaten as a snack. Sunflower oil, which is easily available from grocers and health food stores, is a light, odourless oil used in cooking and salad dressings.

Sunflower is a hardy annual, growing from seed to a great height in one season. It grows best in well dug ordinary garden soil in a sunny, sheltered position. Sow the seed in late April directly into its flowering position, setting in the seeds 2 ft (61 cm) apart. As the plants grow tall they may need staking. Sunflowers should never be sown in the same spot two years running as the soil becomes impoverished.

All parts of the sunflower plant have their uses but in the home it is the seed which is harvested and used. As soon as the seeds begin to ripen the flowerhead can be covered with a muslin or cheesecloth bag to stop them either being eaten by birds and insects or falling to the ground and being lost. Later the heads are cut off to finish drying indoors. They are stored in the usual way.

MEDICINAL USE

A syrup made with sunflower seeds is a delicious way to treat chesty colds and coughs.

To make the syrup: *Put a handful of sunflower seeds into an enamel pan with 2 cups of water. Bring to the boil and simmer for 25 minutes or until reduced by half. Strain and add 4 tablespoons of sugar. Stir until dissolved, bring to the boil and boil hard for 2 minutes. Allow to cool and pour into a stoppered jar. Store in a cool place and take 1–2 teaspoonfuls 3 times a day when the cough is troublesome.*

An infusion of sunflower seeds can help to relieve the distressing symptoms of whooping cough.

To make an infusion: Take a handful of seeds and put them on a baking tray in a slow oven. Leave them in the oven until they are a honey brown. Remove from the oven and when cold grind them to a powder in the coffee mill. Pour ½ cup of boiling water on to a small teaspoonful of powdered seed. Leave to cool and strain through a piece of fine muslin or cheese-cloth into a stoppered jar. Store in a cool place and use within a day or two. Take a teaspoonful at a time.

A decoction of sunflower seeds is diuretic and soothing. It can be a helpful remedy for those suffering from a persistent cough or chronic bronchitis.

To make the decoction: Pour 2 cupfuls of cold water on to 1 large handful of seeds in an enamel pan. Cover and bring slowly to the boil. Simmer for about 25–30 minutes or until the liquid is reduced by half. Remove from the heat and stir. Leave to cool then stir well and strain through muslin or cheesecloth into a stoppered jar. Honey can be added to sweeten. Store the jar in a cool place and use within a week.

Sunflower seeds provide a helpful remedy for coughs, colds and for other chest complaints and they can be taken in the form of a cordial which is soothing and pleasant to taste.

To make the cordial: Add 1 cupful of water to 1 large handful of sunflower seeds in an enamel pan. Bring the mixture slowly to the boil and boil for 25 minutes. Strain the liquid into a jug and add 2 heaped tablespoons of brown sugar. Stir until it has dissolved, then add 2–3 tablespoons of Dutch gin to taste and pour the mixture into a stoppered bottle. Take 1 teaspoonful whenever the cough is troublesome about 3–4 times a day.

BEAUTY CARE

A simple soothing skin cream can be made from sunflower oil and comfrey.

To make a skin cream: Make comfrey infusion by adding ¼ cupful of water to a handful of comfrey in an enamel pan. Bring it to the boil and simmer for 15 minutes. Remove from the heat, strain and leave to cool. Put 1 egg yolk and ½ cup of sunflower oil into a bowl or an electric blender. Beat together and gradually add the comfrey infusion until it is all well mixed together. Pour into pots and store in the refrigerator. Use within a few days.

Sunflower seed oil makes an effective skin cleanser, leaving the skin soft, supple and smooth. Use the fingers to spread oil all over the face then massage it thoroughly into the skin. Remove the oil and the grime with a piece of dry towelling and then wash the face in the usual way to remove any traces of oil.

SUNFLOWER FIRES
Sunflower stems grow thick and hard. When the flower head is removed the stems are cut, stripped of the leaves and left outside to dry. They can be chopped and used as kindling material to start indoor fires. Also, they can be burned outside as part of a garden bonfire. The resulting ash is rich in potash which is a valuable manure and can be spread on flowerbeds.

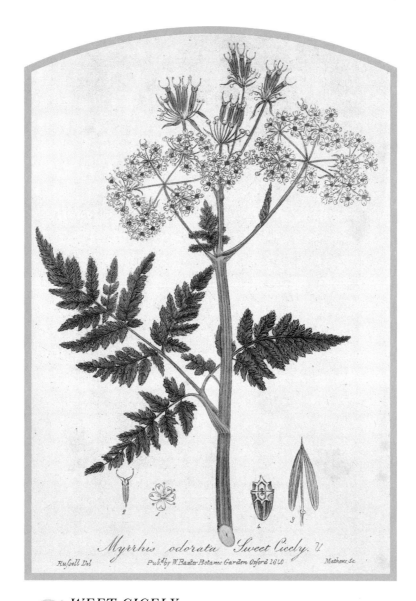

Myrrhis odorata Sweet Cicely. 𝒱

Russell Del.   Pub.ᵈ by W.Baxter Botanic Garden Oxford 1840   Mathews Sc.

SWEET CICELY

In former times the sweet cicely root was more commonly used than the leaf. It was a popular pot herb, being boiled with other root vegetables and eaten with vinegar and oil. Sweet cicely root was believed to prevent infection.

Sweet cicely, *myrrhis odorata*, is a lovely fragrant perennial herb growing up to 2–3 ft (61–91 cm) high. The plant can sometimes be found growing wild on hillsides and high pasture land in northern climates. The soft, lacy leaves are covered with a whitish down on the underside and when crushed have a sweet smell somewhat resembling anise. Early in the season creamy white flowers appear, growing in flat-topped umbels at the top of the stems. The flowers are quickly followed by the characteristic long green seed pods. As the seeds ripen the seed pod turns black. Sweet cicely is an attractive plant to grow in the border, as its leaves appear so early in the year and continue until late autumn.

In the kitchen, sweet cicely is a very useful herb. Chopped fresh leaves or the spicy green seeds add a delightful flavour to salads and salad dressings, any root vegetable and to cabbage. The roots can be sliced, cooked and eaten as a vegetable or grated and eaten raw in salad. The taste is much stronger in the roots than in the leaves and is similar to that of Florence fennel. Because of its ability to cut the acidity when cooked with tart fruits, less sugar is needed and a more healthy diet can be followed. Sweet cicely can be added to the syrup for fruit salads and to fruit drinks. It is a very mild herb and can be used generously wherever a slight anise flavour is required and it is at its best when mixed with other herbs in a dish.

Sweet cicely will grow in ordinary well-drained garden soil in a sunny or slightly shaded spot. It can be propagated either by seed or by division of roots. Sow seed directly into its flowering position in March or April and when large enough thin the seedlings to a handspan apart. Once the plants are established they will self-sow quite readily. The roots of two-year-old plants can be divided in the spring or autumn: plants older than two years are difficult to dig up without damaging the long tap root.

The leaves, roots and seeds are the parts of the herb which are used in the home and to ensure a good supply of fragrant leaves the flowers should be cut off as soon as they appear, unless the seeds are required. The leaves can be gathered for drying any time between February and November and are dried and stored in the usual way. The roots can be dug for eating or drying in the autumn. If some of the flower-heads are left on the plant the seeds can be picked while green for immediate use or left until they have turned black, when they can be gathered and dried in the usual way.

MEDICINAL USE

Sweet cicely reduces the need for sugar when added to foods and so can be helpful to diabetics. It also helps the digestion when taken with meals as a tea.

To make the tea: *Pour 1 cupful of boiling water on to 3 teaspoons of chopped fresh or dried sweet cicely leaves. Leave to infuse for 10 minutes before straining. Drink the tea warm whenever required and make it fresh each time. For the digestion sweet cicely tea can be taken 30 minutes before a meal.*

The tea is also said to cure flatulence and for this distressing complaint a small glassful made from sweet cicely seeds can be drunk hot after meals.

To make the seed tea: *Put 1 teaspoon of crushed seed in an enamel pan and add 1 cup of boiling water. Bring slowly to the boil and simmer for 5–10 minutes. Remove from the heat and strain immediately.*

Sweet cicely tea (seed or leaf) if taken hot will help to ease a troublesome cough. The tea is also an effective tonic and is helpful in cases of anaemia. It is particularly good for the elderly and for teenage girls and the tea, which is very pleasant, can be sweetened with a little honey and taken daily.

Sweet cicely seeds can be chewed as an instant remedy for mild indigestion.

An ointment can also be used as a first aid treatment for cuts and abrasions.

To make the ointment: *Melt 4 tablespoons of white petroleum jelly in an enamel pan and add 1 tablespoon of powdered dried sweet cicely root. Bring slowly to the boil and simmer for 15 minutes. Strain into small pots and cover when cold.*

BEAUTY CARE

Sweet cicely is a useful herb to be included in the diet when following a slimming programme and should be used wherever possible in place of sugar when cooking. It is also mildly diuretic and will help the system to rid itself of excess fluid. A glassful of sweet cicely tea (see Medicinal Use) can be taken first thing in the morning on an empty stomach and to be effective should not be sweetened.

Dried sweet cicely leaves and powdered seeds add a lovely fragrance when mixed with other dried herbs and flowers in a pot pourri. The seeds are particularly useful as they act as a fixative, prolonging the scents of the other herbs. They can be put in a dry pot pourri mixture which is usually put into an open bowl where the scents of all the colourful herbs need to be strong. Ground spices are addee and other fixatives such as the roots of orris or elecampane.

*S*WEET CICELY
For a fruit salad for 4 people, make a syrup by adding 1 sprig of sweet cicely and 1½ tablespoons of sugar and 1½ tablespoons orange juice and ½ cup water. Bring to the boil and boil for 4 minutes. Cool. Discard the sweet cicely. Add the syrup with 1 tablespoon of chopped fresh sweet cicely leaves to thinly sliced fruits such as apples, plums, pears and melon.

S WEET FLAG

Sweet flag was known as sweet rush and highly prized as a strewing herb, covering the floors and filling the rooms with its sweet scent. It was also believed to cure eye trouble.

Acorus Calamus

Sweet flag, *acorus calamus*, is a tall, fragrant, waterside plant growing wild in marshes, by ponds and streams, ditches and lakes. The flat, sword-like leaves are pinkish at the base, very long and very pointed. They grow from a thick round-shaped rhizome. The leaves look rather like those of an iris, but have their own distinctive crimped edges and soft fragrance. The flowers, which bloom in June and July, are stalked and grow in the axils of the leaves. They are a dense spike of tiny, greeny-yellow flowers. The whole plant, including the rhizome, is sweetly scented.

In the kitchen a fresh leaf can be used to flavour an egg custard or a syrup for fruit salad. The leaf should be removed before serving. The dried roots have a strong warm taste and are frequently used in the manufacture of confectionery. The oil extracted from calamus root is widely employed in medicines, perfumes and cosmetics.

The sweet flag only sets seed in India, its country of origin. Elsewhere it is propagated by dividing the rhizomes in early spring and planting in the mud near water. Sweet flag can be grown in the garden where it will need rich moist soil and plenty of watering. It is well worth growing for its fragrance alone, although its exotic appearance makes it a welcome sight.

The rhizomes and leaves are the parts of the plant used in the home. The leaves are used when fresh and have a pleasant sweet taste rather like an orange. The rhizomes are collected in the autumn from two- or three-year-old plants. They are difficult to dry at home because of their high moisture content. The dried calamus root, as it is called, can be purchased from some chemists or health food stores.

MEDICINAL USE

Sweet flag is an invigorating, strengthening herb and helps the stomach to function properly. It stimulates the digestive system and the metabolism and helps to relieve flatulence. It is a good all round tonic and a remedy for nervous complaints such as vertigo, dizziness, fainting and headaches.

To make an infusion: *Pour 1 cup of boiling water over 1 tablespoon of dried calamus root. Infuse for 5 minutes and strain the liquid carefully through fine muslin or cheesecloth.*

The infusion can also be used warm as a gargle to relieve a sore throat.

Candied whole calamus root, chewed or sucked, will help sufferers from indigestion and flatulence.

BEAUTY CARE

Sweet flag can be added to the bath water to provide a stimulating, invigorating bath – which should not be taken at night.

To make a herbal bath: *Add directly to the bath or tie a small muslin or cheesecloth bag of dried root to the hot tap (faucet) when running the bath. Use the bag afterwards to rub on to the skin.*

Origanum Majorana

Published by Dr. Woodville, Sept.r 1. 1792.

SWEET MARJORAM

In ancient times marjoram was used in the preservation of meat for its disinfectant quality. As a medicinal herb it was used both internally and externally for stomach ailments.

Sweet marjoram, *origanum majorana*, is the prettiest of all the marjorams. In cool climates the herb rarely survives the winter and it has to be treated as an annual. The neat, bushy little plant grows up to 12 in (30 cm) high with small, grey-green leaves growing in profusion on the strong woody stems. The flowers bloom from July to September and are small and white, growing closely together in little oblong knots in the axils of the upper leaves. Hence it is often known as sweet knotted marjoram. The whole plant is beautifully fragrant and the sweet spicy flavour makes it a delicious herb to use in the home. There are many other varieties of marjoram, all perennials, which can be used for cooking, but the taste is much stronger and not as delicate as that of the sweet marjoram. The pot marjoram (*majorana onites*), wild marjoram or oregano (*origanum vulgare*) and the Greek or showy marjoram (*origanum pulchellum*) are the best known and all are easy to grow, either from seed or by root division in the spring. It is important that pot marjoram is not eaten by those with kidney disorders or by those who are pregnant.

In the kitchen sweet marjoram, with its sweet aromatic taste, is mainly used with meat, adding a delicious flavour when the meat is rubbed with marjoram before roasting. With rabbit and other poultry and game, marjoram helps to make them more digestible. It can be used in small amounts in soups, casseroles and vegetables. It is a fairly strong herb and needs to be used in moderation to bring out other flavours and not to overwhelm them.

Sweet marjoram seed can be sown during April directly in its flowering position in light soil in a warm sunny spot in the garden. The seed takes time to germinate and the bed should be kept free of weeds and gently watered until the plants appear. When large enough the seedlings should be thinned to a handspan apart.

The leaves and flowering tips of the herb are used in the home, the leaves being picked as required throughout the growing season and the whole herb cut down to the ground for drying in July and August. It is dried and stored in the usual way.

MEDICINAL USE

For a stuffy nose or congestion ground dried marjoram can be used in the form of snuff, clearing the nose by inducing sneezing.

Taken in the form of tea sweet marjoram is an effective herb for colds and sore throats.

To make marjoram tea: *Pour 1 cupful of boiling water on to a small handful of fresh marjoram leaves. Leave to infuse for 5–10 minutes then strain and serve hot. The flavour is improved if a few mint leaves are added and it can be sweetened with honey.* Sweet marjoram is an expectorant and is said to relieve coughs, bronchitis and chronic catarrh. The tea can be taken hot or cold as required.

Sweet marjoram also has disinfectant qualities and the infusion made with fresh or dried herb is helpful as a mouthwash for inflamed gums. Use the tea as an infusion lukewarm.

Taken at the onset of a nervous headache a hot cup of sweet marjoram tea is said to reduce its severity.

At the same time a little oil of marjoram or an ointment can be smoothed over the forehead and temples.

Oil of marjoram can be purchased from some homeopathic chemists (pharmacists) and herb shops and is useful in the treatment of minor ailments. It can be used externally to relieve sprains and bruises. The oil will help to ease rheumatic and muscular pains when lightly massaged on the affected area. Alternatively, a simple oil can be made at home.

To make marjoram oil: *Add 1 cup almond oil to 4 handfuls of sweet marjoram in an enamel pan. Bring very slowly to the boil and simmer gently for 30 minutes or until the leaves are crisp. Strain through a piece of fine muslin or cheesecloth.*

If preferred, make an ointment which will be equally effective.

To make marjoram ointment: *Melt 4 tablespoons of pure lard or shortening in a pan and add 1 heaped tablespoon of dried sweet marjoram. Bring slowly to the boil and simmer gently for 15–20 minutes. Remove from the heat, strain and pour into small pots. Cover when cold.* The ointment and oil can be used slightly warmed if preferred.

A pleasant way to ease rheumatic pains is to pick fresh marjoram leaves, warm them up between 2 plates over a pan of boiling water, and apply them directly on to the affected area.

A poultice will provide greater relief for painful joints and rheumatism as it retains the heat for a greater length of time. It is also said to be very helpful in curing a stiff neck.

To make a poultice: *Pick a large quantity of the herb, wash, and pound to a pulp either by hand or in an electric blender. Dried herb can first be softened in a little water before blending. Spread the pulp thickly on to a piece of lint and heat it thoroughly between 2 plates over a pan of boiling water. Apply as hot as possible to the painful spot. It should be left in place for 10 minutes or until relief is obtained and renewed as necessary.*

Green dried sweet marjoram leaves and flowers can be added to mixtures of other dried herbs for pot pourris and herb cushions. With its strong refreshing aroma it adds an enduring scent. In a herb cushion it can be mixed with peppermint, lavender and sage, lemon verbena, angelica and woodruff for a clean-smelling soothing effect.

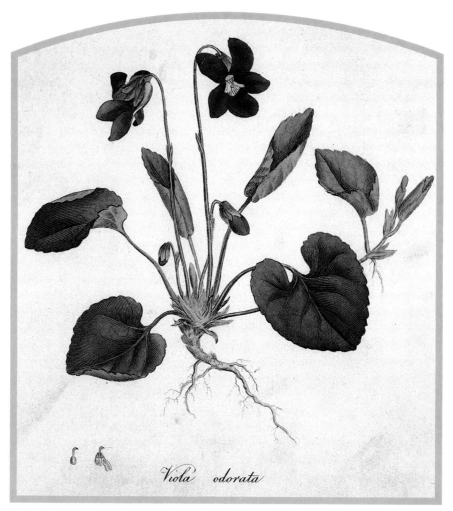

Viola odorata

SWEET VIOLET

In early times violets were much valued as a cure for sleeplessness for which ailment the feet were wrapped in cloths soaked in an infusion and the herb was bound to the forehead. A circle of violets used to be worn round the head to cure dizziness or a headache.

Sweet violet, *viola odorata*, is an attractive perennial plant with soft heart-shaped leaves and sweet-smelling flowers. It is a low-growing herb which gradually spreads over the ground by means of runners. One of the earliest of spring flowers, violets bloom from February to April. The flowers are usually a dark velvety purple, but there are varieties which have pale mauve or white flowers with the same familiar scent. Violets can be found growing wild on hedge banks along country lanes and they can be successfully grown in an open spot in the garden, giving a lovely splash of colour so early in the year.

Nowadays violets are rarely used in the kitchen except as a cake decoration, although they can be used in ice cream and a light syrup made with dried violet flowers adds a delicious flavour to fresh fruit salads and summer drinks.

Violets will grow well in medium to light ordinary soil to which compost has been added. Set out new plants in April a handspan apart and keep them well watered until established, especially in dry weather. Some well-rotted leaf mould set round the plants will help to keep the soil damp. To produce blooms in quantity, feed the plants with liquid manure just before they begin to flower.

The leaves and flowers are those parts of the herb used in the home but only the flowers are dried. These are gathered on a dry day and must be dried carefully to retain their colour and therefore their goodness. They are then stored in the usual way. The leaves are only used when freshly picked.

MEDICINAL USE

Violet flowers taken in the form of a decoction are a helpful remedy for feverish colds. The decoction is soothing and will relieve a headache brought on by too little sleep or too much to drink. It is soothing and pleasant to drink.

To make the decoction: *Add a cup of water to a teaspoon of dried crushed flowers in an enamel pan. Bring slowly to the boil. Immediately remove from the heat and leave to infuse for 10 minutes. The decoction can be taken as required warm or cold and sweetened with honey. It will be found to be slightly laxative so should not be taken for any length of time.*

A syrup of violets is an effective treatment for chest ailments, bronchitis, coughs and chesty colds. Use fresh flowers for the syrup where possible.

To make the syrup: *Put 3 large handfuls of flowers into a bowl and add ½ cup of boiling water. Cover and leave to soak for a whole day. Strain through a piece of muslin or cheesecloth, making sure to get all the liquid out of the flowers. Put the liquid into an enamel pan with 4 heaped tablespoons of honey. Heat slowly to dissolve the honey then bring to the boil. Immediately remove from the heat and when cool pour into a screwtop jar. Store in a cool place. The syrup can be taken 1 teaspoonful at a time. Violet syrup is a good gentle laxative to give to children. It is also soothing for a sore throat.*

Violet ointment made with fresh leaves can be used to soothe and reduce swellings. It is soothing and healing and will soften sore and cracked lips and is good for relieving painful haemorrhoids (piles).

To make the ointment: *Melt 2 heaped tablespoons of pure lard or shortening in an enamel pan and add a handful of chopped leaves. Cover the pan and cook the leaves for 30 minutes over a very low heat. Strain immediately through a piece of muslin or cheesecloth and pour into small pots. Cover when cold.*

A poultice can be applied to bruises and swollen joints to ease the pain.

To make a poultice: *Gather sufficient fresh leaves, wash and mash them to a pulp, either by hand or using an electric blender. Spread the pulp on to a piece of muslin or cheesecloth and heat the poultice between 2 plates over a pan of boiling water. When hot place over the affected area, cover with a dry*

cloth and leave in place until relief is felt. Renew the poultice as necessary.

BEAUTY CARE

A lotion made with violets will help to improve a dull complexion and can be used night and morning to cleanse the skin. It will leave the skin smooth and soft.

To make the lotion: *Pour ½ cup of warm boiled milk on to a handful of dried violet flowers. Leave to infuse for about 2 hours. Strain through a piece of muslin or cheesecloth, pressing all the milk out of the flowers. Store in a stoppered jar in a cool place or in the refrigerator and use within a few days. Dip cotton wool into the lotion to cleanse the face.*

Violets add a lovely perfume to home-made hair rinses. Make a decoction (see Medicinal Use) and leave it to cool before straining. Add the perfumed decoction to rinses made with nettle, horsetail or yarrow, before using on the hair. It adds a lovely fragrance to soft, shining hair.

Violets can be used for a relaxing, aromatic bath which is pleasant and soothing after a tiring day.

To make a herbal bath: *Make up a strong infusion by pouring 2 cupfuls of boiling water over 3–4 handfuls of dried flowers. Leave to infuse for 10–15 minutes then strain and add to the bath water.*

A violet salve will help to keep lips soft and smooth.

To make a lip salve: *Make up a decoction of violets (see Medicinal Use) and leave to cool. Melt 1 tablespoon of beeswax slowly over a low heat. Remove from the heat and add 2 tablespoons of almond oil and 2 tablespoons of violet decoction. Pour into small pots and cover when cold.*

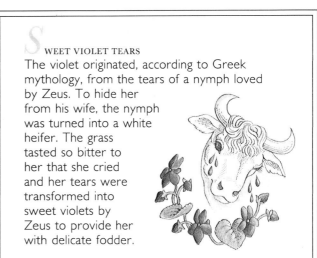

SWEET VIOLET TEARS
The violet originated, according to Greek mythology, from the tears of a nymph loved by Zeus. To hide her from his wife, the nymph was turned into a white heifer. The grass tasted so bitter to her that she cried and her tears were transformed into sweet violets by Zeus to provide her with delicate fodder.

T HYME

The Greeks and Romans would burn quantities of thyme to fumigate their rooms. In medieval times thyme was used in drinks and cordials, and because they were slightly intoxicating the herb came to be regarded as a symbol of courage and bravery.

Thymus vulgaris.

The thyme, *thymus vulgaris*, is the one known as the common or garden thyme. It is an aromatic evergreen perennial herb with small, dark green leaves growing densely on short stalks along the woody stems. A neat bushy plant, thyme grows up to 9 in (23 cm) high, the tiny pale mauve flowers appearing on whorls at the top of the stems. The herb flowers in July. There are many varieties of thyme which can be found growing in the wild and some of these are also cultivated. The garden thyme is closely allied to the wild thyme, but has a better flavour and is more fragrant than the wild. Lemon thyme, also a variety of the wild thyme, has a lovely lemon flavour and scent and is particularly useful in cooking. All the thymes are very good bee plants and thyme honey is quite delicious.

In the kitchen, every bunch of herbs used to flavour meat casseroles, soups and sauces, should contain a sprig of thyme. It is much used in stuffings for poultry and adds a pleasant flavour to meats and some fish when used in the cooking. Thyme is a strong-flavoured herb and should only be used in small amounts. Lemon thyme can be used in similar dishes and also added to fresh fruit salads and creams where the lemony flavour is refreshing. An unusual use for a sprig of thyme is to set it among damp papers, as it is said to prevent them from going mouldy.

Garden thyme can be grown from seed sown in March or April if the weather is mild. Sow the seed thinly in good garden soil in a sunny spot where the plants are to flower and when large enough thin the seedlings to 12 in (30 cm) apart. Established plants can be divided in the spring. The plant has creeping fibrous roots and so needs room to spread. It will act as a fragrant ground cover.

Thyme is a small herb and the stems, leaves and flowering tops are used in the home either fresh or dried. For drying, the herb is cut down when in full flower and dried and stored in the usual way.

MEDICINAL USE

Thyme is used to flavour and perfume commercially-made toothpastes, soaps, deodorants and hair lotions. At home, thyme tea is a pleasant drink and is helpful for digestive upsets and flatulence, loss of appetite and exhaustion.

To make the tea: *Pour 1 cupful of boiling water on to 2 teaspoons of thyme. Leave to infuse for 5–10 minutes. Strain and add honey to sweeten. Make fresh tea each time and drink as required before or after meals.* Warm tea will help to dispel a headache if taken immediately the symptoms appear. Thyme tea can also be taken for mild chest complaints and will help to relieve catarrh.

Thyme is said to be a good herb for easing distressing whooping cough. Thyme syrup can be taken at the onset of the complaint. It is also said to be beneficial for a sore throat if taken a teaspoonful at a time.

To make the syrup: *Add sufficient honey to 3 handfuls of freshly pulped thyme to make a thick syrup.*

Alternatively a decoction can be used.

To make a decoction: *Put a handful of thyme into an enamel pan with 2 cups of water. Bring to the boil and simmer for 20 minutes, or until it is reduced by half. Strain immediately and add honey to sweeten. A tablespoonful can be taken once or twice a day.*

An infusion makes an effective gargle for sore throats and can be used as a lotion for cuts and abrasions.

To make a strong infusion: *Pour 2 cupfuls of boiling water on to 3 handfuls of either fresh or dried thyme. Leave to infuse for 10 minutes, then strain into stoppered jars.*

As a compress the infusion helps to relieve painful joints. Dip pieces of lint in the infusion, place over the affected part and secure in position. Renew the compress as necessary until relief is obtained.

Thyme is said to stimulate the circulation and when added to the bath water provides a refreshing tonic bath for those with rheumatism or sufferers from skin complaints.

To make a herbal bath: *Make a decoction by adding 6 handfuls of thyme to 4 cups of water in an enamel pan. Bring slowly to the boil and simmer for 5 minutes. Remove from the heat and leave for a further 5 minutes before straining and adding directly to the bath water.*

BEAUTY CARE

The strong thyme infusion (see Medicinal Use) is a helpful treatment for acne, spots and pimples. Use the warm infusion to bathe the affected area.

To prevent falling hair and to improve the circulation to the scalp rub the decoction (see Medicinal Use) into the scalp daily.

Thyme mixed with other herbs can be added to a decoction of soapwort (see page 13) and used as a shampoo to improve the condition of the hair and leave it easy to manage.

Thyme acts as a good skin tonic. Used in the form of a face pack it improves a dull complexion, stimulating the circulation.

To make the face pack: *Mix ½ cup of natural yoghurt with 2–3 teaspoons of dried or fresh thyme. Leave it to permeate for 30 minutes. Cleanse the face in the ordinary way and brush the pack over the skin, avoiding eyes and mouth. Cover the eyes with pads of cotton wool wrung out in cold water. Relax for 15 minutes. Wash the face pack off with warm water and finish with a splash of cold water to close the pores.*

Dried thyme flowers and leaves add a lovely scent and colour to pot pourri mixtures. Small muslin or cheesecloth bags filled with the herb can be made for hanging in cupboards (closets) and putting among clothes and linen to give them a pleasing fragrance.

VALERIAN

In the Middle Ages valerian was not only valued for its medicinal qualities but was used as a perfume and a flavouring herb. It is said that rats are attracted by the smell of valerian and that the Pied Piper of Hamelin made the rats follow him by putting valerian in his pockets.

Valeriana officinalis

Valerian, *valeriana officinalis*, is a tall, single-stemmed perennial herb valued for its rootstock. The leaves are made up of numerous lance-shaped leaflets and grow in pairs up the stem. The tiny, almost white, flowers form small umbels and these cluster together on short stalks at the tops of the stem. The flowers bloom from June to September and the whole plant has a strong pungent smell, particularly when the leaves are crushed. Valerian can be found growing wild in damp ditches and on marshy ground.

Valerian can be grown in ordinary garden soil but the roots grow larger in rich moist soil. The herb can be grown from seed sown in April directly ino its flowering position and, when the seedlings are large enough to handle, thin to about 12 in (30 cm) apart. Valerian needs to be well watered at all times and especially in a dry spell. To ensure good thick roots cut off the flowers as they appear.

The roots are harvested in the autumn from two- or three-year-old plants. When they are first dug the roots have very little smell but it becomes pro-gressively stronger as they dry. They are scrubbed and grated or chopped small, then dried in the dark and stored in the usual way.

MEDICINAL USE

Valerian is an excellent remedy for those who cannot sleep due to neuralgia, tension, headaches and over-wrought nerves as a result of continuous strain. In some cases a single dose of valerian tea might be sufficient while with others it may take much longer for the herb to be effective. Valerian tea is soothing and relaxing but it must not be made too strong or taken over too long a period as it will bring on restlessness and a headache. It is always drunk cold.

To make valerian tea: *Use a level teaspoon of the dried grated root and pour on 1 cup of cold mineral water. Cover and leave overnight or for 24 hours if possible before straining. Make fresh valerian tea each time. The taste can be rather disagreeable but the tea can be sweetened with honey. It is most effective when drunk just before going to bed, and it should not be taken every night for longer than 2 weeks.*

Use the tea in the form of a lotion to bathe swollen joints, bruises and contusions to soothe the pain.

Small amounts of valerian can be added to a mixture of fragrant herbs in a herb cushion to relax and help those who cannot sleep.

WATERCRESS

The tangy, pungent taste of the leaves gave rise to the plant's generic name of nasturtium, which comes from the Latin nasi tortium, *meaning 'nose-twisting'. It is rich in Vitamin C and has long been used to prevent scurvy and other skin disorders.*

Nasturtium officinale

Watercress, *nasturtium officinale*, is a peppery-flavoured creeping perennial which always grows near running water, so it can be found in fast-flowing streams and on the edges of rivers. It only grows in or near sweet water. The smooth green leaves are made up of small rounded leaflets and the tiny white flowers, which bloom from July to September, are clustered together at the tops of the stems. Wild watercress can be contaminated by liver fluke which is a dangerous parasite, so watercress should be purchased from a greengrocer or a reputable grower.

In the kitchen watercress is a useful and healthy salad plant and is at its best in May and June. Watercress soup is a delicious start to a meal and its popular use as a garnish is well known as it appears with so many dishes hot or cold.

Watercress is always used fresh and is never dried as this destroys the goodness.

MEDICINAL USE

Watercress should be eaten only in moderation, for too much over too long a period may cause cystitis or other bladder problems. It is an excellent herb for stimulating the appetite and a salad of the herb eaten every other day for a few days is efficacious. Watercress chewed on its own is said to prevent bleeding gums. It is one of the herbs included in a 'spring cure' for toning up the whole system generally and for purifying the blood.

Freshly expressed juice, using either a juice extractor or liquidizer, can be taken mixed with an equal quantity of milk. Drink a small glassful first thing in the morning on an empty stomach every other day for a few days. Watercress juice is also helpful for bronchial ailments; a smaller amount should be taken alone or mixed with clear broth.

A poultice made of crushed watercress leaves is helpful for swollen ankles.

To make a poultice: *Pound the watercress leaves to a pulp and spread carefully on to a piece of muslin or cheesecloth. Heat the pulp between 2 plates over a pan of boiling water and when sufficiently hot lay on the affected part until relief is obtained.*

BEAUTY CARE

Fresh watercress juice is said to be good for spots and other skin blemishes. It can help to fade freckles and to clear the complexion.

To make a skin lotion: *Mix ¼ cup of honey with 10 tablespoons of expressed watercress juice. Mix together well and strain through muslin or cheesecloth into a jar. Cover, keep in the refrigerator and use within a few days. Dab the lotion on to the skin night and morning with a cotton wool pad, taking care to avoid the eyes and mouth.*

WOOD BETONY

Nowadays betony is a little known herb but in classical times it was an important plant used in the treatment of many diseases. It was also believed to ward off evil spirits, and in the Middle Ages betony was planted in churchyards.

Betonica officinalis

Betony, *betonica officinalis*, is a very pretty perennial herb growing wild throughout the country wherever there are woods and copses or damp meadows and dense hedgerows. The whole plant is sweetly aromatic and is of medium height with large, saw-toothed leaves which rise directly from the roots. The flowering stem is hairy and the little red flowers are clustered together in the axils of the leaves. After a bare space on the stem there is another cluster of tiny flowers, all forming an interrupted spike. This helps towards easy identification of the herb in the wild. The flowers bloom in July and August and the whole plant dies in the autumn.

Wood betony is a medicinal and cosmetic herb and the whole flowering herb is picked and dried for winter use. The best time for this is in July, just before the flowers are fully open. They are then dried and stored in the usual way.

MEDICINAL USE

Betony is a tonic herb and good for nervous disorders and stubborn headaches. For these conditions a weak tea should be taken each day at breakfast. The tea can also be given to children as a tonic.

To make the tea: *Pour 2 cups of boiling water on to a handful of dried betony and drink a small glassful once or twice a day.*

For sprains make a strong decoction (see page 13) of betony. Dip pieces of lint into the cooled solution and apply to the affected part. You can also use the leaves strained from the decoction as a poultice, securing it lightly over the injured part.

Bruised betony leaves or the fresh juice of the leaves can be directly applied to boils or thorns and splinters left under skin to draw out the poison and prevent infection.

Betony can be used as a skin ointment which has been found to be very effective in clearing persistent spots and pimples and for acne.

To make the ointment: *Slowly melt 4 heaped tablespoons of white petroleum jelly in a double saucepan. Add a handful of fresh or dried crushed betony plant and stir the mixture well with a wooden spoon. Leave to infuse over a very low heat for about 1 hour. Strain carefully into small pots and leave to get cold before covering.*

BEAUTY CARE

An infusion (see page 13) of betony leaves made fresh each day can be used both night and morning in place of soap and water for cleansing, clearing and softening the skin. It also protects the skin from infection.

WOODRUFF

In the Middle Ages woodruff was valued as a strewing herb, laid over the floor to keep the room smelling sweet. Woodruff was also laid among the linen to keep moths and other insects away.

Woodruff, *asperula odoratum*, is a dainty little herb growing about 12in (30cm) high in shady sheltered spots. It can be found in the wild, growing in damp woods and under hedgerows. Its attractive, bright green leaves grow in whorls around the stems, about six to eight leaves in a group. Woodruff is a perennial herb with a creeping rootstock and grows massed together. The tiny white flowers, which bloom in May and June, grow in great profusion and seen from a distance look like a milky froth. Woodruff has no scent when fresh but when dried or wilted it smells of new mown hay.

In the kitchen, woodruff, used slightly wilted, is added to light wines and apple juice to make delicious and refreshing summer drinks.

Provided a suitable spot can be found for it in the garden, woodruff will grow on for years, gradually spreading over the ground. It looks very attractive under large shrubs. Woodruff can be propagated either by seed or by division of roots in early summer immediately after the plant has flowered. Sow the seed as soon as it has ripened, in good garden soil in a damp shady spot and, when large enough, thin the seedlings to a handspan apart.

Woodruff stems, leaves and flowers are the parts of the herb used in the home. When the flowers are fully out, the whole plant is cut off at the ground and dried and stored in the usual way.

MEDICINAL USE

Woodruff tea is a pleasant flavoured drink and is soothing and calming. The tea is effective for mild digestive troubles and will help to relieve a headache or a migraine. Woodruff is a delicate herb and when making the tea, hot rather than boiling water should be used, otherwise its properties will be destroyed.

To make woodruff tea: *Pour I cupful of hot water on to I teaspoon of dried woodruff. Cover and leave to infuse for 30 minutes. The tea can be reheated by standing the cup in a bowl of hot water.* Woodruff tea taken hot last thing at night will help those who cannot sleep or who suffer from vertigo or nervous tension. One or two cups a day will help to restore the nerves and purify the blood.

Fresh crushed leaves laid over the affected part will relieve the pain of a headache.

Dried and powdered woodruff can be added to other herbs in a pot pourri mixture. The dried crushed herb either used on its own or mixed with other herbs such as elderflower, chamomile flowers or bergamot and made into a herb cushion will be found soothing and relaxing.

YARROW

Yarrow was highly prized as a wound herb. It is said that Achilles used the fresh herb to stop the flow of blood from the wounds of his soldiers. Later yarrow was made into an ointment and used for the same purpose. One of its country names is nosebleed, derived from the use of its leaf as a plug to the nostril.

Achillea Millefolium.

Published by Dr Woodville Jan.y 1, 1792.

Yarrow, *achillea millefolium*, is a very familiar wild herb. It can be found growing almost everywhere, in fields, by hedgerows and along country lanes. It is an attractive small plant, growing up to 12in (30cm) high. The square erect stem carries longish very finely cut feathery leaves which are deep green. The flowers, which bloom from June to September, are white or pale pink, very small, and grow massed together in a flat-topped cluster which stands out prettily among other hedgerow plants. The whole plant is covered with fine silky hairs and has a pungent, rather spicy scent, while the taste is strong and slightly bitter. Yarrow has a creeping rootstock and sets many seeds so it is readily available in the wild. It is very easy to grow in the garden and, far from becoming a troublesome weed, will help to keep plants growing nearby free from disease. It is also a safer way to provide yarrow for use in the home, because of possible contamination of the wild plants by chemical spraying.

Yarrow can be planted in any garden soil in sun or in shade. Set the plants in during the spring or autumn. Once established, yarrow will need to be periodically cut back to prevent it from spreading into the other plants in the border.

Both flowers and leaves can be dried for winter use. The leaves are picked at any time during the growing season and the flowers when they are just coming into bloom. Leaves and flowers are usually dried separately, but can be mixed together for storing.

MEDICINAL USE

Yarrow is a useful remedy for a feverish cold, especially if taken as soon as the symptoms appear. Taken in the form of a tea, yarrow increases perspiration, helping to bring down a fever. Combined with elderflower or peppermint the tea can bring speedy relief to the sufferer.

To make yarrow tea: *Pour ½ cup of boiling water*

over 1 teaspoon of fresh or dried yarrow. Leave to infuse for 5–10 minutes. Strain and add honey to sweeten if preferred.

The tea made purely with the flower can be taken in cases of chronic catarrh. It is also beneficial to those with indigestion and flatulence and is a gentle laxative. Taken warm 30 minutes before a meal, yarrow tea will help to stimulate the appetite.

For external use, an ointment using the fresh herb will soothe painful haemorrhoids (piles). It can also be used to ease painful joints, and for cuts and abrasions.
☞To make the ointment: *Melt 4 heaped tablespoons of white petroleum jelly in an enamel pan. Stir in 1 good handful of chopped fresh herb. Bring it slowly to the boil and simmer gently for 15–20 minutes. Strain and pour into small pots. Cover when cold.*

A poultice made from fresh yarrow leaves is said to relieve painful rheumatic joints.
☞To make a poultice: *Pick and wash enough leaves to make into a pulp, either by hand or in the electric blender. Spread the pulp on to a piece of muslin or cheesecloth and heat it between 2 plates over a pan of boiling water. Place over the affected part as hot as possible and leave until the poultice has cooled. Renew as necessary until relief is felt.*

BEAUTY CARE

Yarrow is an excellent cosmetic herb when used wisely. It is important to note that when using yarrow on the skin over a long period of time, the skin may become sensitive to sunlight and discoloration of the skin may occur. Yarrow lotion is an infusion made from the flowers and is a good cleanser for oily skin. It is an astringent herb, so a weak infusion will be found quite effective.
☞To make yarrow lotion: *Pour 2 cups of boiling water on to 1½ tablespoons of fresh herb or 3 teaspoons of dried herb. Leave to infuse for at least 1 hour then strain into a screwtop bottle. Keep the bottle in the refrigerator and use within a few days. Dip cotton wool into the lotion and wipe over the face night and morning. As soon as a beneficial effect is noticed the treatment should be discontinued.*

For blackheads in an oily skin, a facial steam will help to cleanse and stimulate the skin.
☞To make a facial steam: *Into a bowl put 2 handfuls of yarrow and pour boiling water over them. Cover the head and bowl with a towel and let the steam cleanse and soften the skin for 10 minutes. Afterwards carefully wipe the face and finally splash the skin with* cold water to close the pores. *The addition of other herbs in the facial steam will help to make it more effective. Use herbs such as chamomile flowers, nettle, lime flowers and salad burnet for a fragrant steam.*

A useful treatment for oily skin is to have a yarrow face pack. It will help to close large pores and improve the texture of the skin.
☞To make the face pack: *Gather fresh leaves and flowering tops, wash and finely chop them. Put into an enamel pan with sufficient water to prevent burning. Bring to the boil and simmer gently for 10 minutes until a thick pulp is formed. Cleanse the face thoroughly and spread the mixture on to a piece of gauze. Put the warm pack on to the face, avoiding eyes and mouth. The eyes can be covered with cotton wool pads wrung out in cold water. Lie down and relax for 15 minutes. Wash off with tepid water. The face pack will also help to heal spots and pimples and will generally improve the complexion. To make the treatment more effective a cup of yarrow tea (see Medicinal Use) can be taken.*

Yarrow infusion can be used as a hair rinse, when it will help to clear mild cases of dandruff. The infusion can also be used as a hair lotion and rubbed into the scalp three or four times a week to stimulate the growth and leave the hair soft and shining.
☞To make the infusion: *Pour 4 cups of boiling water on to 3 tablespoons of fresh crushed yarrow in a jug. Leave to stand for 2 hours, then strain and reheat by placing the jug in a pan of hot water until the infusion is sufficiently warm. Shampoo and rinse the hair in the ordinary way. Finally pour the yarrow rinse over the hair several times, massaging it well into the scalp. The infusion may be poured into a stoppered jar and used within a few days. Store in a cool place or in the refrigerator.*

The infusion makes an effective lotion for chapped hands when used on an occasional basis. Pour some lotion into a bowl and soak the hands for 5–10 minutes. Alternatively use as a compress; dip pieces of lint into the lotion and spread over the hands. Leave for 10–15 minutes.

As a bath addition yarrow provides a soothing relaxing soak which is at the same time good for the skin.
☞To make a herbal bath: *Make a strong infusion by pouring 2 cups of boiling water over 3–4 handfuls of the herb. Leave it to infuse for 15–20 minutes then strain and add to the bath water. The addition of a highly perfumed herb such as lavender will make it more fragrant and increase the pleasure of the bath.*

A HERBAL CALENDAR

JANUARY

Plan the herb garden. Where a new herb bed is being started choose one facing south with protection from the north and east. A sloping bed is the ideal site. Decide on herbs to be grown and order seeds. Decide which perennials are to be bought as plants and which can be raised from seed. Make a sketch of the herb bed and place the plants, remembering their height when fully grown and sun, part shade and other requirements. Herbs which were brought indoors for the winter months need careful watching. Do not over water but keep the soil just moistened. Sow parsley seed under glass for an early crop.

FEBRUARY

Where weather permits prepare new herb bed by digging in compost and six weeks later adding lime. Provide shelter from the wind using screening herbs. Sow feverfew under glass, parsley seed in the open in a damp shady spot and chervil in the frame or cool greenhouse. Divide mint roots setting new runners in rich, moist soil. Set new roots one foot apart, placing root tiles in the earth to stop mint growing into other plants. Plant hawthorn trees. Set garlic cloves into the ground. Plant rooted cuttings of horseradish. Lift and divide roots of established salad burnet. Plant honeysuckle bushes. Lift orris root for drying.

MARCH

As soil warms up, prepare seed bed by raking soil to fine tilth. Sow annual seeds of cornflower, fumitory, marigold and nasturtium in full sun in flowering position. Sow annual coriander and perennials rosemary, thyme and sage under glass. Sow perennials fennel and solidago in flowering position. Plant sweet flag in mud or damp spot near water. Lift and divide lovage, hyssop, catnep, St. John's wort and costmary plants. Take stem cuttings of mugwort and root cuttings of calamint. Lift and divide sweet cicely roots of two year old plants, keeping some for drying. On a dry day collect lesser celandine plant and coltsfoot flowers for drying. Sow a small amount each of dill and chervil seed in the open.

APRIL

Sow biennial caraway seeds in a sunny spot. Set out bought plants angelica, perennials costmary and bergamot. Plant comfrey in a damp position. Sow annuals anise, borage, flax, purslane, summer savory and sweet marjoram in the open ground. Sow arnica, mullein and sunflower under glass. Set out sage, yarrow and new violet plants. Sow biennial burdock in the sun. Sow perennials calamint, catnep, salad burnet, self heal, motherwort, valerian in the open. Sow seed or plant rooted cuttings of wild honeysuckle. Sow perennials in pots for transplanting later of hyssop, lavender, lovage, mint, rosemary, sage and thyme. Thin out seeds sown in March. Plant rooted cuttings of lavender, hyssop, sage. Hoe the herb bed.

MAY

Thin out seedlings when large enough. Divide old straggling thyme plants. Layer creeping thyme stems. Sow annuals Blessed Thistle and coriander in the open and the biennial clary in a seed bed. Sow perennials chicory, elecampane, lemon balm, lady's mantle, parsley, St. John's wort and white horehound. Set out bought plants elecampane, hyssop and lemon verbena. Plant out rosemary and sage seedlings. Take stem cuttings of established lemon balm and sage. Pick coltsfoot leaves for drying. Gather hawthorn flowers for drying. Cut heartsease for drying if flowers are almost out. Cut woodruff for drying when flowers are fully open. Sow annual chamomile in flowering sunny position. Sow more seeds of dill, chervil and parsley.

JUNE

Make further sowings of borage and chamomile. Thin out seedlings, grown in their flowering positions, to their correct width apart. Sow perennial cowslip. Plant out feverfew seedlings. Sow woodruff seeds as soon as ripe. Cut cornflowers for drying as the flowers open. Start gathering damask rose petals for drying. Gather elderflowers for drying or syrup. Cut melilot leaves and flowers. Dry salad burnet leaves. When damp lift, divide and replant primroses. Continue to keep the herb garden free of weeds by frequent hoeing. Cut herb leaves for drying when at their best. Take cuttings of rosemary and southernwood.

JULY

Gather honeysuckle flowers for drying. Pick horehound for drying as flowers appear. Cut both lady's mantle flowers and leaves for drying. Take stem cuttings of lemon verbena. Pick lime flowers and solidago as they come into full flower. Gather leaves and flowers of meadowsweet for drying and cut down stems of southernwood for drying. Dry all herbs separately and continue to dry leaves and flowers of all herbs when they are at their best. Gather lavender flowers when in full bloom cutting them with long stems. Make sure the herbs are gathered when the weather is dry. Make further sowings in small amounts of chervil and dill. Continue to hoe the herb garden and water plants in a dry spell. Watch out for signs of pests or diseases. Treat greenfly, spraying plants with soapy solution.

AUGUST

Sow parsley seed in the first week in the open or a frame for winter use. Take cuttings of lavender, hyssop, rosemary and sage. Set them in sandy soil in the frame and spray with water during the day until roots are formed. Collect clary seeds for drying from second year plants. Lift clary roots for drying. Pick costmary flowers for drying and harvest flax seed. Collect dill seeds for drying and dig up garlic bulbs. Sow lovage seed as it ripens or leave it to fall and grow around the plant. Gather marshmallow flowers for drying and flowering tips of mugwort. Take cuttings of mugwort. Weed and water in dry spells.

SEPTEMBER

Sow freshly ripened caraway seed in a sunny spot. Sow chervil seed to provide leaves in early spring. Lift chicory roots for drying. Set clary plants into flowering position. Gather fennel seeds as they ripen. Sow fumitory seed. Collect hawthorn berries. Gather hop cones for drying, set out new hop plants. Sow marshmallow seeds when ripe. Divide roots of meadowsweet to increase stock. Sow melilot seed in flowering position and plant out mullein seedlings. Lift and divide soapwort plants. Divide and replant old bergamot plants using only the outside shoots of the plant. Take and set more lavender cuttings.

OCTOBER

Buy and set out barberry plants. Layer suckers on existing plants. Lift and divide costmary, setting plants out a foot apart. Divide lady's mantle roots. Plant lesser celandine bulbsets. Sow mullein seeds as they ripen. Set out primrose plants for flowering in the spring and dig up roots of two or three year old plants for drying. Prune sage bushes. Divide solidago plants which are too large. Collect sweet flag rhizomes for drying for two or three-year-old plants. Set out yarrow plants. Lift and divide some mint replanting one or two pieces in greenhouse. These can be forced for a supply of mint leaves throughout the winter months. Start to clear up the herb garden generally removing all the dead leaves and flowers.

NOVEMBER

Clear away dead and dying annuals and second season biennials such as parsley and mullein. Remove old and straggly herbs to the compost. Cover parsley and chervil seed sown in August or September with cloches. Protect lemon verbena for the winter with straw and sacking. Lift marshmallow and divide the roots keeping some back for drying. Replant roots one foot apart. Plant out rooted cuttings of honeysuckle and bare rooted rose trees in first weeks of November. Where the ground is cleared start the digging to get it completed by the end of the month. Sow fresh sweet cicely seed and angelica in seed trays in open ground, cover with netting. Prick out seedlings at four leaf stage the following year.

DECEMBER

Lift horseradish roots of first or second-year plants. In cold areas and where danger from frost is prevalent protect rosemary bushes with layers of straw and leaf mould or peat. Protect small bushes by enclosing them in wire netting. Perennial herb plants such as bergamot, marshmallow and mint die right down in winter. Continue to keep the herb garden free of old leaves and other rubbish. Any herb brought into the greenhouse earlier should be kept watered. Herbs such as parsley, chervil and mint growing in frame or greenhouse can be used as required. Finish clearing away old unwanted plants ready for next year.

A DICTIONARY OF AILMENTS

For any condition of a serious nature which shows signs of complication, a doctor should be consulted. The following remedies are culled from old herbals. All should be taken or applied in moderation.

ACNE
Acne is an inflammation of the sebaceous glands, usually on the face. It is most common in adolescence and often clears up later. Stress and unbalanced diet can aggravate it. Try to keep the skin clean and do not pick or squeeze the spots.
Compress (see page 13): made with an infusion of marigold petals to heal scars left behind when acne is cured.
Face Pack (see page 13): mix Fuller's earth with a strong infusion of coltsfoot or yarrow to a thick paste. Use once or twice a week.
Lotion: make up an infusion (see page 15) of burdock, chamomile flowers, elderflowers, marigold petals, plantain, lavender flowers or yarrow. Bathe the face in the lotion daily, and use as a compress on badly affected areas.
Ointment (see page 14): make from marigold or yarrow and apply at night to soothe and heal.
Poultice (see page 16): make from fresh cleavers, honeysuckle, sweet violets or plantain, or use poultices made from chickweed, hops, marsh mallow or thyme. Use as necessary.

ATHLETE'S FOOT
Athlete's foot is a fungoidal infection which attacks the feet and mainly lodges between the toes. This results in itching and unpleasant odour. It is often caused by excessive sweating or not drying between the toes. It can be avoided by keeping the feet clean and dry, using a foot powder and changing socks and stockings frequently.
Footbath (see page 14): make up a strong infusion of agrimony, lovage,

comfrey or mugwort and use hot.
Fresh comfrey leaves can be placed between the toes until the trouble is over.

BAD BREATH
This can be caused by a number of reasons. Chronic bad breath can indicate a poor digestion, that the teeth are in need of attention or that the gums may be infected. In these cases a doctor or dentist should be consulted. For occasional bad breath and to help chronic sufferers the following can be tried.
Chew a small piece of dried orris root slowly in the mouth to scent the breath with violets. Chew fresh parsley leaves to remove the smell of garlic. Chew fresh leaves of either garden mint or peppermint.
Infusion (see page 15): make up with lavender flowers, lemon balm leaves or flowering tips of rosemary. Use warm or cold infusion as a mouthwash whenever required. Occasionally drink a glassful of the infusion to make the treatment more effective. Make up an infusion using angelica seeds (see page 21) to sweeten the breath.

BLISTERS
Blisters are thin bubbles on the skin which contain a watery substance and are caused by constant rubbing on the same spot. Remove the source of the rubbing and try one of the following.
Compress (see page 13): make a strong infusion of either cleavers or costmary. Apply when cold.
Infusion (see page 15): make up with cleavers or costmary and bathe the affected part until relief is felt.
Ointment (see page 14): make it with cleavers or costmary. After applying compress pat dry and smooth on the ointment.
Poultice (see page 16): make it with cleavers. Place gently over the blisters to ease the pain.

BOILS
These are painful inflamed swellings which can occur when the body is run down, or where there is a shortage of mineral salts, or because of constipation or lack of exercise.
Fomentation (see page 14): make up strong infusions of any of the following herbs: hops with chamomile flowers, lady's bedstraw or marsh mallow leaves. Apply to affected part as hot as possible and renew as necessary.
Juice Use freshly expressed juice of lady's bedstraw or wood betony and paint on to the boil.
Ointment (see page 14): make from clary leaves. Smooth over boil to draw it to a head.
Poultice (see page 16): use leaves of lovage, mullein, lady's bedstraw; marsh mallow roots or nasturtium seeds.

BRONCHIAL CONGESTION
This complaint is brought about by infection of the air passages (usually of the chest) which become clogged and painful. To relieve the discomfort and ease the pain the following remedies may be helpful.
Fomentation Make up with dried marsh mallow leaves (see page 96). Wring out pieces of lint in the solution and apply to the chest; breathe deeply, until relief is felt.
Inhalation Make up with dried crushed marsh mallow leaves (see page 96) and breathe in the steam for ten minutes. Make up with mullein flowers (see page 102) and use for ten to fifteen minutes to ease congestion.
Oil (see page 14): make up using lavender flowers and gently smooth the warm oil on to the chest both back and front.
Poultice (see page 102): make up with fresh mullein leaves and apply to both sides of the chest as warm as possible. Leave in place until relief is felt. Renew as required.

BRONCHITIS

Bronchitis is a painful inflammation of the bronchial tubes. Mild cases only can be treated in the following ways.

Cordial (see page 13): use sunflower seeds and take a teaspoonful whenever complaint is troublesome.

Infusion (see page 15): make up with mullein flowers, horehound or plantain leaves and flowers. Drink a small glassful two or three times a day.

Inhalation (see page 13): make from lavender flowers, rosemary or garden mint leaves. Inhale for ten minutes once or twice a week.

Oil (see page 14): use garlic cloves and rub on to back and front of chest.

Syrup (see page 15): make with elderberries or horehound. Sip as required.

Decoction (see page 13): use coltsfoot flowers. Drink warm once or twice a day.

BRUISES

Bruises are injuries to the skin caused by a heavy blow or blows producing discolouration and some pain according to the severity of the blow.

Compress (see page 13): use dilute tincture of arnica. Renew compress until relief is obtained.

Lotion Make up infusions (see page 15) of solidago or valerian leaves. When cold bathe bruise to reduce pain and discolouration.

Oil (see page 14): use rosemary leaves and flowering tips and gently smooth over the bruise.

Ointment (see page 14): use fresh or dried chickweed. Pat on to bruise.

Poultice (see page 16): make from fresh leaves of sweet violet. Lay it lightly on to the bruise and renew as necessary until pain has subsided.

BURNS AND SCALDS

Burns are injuries caused by fire or great heat. Scalds are injuries caused by hot liquids. Minor burns and scalds can be treated in the following ways.

Extract (see page 96): make with fresh or dried marsh mallow leaves. Use in the form of a cold compress (see page 13) and place over affected part until relief is felt.

Lotion Make up a strong infusion (see page 15) of mullein leaves (page 102) or chamomile flowers. When cold bathe the affected part copiously until the pain has decreased.

Oil (see page 14): make with comfrey leaves, lavender or St John's wort flowers. Use in form of compress and renew as necessary.

Ointment (see page 14): use cleavers, marigold petals or extract of marsh mallow. Smooth very gently over burn or scald.

CATARRH

This is a discharge of fluid from the nose caused by inflammation of the lining of the air passages. It can be in the nose or on the chest.

Decoction (see page 13): make up with flowering tips of hyssop or coltsfoot leaves and flowers. Take a small glassful once or twice a day until relief is obtained.

Infusion (see page 15): use yarrow or fennel leaves, thyme, honeysuckle, elderflowers, sweet marjoram. Drink a small glassful as required.

Inhalation (see page 13): make with peppermint leaves, chamomile flowers, thyme or sage, or use a mixture of herbs. Use once or twice a week.

Oil (see page 14): use garlic cloves, lavender flowers or rosemary. Rub oil over back and front of chest to ease bronchial catarrh.

CHILBLAINS

Chilblains are painful red swellings which appear on extremities, hands, feet and ears in cold weather.

Decoction (see page 13): make up with elderflowers or marigold petals. Use while warm and bathe affected part frequently.

To prevent chilblains forming, the hands and feet can be bathed in a decoction made with marigold petals. Add a little sea salt to the cooled decoction and carry out the treatment night and morning.

Fomentation (see page 14): use a strong decoction of elderflowers. Bathe affected areas when required to ease pain.

Oil (see page 14): make from mullein flowers and smooth over painful areas.

Ointment (see page 14): make up using chickweed, marigold petals or elderflowers. Gently massage chilblains at night.

Poultice (see page 16): make up using chickweed, marigold petals or mullein leaves. Use as often as required to bring relief.

COLD SORES

Cold sores are clusters of little blisters which usually appear on the face at the onset of a cold. The virus lives in the system and if the cold sores appear too often a doctor should be consulted. For the occasional sore the following herbal remedy can be tried.

Compress (see page 13): make a strong decoction using elecampane root. Use cooled or just warm for compress, renewing as necessary.

COLDS

A cold is an inflammation of the lining of the nasal passages and most often starts when the body's resistance is low. A cold can lead to catarrh, cough or influenza. Some herbs can help to ward off a cold, others help to relieve the symptoms.

Candy To prevent a cold going down to the chest suck pieces of coltsfoot or horehound candy (see pages 42 & 74).

Infusion (see page 15): make up any one of barberries, burdock, cleavers, coltsfoot, elderflowers, limeflowers, rosehips or yarrow. Drink a small glassful of the infusion two or three times a day. Take one cup of meadowsweet tea per day.

Inhalation (see page 13): choose from limeflowers, marsh mallow leaves, nettle or peppermint to clear a stuffy head. Use inhalation for ten minutes once or twice a week.

CONSTIPATION

This is an irregular action of the bowel when the body fails to rid itself of waste matter. A poor diet is often the cause. Try to eat more roughage in the form of fresh fruit, raw vegetables and wholewheat bread and to take regular exercise. For mild cases try one of the following.
Infusion (see page 15): make up with either centaury, chickweed, dandelion leaves, flax seeds, purslane or yarrow. Take a small glassful as required once or twice a day.
Seed Take two teaspoons of flax seed swallowed with a large glass of water at night or in the morning.
Syrup (see page 15): make up with elderberries and take a teaspoonful on an occasional basis only. It is best when taken at night.

CORNS

These are small, hard growths of dead tissue which usually appear on the toes or foot and are caused by continuous pressure or friction. Ill-fitting shoes are the worst offenders. A chiropodist should be consulted if the corn is large and painful, otherwise try the following.
Juice Express juice from the marigold plant and apply morning and evening until relief is obtained.

COUGHS

A cough is an irritation in the throat or chest caused by inflammation of the air passages.
Candy Make horehound candy (see page 74) and suck a piece to soothe.
Cordial (see page 13): make up with sunflower seeds and sip a teaspoonful when cough is troublesome.
Extract Make up with marsh mallow root (see page 96) and take a teaspoonful as required.

Infusion (see page 16): make up with agrimony, aniseed, coltsfoot, elecampane root, fennel, horehound, parsley or sweet cicely. Sip a small glassful whenever the cough is troublesome.
Inhalation (see page 13): make with elderflowers, nettle, lavender or limeflowers or a mixture of herbs. Inhale the steam as and when required.
Poultice (see page 16): make up with mullein using fresh leaves. Apply to chest to loosen a stubborn cough.
Syrup (see page 15): use any one of barberries, dried angelica roots, fennel, honeysuckle, horehound or thyme. Take a teaspoonful as required.

CUTS

Cuts and abrasions are shallow wounds where skin is grazed maybe by a fall or scratched by a sharp object. Deep cuts should be seen by a doctor. For minor cuts and grazes try one of the following treatments.
Compress (see page 13): make a strong infusion of mullein or use St John's wort oil. Cleanse wound thoroughly before applying compress. Secure in place until relief is felt.
Decoction (see page 13): make a strong decoction of marigold petals

or sage and use as described above.
Fresh parsley leaves applied at once provide an instant remedy for minor cuts and grazes.
Infusion (see page 15): make up with lady's mantle or meadowsweet. Bathe cuts and grazes with cool infusion until clean and bleeding stops.
Ointment (see page 14): make up with primrose flowers, sweet cicely or yarrow and smooth over the cleansed wound and keep it covered.

DIARRHOEA

Mild cases of diarrhoea occasionally occur when the body needs to rid the system of toxic matter as quickly as possible. In cases of chronic diarrhoea and where there is pain and fever, a doctor should always be consulted. To help relieve the discomfort and soothe the inflammation the following can be tried.
Decoction Make up with dried comfrey root (see page 44). When cool take a small glassful three or four times a day until relief is felt.
Infusion (see page 15): make up with cleavers or lovage. Drink a warm infusion a glassful at a time as required. Lovage should not be taken by those with a kidney complaint or during pregnancy.

DIZZINESS

Dizziness, fainting and vertigo are all varying degrees of giddiness or swooning. These unpleasant complaints can be helped in a minor way by the following.
Infusion (see page 15): make up with blessed thistle, garden mint or woodruff. For vertigo drink warm last thing at night.
Oil (see page 14): make it with lavender or rosemary. For dizziness take five drops of lavender oil on a lump of sugar, or pour a few drops of rosemary oil on to cotton wool and hold under the nose.
Syrup (see page 15): use cowslip flowers. Sip a teaspoonful when

required or dilute with water and take a small glassful.

Fresh leaves of calamint lightly crushed can be held under the nose.

Eczema

This is a skin disease which affects young and old and is often caused by tiredness and stress, or by an allergy to a certain food. Small red patches appear on the skin which are extremely itchy. These turn into little blisters and become dried and scaly.

Compress (see page 13): make up a strong infusion of chamomile flowers, heartsease or a strong decoction of sage. Renew as required and until itching is relieved.

Decoction (see page 13): make it with dandelion root or leaves and drink a small glassful three or four times a day. Add decoction to bath water at night to ease the itching.

Ointment (see page 14): make up with marigold petals or sage leaves and smooth over red patches to stop irritation.

Flatulence

This is caused by the formation of gases in the stomach or bowel during the digestion of food.

Infusion (see page 15): make up with any one of the following herbs: angelica, aniseed, caraway seeds, catnep, fennel, garden mint, lemon balm, motherwort, peppermint, summer savory, sweet flag or thyme. Take a small glassful of warm infusion after a meal or as required.

Haemorrhoids

Haemorrhoids, or piles, are enlarged veins which occur around the anus. If they become very painful and swollen, with bleeding, a doctor should be consulted. For a mild attack of piles the following can be tried.

Fomentation (see page 14): make a strong decoction of lesser celandine and use as hot as possible to bring relief.

Infusion (see page 15): make up with

parsley and take one or two warm cups a day or as required.

Oil (see page 14): make up with mullein flowers. Smooth oil over painful area as required.

Ointment (see page 14): use either lesser celandine, plantain, sweet violet or yarrow and gently rub on to affected part.

Headache

This is a pain in the head. For a serious headache which keeps recurring a doctor should be consulted. A headache can be caused by tiredness, indigestion, eye strain and for many other reasons. Any of the following herbs may help to reduce a headache.

Infusion (see page 15): make up with elderflowers, lavender, lemon balm, sweet marjoram, sweet violet, sage or wood betony. Drink a cup of warm infusion at the onset of a headache.

Compress (see page 13): make a strong decoction of fennel seeds and when lukewarm use compress on temples and forehead.

Herb Cushion Fill a cushion with any of these to soothe and disperse a headache: lavender, sage, peppermint, wood betony or valerian.

Mentha piperita

Hiccups

These are the periodic involuntary contraction of the diaphragm while the glottis is spasmodically closed.

Infusion (see page 15): make up with dill or fennel seeds, garden mint or peppermint and drink warm as required.

Hoarseness

This is a condition of the throat which produces a rough husky voice; often brought on by a cold or by straining the voice. To relieve the accompanying discomfort and soreness try one of the following remedies.

Decoction Make up with mullein flowers (see page 102). Use the decoction as a warm gargle as often as required to obtain relief. A decoction of sage leaves can also be used as a gargle (see page 119).

Syrup Make up with garlic cloves (see page 68) adding a few caraway seeds to soften the flavour and smell. Take a teaspoonful two or three times a day.

Hot flushes

Hot flushes are a distressing, embarrassing symptom of the menopause, when a sudden feeling of heat rushes to the head and the face reddens. It is often accompanied by immoderate perspiration over the whole body. The flushes are usually of short duration but can arise at any time. A sensible diet and a correct intake of vitamins and minerals are important. Exercise and keeping the weight down may lessen the frequency of the flushes. The following may also prove beneficial.

Infusion (see page 15): make up with crushed hawthorn flowers or lady's mantle leaves and sweeten with a little honey. Take a small glassful once or twice a day.

A most effective treatment is to take oil of evening primrose in capsule form. These can be purchased from health food stores and directions on the label should be closely followed.

INDIGESTION

This is the painful digestion of food and there are many possible causes. The pain is a warning signal that the stomach cannot cope. For minor digestive problems the following can be tried and each is pleasant to take.
Chew caraway seeds for quick relief at onset of indigestion.
Infusion (see page 15): make up with angelica, aniseed, caraway or dill seeds, lemon verbena, chamomile flowers, chervil, melilot, mugwort, peppermint, sage or solidago. Drink a small glassful of warm infusion after a meal or as required.

INFLUENZA

Influenza is a virus which attacks the upper respiratory tract and produces aching head and body, fever and high temperatures. Mild cases of influenza can be helped with herbs which increase perspiration and bring down a fever.
Infusion (see page 15): make up with any of the following: angelica, borage, hyssop, limeflowers, meadowsweet or yarrow. Take a hot cup of infusion as required.

INSECT BITES

Insect bites and stings can cause a severe reaction in some people and these should be treated by a doctor.
Fresh aloe leaves split open. Use juice on insect bite.
Fresh crushed plantain leaves on nettle sting, mosquito and other bites.
Fresh crushed sage leaves on insect bites to reduce irritation.
Fresh crushed summer savory herb on bee and wasp stings to relieve pain.

MIGRAINE

Migraine is a prostrating headache often accompanied by nausea. Severe cases require professional advice. For those who suffer a migraine only occasionally the following herbs may be of help.
Eat three or four feverfew leaves a day on a regular basis.

Infusion (see page 15): make a strong infusion of chamomile flowers. When cold drink it freely. Try limeflowers or feverfew, taking it once or twice a day regularly.
Juice Express juice of blessed thistle leaves and rub gently over forehead and temples.
Oil (see page 14): make up with lavender flowers and take five drops of oil on a lump of sugar at the onset of a migraine.

MUSCLE ACHES

Muscle aches and pains occur when little-used muscles are suddenly overworked by exertion at sport or gardening, cycling etc. Herbs can help to soothe and ease.
Oil (see page 14): make up with fennel, peppermint, sweet marjoram or thyme. Massage a little oil on to the muscle as necessary.
Poultice (see page 16): make up with fresh or dried comfrey leaves, hyssop or yarrow. Place gently over the affected part to relieve.

NEURALGIA

Neuralgia is a sharp intermittent pain which runs along the course of a nerve and is usually in the head or face.

Infusion (see page 15): make up with feverfew flowers and take a glass of cold infusion once or twice a day. Try an infusion of warm lemon balm or lavender flowers at night and in the morning. Take a glass of cold valerian last thing at night for a few days.
Oil (see page 14): make up with peppermint leaves and gently smooth over painful area.

SKIN COMPLAINTS

These include skin eruptions such as heat rash and irritations caused by prickly clothing or hard water. Shingles is a painful itching skin eruption which follows the line of a nerve.
Compress (see page 13): make up a decoction of hyssop or an infusion of marigold. For shingles make up a strong infusion of plantain. Renew the compress until relief is obtained.
Decoction (see page 13): make up with hyssop and bathe affected parts to ease the itching.
Infusion (see page 15): make up with plantain to bathe itching skin.
Oil (see page 14): make up with St John's wort and smooth on to shingles when skin is unbroken to ease the pain.
Ointment (see page 14): use marigold petals and smooth the ointment over all skin eruptions.

SLEEPLESSNESS

Sleeplessness can be caused by tension and strain, feeling overtired and run down or it may be due to digestive problems. There are many herbs which can be helpful for occasional spells of sleeplessness.
Infusion (see page 15): make up with one of the following: catnep, cleavers, dill seeds, hawthorn flowers, hops, lemon verbena, melilot, motherwort and valerian. Take a glassful of warm infusion in the evening. Do not take valerian for longer than two weeks.
Herb pillows Fill small decorative bags with hops, lemon verbena or a mixture of sleep-inducing herbs. Use

the pillows at night.

SPRAINS

Sprains and strains and swollen joints can all cause a great deal of pain and discomfort. For mild cases there are herbs which can help to reduce the pain and the swelling.

Fomentation (see page 14): make up a decoction of hyssop and use on sprains and strained muscles. Make an infusion of comfrey leaves and use in the same way.

Infusion (see page 15): make up with melilot and bathe the affected parts.

Oil (see page 14): make up using comfrey or sweet marjoram and smooth over painful areas.

Ointment (see page 14): make up using comfrey or sweet marjoram and gently rub on to affected area.

Poultice (see page 16): make up with comfrey, coltsfoot leaves or fresh meadowsweet flowers. Renew as necessary.

Tincture (see page 16): make up with arnica flowers and dilute with warm water for bathing affected areas.

STIFFNESS

Stiffness of muscles and joints can be painful and inhibiting and is due to various causes.

Compress (see page 13): make up an infusion of heartsease or a strong infusion of thyme and renew as required.

Oil (see page 14): make up with lavender flowers or mugwort flowering tips and smooth over painful areas.

Ointment (see page 14): make up with sage leaves or yarrow and gently apply to muscles or joints.

STYES

These are small inflamed swellings which appear on the eyelids and often occur when the body is in a run-down state. They may be attributed to the diet if it includes too much sugar and starchy foods. Bathing the eye with warm water to which some bicarbonate of soda has

been added may reduce the stye or bring it to a head. The following treatments can also be tried.

Compress (see page 13): make up a weak decoction of cornflowers using distilled water and use to soothe inflamed eyelid. A horsetail decoction with distilled water may be used in the same way.

Infusion (see page 15): make up with plantain and while warm bathe the eyelids until relief is felt.

Melissa officinalis

TENSION

Tension or strain can be caused by pressure and stress. Try any of the following in an infusion as for Sleeplessness: lemon balm, limeflowers, primrose, woodruff and valerian.

THORNS AND SPLINTERS

Thorns and splinters can lodge deeply into the flesh and can be unpleasant. To help draw out the inflammation try the following.

Ointment Make a soft ointment of crushed fresh clary leaves (see page 14) and smooth on.

Juice Use freshly expressed juice of wood betony leaves directly on to thorns and splinters to draw out the poison.

THROAT INFECTIONS

These cause inflammations of the lining of the throat and can take the form of a sore throat, tonsillitis, laryngitis, hoarseness or loss of voice. There are many herbs which may help to ease these problems.

Candy Make up horehound candy (see page 74) and suck a piece for hoarseness.

Compress (see page 13): make up an oil using chamomile flowers and use a warm compress on the throat for loss of voice.

Decoction (see page 13): make up with hyssop and sip a teaspoonful to ease a sore throat. Make with mullein flowers and use as a gargle for all throat complaints.

Infusion (see page 15): make up with coltsfoot, selfheal or sage. Sip warm selfheal for a relaxed throat. Use sage or selfheal as a gargle for sore and inflamed throat. Sip warm coltsfoot to ease laryngitis.

Syrup (see page 15): make up with angelica, barberries, sweet violet or horehound and use for sore throats and tonsilitis.

TOOTHACHE

A dental surgeon should be consulted for all cases of toothache. While waiting for the appointment one or two herbs may help to reduce the pain and discomfort.

Chew fresh catnep leaves for an instant remedy.

Infusion (see page 15): make up with lemon balm and use warm as a mouthwash to ease a bad tooth.

Oil (see page 14): make up with peppermint, or use the stronger oil bought from a chemist, and paint on to the offending tooth.

WARTS

Warts are caused by a virus and form small, hard protuberances on the skin. Crush fresh mullein flowers and immediately bind them over the wart.

Juice Express the juice from marigold plant or dandelion and paint on to the wart.

A DICTIONARY OF BEAUTY CARE

BLACKHEADS

Blackheads are the result of the pores of the skin becoming clogged with oil which turns black once open to the air. To prevent them forming, thorough cleansing of the skin is required. To help remove a mild outbreak of blackheads try the following herbs.

Facial Steam Make up with chamomile, limeflowers or yarrow. For a more effective facial steam use a mixture of the herbs as above and include nettle and salad burnet. Cleanse the face thoroughly, use the steam for ten minutes, then gently press out the blackheads with two pieces of cotton wool. Dab the skin with cold water or an astringent to close the pores.

CALLUSES

Calluses are local thickening of the skin and usually appear on the heels, elbows and the palms of the hands, places which are abraded by constant friction. They are unsightly, dry, hard patches on the skin. To remove them and to ensure the skin remains smooth and supple the following treatments can be tried.

Extract (see page 96): make up with marsh mallow leaves and use daily to soften rough skin.

Juice The freshly expressed juice of the marigold can be gently massaged into the affected area once or twice a day.

Ointment (see page 14): make up with marigold petals and rub on to the calluses each night, massaging well into the skin to lubricate and soften.

DANDRUFF

Dandruff is a disorder of the scalp which results in dry dead tissue flaking off the scalp. Mild cases can be dealt with in the home where the diet should consist of lean meats, salads, vegetables and plenty of fresh fruit. At the same time try the following herb treatments.

Decoction (see page 13): make up with fresh or dried burdock root and leave to cool. Use every day, massaging the lotion into the scalp.

Infusion (see page 15): make up with either garden mint, nettle or yarrow and use as a final rinse after shampooing the hair. Use as a lotion, rubbing it into the scalp with pieces of cotton wool two or three times a week.

EYES

Puffiness around the eyes is often caused by tiredness, reading and sewing in a bad light.

To help reduce the swellings the following herbs can be tried.

Compress (see page 13): make up an infusion with one of the following herbs: chamomile, chervil, coltsfoot, fennel, horsetail, lovage or rosewater. When cold use as a compress over closed eyes for fifteen minutes while lying down and relaxing.

Infusion (see page 15): make up with rosemary and use cold infusion on cotton wool pads to smooth over the skin, pressing lightly on to the puffiness. Use in the mornings after washing the face.

FEET

Tired, weary and aching feet are mainly the results of standing overlong, ill-fitting shoes, walking too far or when the weather is very hot. Good comfortable shoes are important and foot exercises can help to get feet into shape again. The following treatments may also help.

Decoction (see page 13): make up with chamomile flowers and when lukewarm sponge the feet well. Dry carefully and lie down for twenty minutes with feet higher than the head.

Footbath Make up a strong infusion (see page 15) of limeflowers, marigold petals or mugwort and soak the feet for fifteen minutes. Dry carefully and powder the feet with dried ground mugwort.

Tincture (see page 16): make up with arnica flowers (see page 23) and dilute with warm water. Immerse the feet for ten to fifteen minutes.

FRAGRANCES

Many herbs possess a natural fragrance delightful in its freshness and surprising in its vigour. Traditionally a posy of sweet-smelling herbs was carried to ward off the offensive smells associated with insanitary conditions. Today the fragrant herbs may be used as perfumes in the form of an oil or a toilet water. The strongly scented herbs make longer lasting perfumes, but some of the milder scents can linger on the skin and are a delight to use. Most of the herbs which are suitable for adding to pot pourri are sufficiently scented to be made into perfumes. An atomiser can be purchased for spraying the skin with toilet water.

Chamomile Make up a decoction of the flowers (see page 35) and store in a cool place. Smooth over the face and neck after washing in the morning for a soft fragrance.

Damask rose Make rose oil (see page 50) and gently smooth a little on the eyelids to make them shine and add a lovely scent. Make toilet vinegar (see page 50) and add to the washing water. Smooth bought rosewater over the skin each day for a scent that lingers.

Elder Make up a strong infusion (see page 15) of elderflowers and use the lotion to soften and perfume the skin of the face and neck.

Honeysuckle Make up a strong infusion of honeysuckle flowers (see page 71) and use to perfume the body after a bath, rubbing it over the skin.

Lavender Make up a bottle of lavender toilet water (see page 84) or purchase from a chemist and dab it over the skin for a long-lasting perfume. Make up a strong infusion of fresh flowers (see page 84) and use to freshen the skin during the day.

Lemon verbena Make up an infusion (see page 87) and add a little to the washing water to refresh the skin. Lemon verbena is a strongly lemon scented herb and it should be used sparingly.

Limeflower Make up a strong infusion of limeflowers (see page 90) for a relaxing scent. Use in the washing water night and morning.

Rosemary Make up an infusion of the flowering tips (see page 116) and use in the washing water or use cotton wool to smooth the lotion over the skin. Rosemary toilet water may also be purchased from a chemist.

Sweet violet Make up a decoction (see page 137) with violet flowers and add to the washing water. The lotion is good for the skin and the light fragrance is pleasant and soothing.

Thyme Make up a decoction (see page 139) and dilute with distilled water before spraying over the skin or adding to the washing water.

Perfumes from herbs described above are completely natural and as they contain no alcohol or other fixative will not keep for longer than two or three days.

FRECKLES

Freckles are small, brownish-yellow spots on the skin which appear on face and arms. There is a number of herbs which can be tried and which may help to fade the freckles.

Decoction (see page 13): make up with dandelion flowers or use fumitory boiled in milk (see page 64). When cold bathe the freckles night and morning.

Fresh honeysuckle flowers steeped in cold milk make a lotion to be dabbed on to freckles at night.

Fresh horseradish root pulped and mixed with a little lemon juice can be brushed on to freckles on hands and arms only.

Fresh expressed parsley juice can be used directly on to freckles. Dab on the juice night and morning.

HAIR

Thick, shining, bouncy hair is healthy and in good condition and proper care will keep it that way. Regular treatment can prevent falling or brittle hair and split ends and will condition dry or oily hair.

Hair rinses

Used after shampooing to promote healthy hair.

Cleavers Make up hair tonic (see page 40) and use as a final rinse to make the hair shine.

Fennel Make up the rinse (see page 61) using fennel on its own or mixed with limeflowers and chamomile flowers. This rinse helps to stimulate the scalp and strengthen the hair. Pour it over hair several times as final rinse.

Lavender Make the infusion using lavender flowers and rinse hair several times after shampooing to leave the hair shining and soft.

Rosemary Use a decoction of rosemary on dark hair, rinsing several times to leave the hair soft, shining and easy to manage.

Southernwood Mix with equal quantities of other herbs such as rosemary, parsley and yarrow. Make up infusion and use after shampooing hair to keep it in good condition.

Hair shampoos

Aloe vera shampoo can be bought and used on dry, brittle hair.

Chamomile Make up rinse (see page 35) and use once or twice a week on blond hair.

Rosemary Make up a strong decoction and add to soapwort shampoo (see page 125). Use once or twice a week on dark hair.

Soapwort Make up decoction (see page 125) and add to it a concentrated infusion of any herb good for hair. It leaves hair soft and shining and easy to manage.

Southernwood makes a good dry shampoo useful for oily hair. Make up shampoo (see page 127) and leave for five to ten minutes, then brush well to remove. Add southernwood to a strong soapwort solution for a wet shampoo to keep hair shining and soft.

Hair tonics

Burdock Make up decoction of the root and use as a lotion for mild cases of falling hair and dandruff. Apply daily, massaging gently into the scalp. Do not use if scalp is sore.

Nettle Make up a decoction (see page 13) of nettle tops and use the lotion two or three times a week massaging it into the scalp. This stimulates the circulation to the scalp and stimulates the growth of the hair.

HANDS

Rough, chapped hands often result from gardening or cooking. Contact with detergents will remove natural oils and dry the skin. Regular use of creams and lotions will help soften and smooth the skin and prevent the problem recurring.

Extract Use dried marsh mallow roots to make extract (see page 96). Add extract to glycerine and use at night to soften rough skin and relieve painful chapped hands.

Infusion Make up with chamomile flowers or plantain (see page 112) and smooth over hands after washing them. Make up an infusion with yarrow. When cold soak hands for five to ten minutes. Make up an infusion with damask rose petals. When cold mix with cream and smooth over hands. Make up a strong infusion of elderflowers and mix with glycerine. Shake well before use.

Oil Make up with lavender flowers and mix with glycerine. Shake the bottle well before using.

Ointment Make up with marigold petals and smooth over hands.

Lips

In cold weather or in a dry atmosphere created by central heating the lips can become dry, chapped and sore. To help prevent this and to keep the lips soft and smooth there are some herbal remedies.

Cream Make up with sage (see page 120) and smooth on to chapped lips as required.

Ointment (see page 14): use fresh leaves of sweet violet to make up ointment and use to soften sore, painful, chapped lips as often as needed.

Nails

When nails become dried from whatever cause they are brittle, they break easily and tend to split lengthways down the nail which can result in much discomfort. Nails need to be kept strong and well lubricated.

Decoction (see page 13): make up with horsetail (see page 76). Twice a week soak the nails first in warm oil and then in horsetail decoction. Soak for ten minutes in each bowl.

Infusion (see page 15): make up with horsetail. Drink a cup night and morning to assist the treatment described above.

Pores

Large pores mostly appear on patches of oily skin on the face. To shrink the enlarged pores there are various treatments which can be tried. Regularly applied, the following herbal remedies may be of help.

Compress (see page 13): make up infusion with marigold petals or peppermint leaves. Cleanse the face and apply the compress for ten to fifteen minutes.

Face pack Make up with fresh or dried plantain (see page 112), with horsetail or with sage leaves. Leave on the face for fifteen minutes, then wash off with tepid water and end by splashing the skin with cold water. A face pack made with yarrow (see page 145) is especially

effective for oily skins but should only be applied on an occasional basis.

Juice Freshly expressed plantain juice can be added to a soft plain proprietary cream. Alternatively mix the juice with a little milk. In both cases clean the face well, then smooth or dab the preparations on to the skin. Dab lady's mantle juice on to the pores and leave to dry on the skin.

Skin

Skin is the body's protective covering. A normal healthy skin is smooth and firm. It has a natural elasticity and moistness. To keep the skin in healthy working order a good wholesome diet should be followed with plenty of fresh air, exercise and sleep.

To help the skin it is necessary to care for it properly by keeping it scrupulously clean and well moisturised and to protect it from the elements.

Skin Cleansers

Centaury Make up a decoction of the herb and leave it to cool. Wash the face in the decoction each day and leave it to dry.

Salvia officinalis

Published by D. Woodville Aug.* 1.1790.

Elder Make up elderflower infusion and use the lotion night and morning to cleanse and tone the skin. Good for oily skins and can be used over thread veins. To deep cleanse the skin make up a facial steam and finish by splashing the skin with cold water.

Elecampane Make up a weak decoction with root (see page 58) and use as a cleansing lotion especially where there are spots and pimples.

Astringent and Toning Lotions

Chickweed Make up an infusion (see page 37). When cooled use on a cleansed face night and morning to clear the skin and to improve the texture.

Coltsfoot Make up a strong infusion (see page 42) and use when cold. Cleanse the face and smooth or pat the lotion over the skin. Leave to dry. This will tighten and help to tone a flabby skin.

Cornflower Make up a weak decoction (see page 46). Use the refreshing lotion daily for toning and firming the skin.

Fumitory Make up the lotion in milk (see page 64) and use as a refreshing toning lotion after cleansing the skin.

Lady's mantle Make up a strong infusion and use night and morning after cleansing the face to tone the skin.

Marigold Make up an infusion of marigold petals and use the lotion as an astringent on oily skins.

Salad burnet Make up an infusion and use daily on the skin to improve the texture.

Skin Softeners

Chamomile Make up a decoction (see page 35) and bathe the face night and morning.

Chervil Make up an ointment and smooth over the skin at night to soothe and soften.

Flax Make up a face pack (see page 63) and leave on face for fifteen minutes. After washing it off with warm water smooth chamomile lotion over the skin to soften.

Wood betony Make a fresh infusion each day and use night and morning after cleansing for clearing and softening the skin.

Moisturisers

Damask rose Make up the moisturising cream (see page 49). A soothing cream for dry skins, it can be used at night and in the morning.
Evening primrose Use oil of evening primrose and smooth over the skin at night after cleansing and washing.
St John's wort Make up an infusion and apply as a compress to the skin after cleaning. *But only* at night.

Spots and pimples
Spots and pimples are unsightly eruptions which appear mainly on the face and cause discomfort and irritation. Care should be taken not to pick or scratch the spots as this can cause further infection. Try one or other of the following remedies.
Decoction (see page 13): make up with burdock root and use to bathe the spots and pimples night and morning.
Face pack Make up with coltsfoot (see page 42) and leave on the face for fifteen minutes. Remove with tepid water and wipe the face with coltsfoot infusion. Make up face pack with dandelion and nettle mixed (see page 53). Use every two or three days for a fortnight to help clear the skin and improve the circulation.
Infusion (see page 15): make up a strong infusion of thyme and use when cold to bathe affected areas.
Juice Use freshly expressed juice of borage, dandelion and watercress and dab on the spots at night.
Ointment (see page 14): make up with cowslip flowers and use each night on the affected area.

Sunburn
This is the result of over long exposure of the skin to strong sunlight. Sunbathing for most people should be limited to fifteen minutes per day. For mild cases of sunburn

Rosa centifolia

there are remedies which will help to soothe and ease the sunburn.
Decoction (see page 13): make up with chamomile flowers (see page 35). When cold bathe the affected part until relief is felt.
Infusion (see page 15): make up with cleavers and when cool sponge the area until burning sensation is relieved.
Juice Break off a leaf of the aloe plant and immediately smooth the juice over the affected part.
Ointment (see page 14): make up with comfrey or elderflowers and smooth over sunburnt area to soothe and ease the discomfort.

Thread veins
Thread veins usually appear on the face and legs and are difficult to remove. The skin should be protected at all times from extreme temperatures by the use of creams and lotions. The following herbal treatments may be helpful.
Compress Make up an infusion with coltsfoot leaves or flowers (see page 42). Twice a day use a lukewarm infusion, leaving the soaked cotton wool pads on the skin until cold.

Lotion Make up with elderflowers (see page 57) or plantain (see page 112). Use the lotion night and morning, dabbing it gently over the thread veins.

Wrinkles
Wrinkles often appear earlier on a dry skin than they do on an oily skin. But wrinkles usually come with the advancing years because the processes whereby the skin casts off the dead cells which rise to the surface slow down. Treatment can help to ward off early wrinkles and reduce and soften others.
Compress (see page 13): make up an infusion of limeflowers and when cooled use compress on wrinkles for ten minutes. Alternatively use the lotion to pat on to wrinkles and leave to dry.
Cream Use a proprietary aloe vera cream every night to help reduce wrinkles.
Decoction (see page 13): make up with cowslip flowers, chervil or with rosemary. Soak cotton wool pads in the decoction and press lightly over the wrinkles. Use night and morning, leaving it to dry on the skin.
Face pack (see page 13): make with a strong infusion of fennel. Leave on the face for twenty minutes and wash off with warm water.
Infusion (see page 15): make up with cowslip or primrose flowers and use as described above.
Ointment (see page 14): make up with cowslip flowers and use at night, smoothing it gently over the wrinkles.

INDEX